GEORGE WHITEFIELD

Evangelist for God and Empire

LIBRARY OF RELIGIOUS BIOGRAPHY

Mark A. Noll and Heath W. Carter, series editors

The Library of Religious Biography is a series of original biographies on important religious figures throughout American and British history.

The authors are well-known historians, each a recognized authority in the period of religious history in which his or her subject lived and worked. Grounded in solid research of both published and archival sources, these volumes link the lives of their subjects—not always thought of as "religious" persons—to the broader cultural contexts and religious issues that surrounded them. Each volume includes a bibliographical essay and an index to serve the needs of students, teachers, and researchers.

Marked by careful scholarship yet free of academic jargon, the books in this series are well-written narratives meant to be read and enjoyed as well as studied.

Titles include:

Emily Dickinson and the Art of Belief • Roger Lundin

A Short Life of Jonathan Edwards • George M. Marsden

Sworn on the Altar of God: A Religious Biography of Thomas Jefferson
Edwin S. Gaustad

The Religious Life of Robert E. Lee • R. David Cox

Abraham Lincoln: Redeemer President • Allen C. Guelzo

The First American Evangelical: A Short Life of Cotton Mather • Rick Kennedy

Harriet Beecher Stowe: A Spiritual Life • Nancy Koester

Assist Me to Proclaim: The Life and Hymns of Charles Wesley • John R. Tyson

For a complete list of published volumes, see the back of this volume.

George Whitefield

Evangelist for God and Empire

Peter Y. Choi

WILLIAM B. EERDMANS PUBLISHING COMPANY
GRAND RAPIDS, MICHIGAN

Wm. B. Eerdmans Publishing Co.
2140 Oak Industrial Drive N.E., Grand Rapids, Michigan 49505
www.eerdmans.com

Published 2018
Printed in the United States of America

27 26 25 24 23 22 21 20 19 18   1 2 3 4 5 6 7 8 9 10

ISBN 978-0-8028-7549-5

Library of Congress Cataloging-in-Publication Data

Names: Choi, Peter Y., author. | Noll, Mark A., 1946- writer of foreword.
Title: George Whitefield : evangelist for God and Empire / Peter Y. Choi ;
    foreword by Mark A. Noll.
Description: Grand Rapids, Michigan : Eerdmans, 2018. | Series: Library of
    religious biography | Includes bibliographical references and index.
Identifiers: LCCN 2018001803 | ISBN 9780802875495 (paperback)
Subjects: LCSH: Whitefield, George, 1714-1770. | Evangelists—Great
    Britain—Biography. | Evangelists—United States—Biography. | United
    States—Social conditions—To 1865. | Great Britain—Colonies—America. |
    BISAC: BIOGRAPHY & AUTOBIOGRAPHY / Religious. | HISTORY / United States /
    Colonial Period (1600-1775).
Classification: LCC BX9225.W4 C53 2018 | DDC 269/.2092 [B] —dc23
    LC record available at https://lccn.loc.gov/2018001803

The author and publisher gratefully acknowledge permission to reprint extracts from
Peter Y. Choi, "Whitefield, Georgia, and the Quest for Bethesda College," from *George White-
field: Life, Context, and Legacy*, edited by Geordan Hammond and David Ceri Jones (2016).
Used by permission of Oxford University Press.

For Minsun

Contents

Foreword

In 2014 scholars and an impressively large number of lay people gathered at several locations in North America and the United Kingdom to
commemorate the 300th anniversary of the birth of George Whitefield.
These meetings offered learned papers on many different aspects of
Whitefield's momentous career—life-changing conversion as an Oxford undergraduate, spectacular fame (and notoriety) as a preacher in
England and Scotland, dramatic scenes of spellbound crowds in the
much sparser populations of colonial America, celebrated controversy
with his friends John and Charles Wesley over Calvinism (his position)
versus Arminianism (theirs), and more. The meetings also featured
full attention to themes that have continued to keep Whitefield alive
in reaches far beyond the academy—his laser-like focus on the need for
sinners to be born again, his all-out dedication to a preaching vocation,
his mind-bending capacity for travel that took him to the colonies seven
times and to ceaseless itinerations in the British Isles, and still more
of the heroic qualities that have distinguished him in some circles as a
paragon of self-giving godliness.

It was no surprise that these tercentennial commemorations and
the publications that followed concentrated on Whitefield's career
from 1736 through 1742.[1] In the former year he emerged in England
as a preaching phenomenon; in the latter year a combination of his re-

---

1. For example, *George Whitefield: Tercentenary Essays*, ed. William Gibson and
Thomas W. Smith, a special issue of *Journal of Religious History, Literature and Culture*
1, no. 2 (2015): v–106; and *George Whitefield: Life, Context, and Legacy*, ed. Geordan
Hammond and David Ceri Jones (Oxford: Oxford University Press, 2016).

nown and the power of his message riveted much of Scotland (reliable witnesses reported as many as thirty thousand auditors harkening spellbound in the twilight on July 11, 1742, at Camsbuslang, near Glasgow, as he preached on the text "for thy Maker is thine husband; the Lord of hosts is his name"). Between 1736 and 1742 also took place Whitefield's voyages to the New World, where from Georgia in the South to Maine in the North he drew audiences by the thousands, sparked the colonial Great Awakening, and in so doing all but singlehandedly created an ongoing evangelical tradition that may also have exerted an indirect influence leading to the American Revolution.

Peter Choi's *George Whitefield: Evangelist for God and Empire* begins with what might be called the Spectacular Whitefield of those uniquely luminous years. Yet his widely researched and beautifully written book makes its fresh contribution by turning away from the years 1736–1742 to pursue other questions. For example, what do we learn about Whitefield the person and the message he preached if we examine the twenty-eight years of his life *after* 1742 with the same care that so many have lavished on his early public career? Or, what happens when we shift focus from viewing Whitefield bestriding the British Empire of his day to examine the effects of the empire on his ministry? Again, what fresh insights come from treating Whitefield's efforts to sustain an orphanage in the frontier of colonial Georgia as the centerpiece of his life instead of merely a sideshow to justify his travels as fundraiser for this orphanage? Or again, do we add important dimensions to understanding Whitefield and his age if we find out why he could so adamantly condemn slave owners for abusing their human property in 1740 but less than ten years later lead the charge to legalize slavery in Georgia, where other evangelicals who founded that colony had prohibited the institution?

As the book before you addresses these questions, we gain a much fuller picture of George Whitefield's entire life. We learn how directly the events of British imperial history—especially wars with France in the mid-1740s and then from 1754 to 1763—affected his preaching. We learn why Whitefield, himself an Anglican minister, quarreled so contentiously with other leading Anglicans in the 1760s. Most of all, these pages provide an unusually clear account of Whitefield's gospel message understood first as a message in its times and for the places where he traveled. For these historical and religious purposes, in other words, Peter Choi provides a Whitefield of flesh and blood. His portrait confirms the Grand Itinerant as a great preacher and a positive force in promoting evangelical faith, but also as a man embedded in his times who, as a feature of that embeddedness, combined God-honoring service with morally questionable flaws—just like all the rest of his eighteenth-century evangelical peers, and all of their spiritual descendants today.

More than a quarter of a century ago, as one of the first volumes in the Eerdmans Library of Religious Biography, Harry Stout published an unusually effective biography of Whitefield focused on his spectacular early career. By placing Whitefield in the context of an age fascinated by the power of the stage and accepting the marketplace as the key arena for truth claims, Stout advanced understanding of Whitefield so effectively that the book continues to be read (and assigned in classes) to this day. Peter Choi has done something similar for the latter decades of Whitefield's life. Stout and Choi both acknowledge that conventional accounts have much to offer about Whitefield as a faithful preacher, dedicated itinerant, and heroic Christian exemplar. In addition, however, Choi's *George Whitefield: Evangelist for God and Empire* now joins Stout's *The Divine Dramatist: George Whitefield and the Rise of Modern Evangelicalism* by demonstrating that the world in which Whitefield lived shaped him just as much as Whitefield's larger-than-life career shaped that world. Readers now, as then, are in for a feast of historical insight and spiritual wisdom.

MARK A. NOLL

Acknowledgments

Writing this book would not have been possible without the support of numerous institutions, teachers, friends, and family. It is a joy to write this note of thanks and to remember the many gifts I have received along the way.

I am grateful for the generous support of many foundations and institutions. The Lynde and Harry Bradley Foundation, the Andrew W. Mellon Foundation, the Huntington Library, and the Institute for Scholarship in the Liberal Arts at the University of Notre Dame provided funding that made the research for this project possible. Thanks to their generous support, I was able to spend extended periods of time at the Massachusetts Historical Society, the New York Historical Society, the American Philosophical Society, the Historical Society of Pennsylvania, the Library Company of Philadelphia, the Georgia Historical Society, and the Huntington Library. Newbigin House of Studies provided funding for research at Lambeth Palace Library toward the end of this project. Visits to these many archives afforded the time to read rare manuscripts as well as a place for stimulating conversations with colleagues that yielded directions for this study beyond what I could have imagined at the outset.

This project benefited from the many excellent contributions at "George Whitefield at 300: An International Tercentenary Conference at Pembroke College, Oxford University." During this conference at the college where young Whitefield himself was a student, I met many of the leading lights who have illuminated my study of Whitefield's life and early evangelicalism. It was a special delight to meet the organizers, Geordan Hammond and David Ceri Jones, and I thank them for including my chapter on Whitefield's quest for Bethesda College in their edited volume *George Whitefield: Life, Context, and Legacy* (Oxford University Press, 2016). Their skillful feedback and probing questions strengthened my argument in chapter 6 of this book. I also want to thank Tommy Kidd for inviting me to present a paper on Whitefield and slavery at the Institute for Studies of Religion at Baylor University, during another tercentennial conference. The opportunity to discuss Whitefield with thoughtful scholars like Kidd, David Bebbington, and Bruce Hindmarsh provided stimulating insights for this project, and many ideas from conversations over those few days in Waco still linger in my mind today.

Owing a debt of gratitude to so many institutions and persons is a humbling reminder that studying the past is an enormous undertaking that depends on the generosity of others. I have benefited immensely from many historians. During my years at Calvin Theological Seminary, Lyle Bierma, Richard Muller, and Henry Zwaanstra showed me the spiritual significance of studying church history. They imparted not only wisdom but also gnawing questions that would eventually drive me back to further graduate work in history. At an early stage of this journey, when the paucity of manuscripts from Whitefield's later years could easily have led me to abandon course, David Ceri Jones shared a veritable treasure map pointing to hundreds of Whitefield documents in far-flung repositories. James Bradley, during a conversation in Pasadena, encouraged me to think more broadly about the Hanoverian context. On a wintry morning in Grand Rapids, George Marsden didn't pull any punches in offering incisive questions that eventually sharpened my analysis of the relationship between Whitefield and Catholicism.

I am deeply thankful for members of the committee supervising my dissertation, from which this book originated. James Turner challenged me to expand my understanding of the British Atlantic world. Tom Kselman encouraged me to ask good social and cultural questions in the study of religious history. Patrick Griffin showed me that the historian's craft is a painstaking art and that clear thinking is the essential labor of writing well.

Above all, Mark Noll provided wise counsel and ongoing encouragement from start to finish. He always modeled genuine and enthusiastic curiosity about the past, challenged me to let discordant voices speak for themselves, and taught me to venture interpretation with precision and charity. He listened to and read my words so carefully that he often knew what I was trying to say better than I did. Ever the patient teacher, he also knew when to give time and space when I needed to learn for myself. I am still rediscovering Post-it notes with profundities in barely legible script on books and articles he has shared with me over the years. I have learned so much from him; it is hard to imagine a mentoring experience more formative and inspiring.

Somewhere in the middle of this endeavor, Jul Medenblik and Ronald Feenstra took a chance on a doctoral candidate in the throes of dissertating and welcomed me back to Calvin Seminary, where, as a former student turned teacher, I had the blessing of working alongside many incredible people. I am indebted to the Reformed tradition I learned at Calvin for pointing the way to hermeneutical humility and patience.

I currently have the tremendous privilege of working at not one but two institutions that help my scholarly endeavors to integrate spiritual questions. My work at Newbigin House of Studies and City Church San Francisco challenges my study of history to include a concern for the common good and human flourishing. I owe a special debt of gratitude to Scot Sherman and Fred Harrell for their encouragement of my work and for providing leadership that courageously pushes boundaries.

It has been a great pleasure to work with a wonderful team at Eerdmans. David Bratt as editor guided the whole process with a deft hand. Jenny Hoffman gave painstaking attention to details with grace and professionalism. As a first-time author with little clear sense of what to expect, this process showed me once again the value of collaboration and exceeded my expectations at seemingly every turn.

Many friends and family gave support and encouragement throughout the writing of this book. Young Kim shared his contagious love of history. Rachel Lee and Andrew Kim helped me to see things I would not have seen on my own. Jordyn Cho, Abe Cho, Jason Wallace, and Kathy Wallace offered hospitality during what seemed like interminably peripatetic jaunts from archive to archive, coast to coast. Throughout this process, as always, my parents provided unconditional encouragement and the unmatched gift of their prayers. Elijah, Zachary, and Josiah not only put up with a dad who too often had the eighteenth century on his mind but even evidenced interest on occasion by asking, "Can you tell us more about that Whitefield guy?"

Acknowledgments

I have saved the best for last, for the end of this project is a fitting time to thank the person who means most in my life. It is a testament to her spirit that my affection for Minsun deepens with each passing day. Without her, not only this work but so much else would not have been possible. Her love and support mean more to me than words can express, but I look forward to many years of trying.

Introduction

The longing for revival has long marked evangelicalism, a movement forged in the fires of the Great Awakening. While fragments of the story of its dramatic origins abound, a great deal about the long trajectory of evangelical revivals remains obscure. Historians have generally acknowledged that a movement of Protestant renewal erupted across the eighteenth-century Atlantic world.[1] Eyewitness accounts corroborate the claim that a period of sustained religious fervor turned the British Empire upside down.[2] But then the narrative turns murky and historical consensus proves evasive beyond the basic story: after a period of heightened religious activity during the early 1740s, the revivals fizzled out or ebbed only to flow again later.[3] Step past this limited area of agreement and divergent

---

1. Even on this fundamental point, however, there is considerable debate. See for example, Jon Butler, "Enthusiasm Described and Decried: The Great Awakening as Interpretative Fiction," *The Journal of American History* 69, no. 2 (1982): 305–25.

2. Evaluations of the revivals' effects run the gamut. Charles Chauncy, a pastor in Boston, issued vehement denunciations. Charles Chauncy, *Enthusiasm Described and Caution'd Against. A Sermon. With a Letter to the Reverend Mr. James Davenport* (Boston: S. Eliot & J. Blanchard, 1742). For a more favorable contemporary assessment, see Benjamin Franklin, *Autobiography* (Boston: Houghton Mifflin & Company, 1906), 111–13. For a broader survey, which claims that no other event received as much newspaper coverage, see Lisa Smith, *The First Great Awakening in Colonial American Newspapers: A Shifting Story* (Lanham: Lexington Books, 2012).

3. Kidd argues for a long season of revival that stretches into the nineteenth century. Marini traces the continuation of Whitefieldian revival in radical sects. Westerkamp extends the Great Awakening into at least 1765. Thomas S. Kidd, *The Great Awakening: The Roots of Evangelical Christianity in Colonial America* (New Haven: Yale University Press, 2007); Stephen A Marini, *Radical Sects of Revolutionary New England* (Cambridge: Har-

narratives abound. The chorus of confusion around interpretations of the Great Awakening ranges from its dismissal as historical fiction to its revision into socioeconomic protest to the valorization of its leading figures as saints and heroes.[4] Put one way, we do not have the whole picture of the Great Awakening due to a woeful lack of attention to the aftermath of revival. Despite the profusion of studies on the beginning and middle years of the awakenings, there have been few corresponding efforts to examine its later stages.[5] It is a question few think to ask, but one which opens up a crucial avenue of inquiry, a strategy for understanding the whole by careful examination of all its parts: what happened after revival?

My book pursues this question in the form of a character study as I argue that a view of empire shaped the Awakening in its early phases and absorbed the revivals in their later stages. By examining the beginning, middle, and especially the later years of George Whitefield's itinerant life, this study reconceptualizes the Great Awakening in its relationship to a fast-growing British Empire. Viewing the whole of Whitefield's public career, and not only the early stage of revival success, reminds us that he lived and ministered in the context of an expansive imperial culture. As a culturally embedded religious message, his revival agenda could not resist imbibing the values of British state formation in the middle of the eighteenth century. The relationship between George Whitefield's religious and imperial agendas represents the central focus of this study.

---

vard University Press, 1982); Marilyn J. Westerkamp, *Triumph of the Laity: Scots-Irish Piety and the Great Awakening, 1625–1760* (Oxford: Oxford University Press, 1988).

4. Butler, "Enthusiasm Described and Decried"; Jon Butler, *Awash in a Sea of Faith: Christianizing the American People,* Studies in Cultural History (Cambridge: Harvard University Press, 1990); Gary Nash, *The Urban Crucible: The Northern Seaports and the Origins of the American Revolution* (Cambridge: Harvard University Press, 1986). Joseph Tracy's work, one of the earliest historical studies of the Great Awakening, is a key primary source in the development of the Awakening as a historical concept: Joseph Tracy, *The Great Awakening: A History of the Revival of Religion in the Time of Edwards and Whitefield* (Boston: Charles Tappan, 1845).

5. In a telling example, Thomas Kidd's recent biography of Whitefield provides a thorough study of the preacher's early and middle life, offers rich primary source engagement, and successfully establishes Whitefield as "the key figure in the first generation of Anglo-American evangelical Christianity," but it arrives at these achievements by focusing primarily on the first two decades of the itinerant's public career. In a twelve-chapter book, the narrative does not reach the 1750s in any substantial measure until the middle of the penultimate chapter and therefore provides only cursory treatment of the last twenty years of Whitefield's life. Thomas S. Kidd, *George Whitefield: America's Spiritual Founding Father* (New Haven: Yale University Press, 2014).

Though best known as the Grand Itinerant who traveled far and wide proclaiming a religion of new birth, Whitefield was more than a famous revival preacher. He was an agent of British culture who used his potent mix of political savvy and theological creativity to champion the cause of imperial expansion. This book seeks to show that the significance of George Whitefield's evangelistic ministry lies not only with his traditional reputation as the single most important preacher of the eighteenth-century Protestant awakenings. More specifically, his life from 1714 to 1770 offers a case study in the transition that occurred over the course of the eighteenth century from centripetal British expansionism to an increasingly diffuse culture. That this dynamic movement in the culture of empire coincided with the rise and decline of revival serves to highlight the essential relationship between evangelicalism and imperialism.

When Whitefield set foot in America for the first time in 1738, both religion and politics were unsettled in the colonies. Religious life was in disarray because of the great variety in colonial religious successes and failures. The political direction of the colonies was subject to forces that were pulling the colonies closer to the mother country but were also setting up the path to revolution. Over the course of the next thirty-three years, Whitefield became a dominant fixture on this shifting American landscape, making a total of seven trips to the colonies, preaching over twenty thousand sermons, befriending social elites and government officials, and winning the hearts of commoners everywhere. Declaring the world to be his parish, moreover, he journeyed fourteen times to Scotland, three times to Ireland, with stopovers in places as far afield as Holland, Portugal, and Bermuda. By the middle of the eighteenth century, he had become a household name on both sides of the ocean and one of the first international celebrities, recognized not only by evangelical peers but by admirers as diverse as Benjamin Franklin and David Hume. His outsized personality left an indelible imprint on his world. Though Whitefield stepped onto a troubled and crumbling stage in the mid 1730s, by the time of his death in 1770, a new world was emerging, one he had contributed much to remaking.[6] In short, to understand

6. Though Alan Heimert's thesis connecting the awakenings to revolution has been much disputed, echoes of his argument remain. Recent scholarship has moved away from direct links between the revivals and revolution; for instance, Patricia Bonomi argues for the role of denominational politics in contributing to a more contentious civic discourse. Alan Heimert, *Religion and the American Mind: From the Great Awakening to the Revolution* (Cambridge: Harvard University Press, 1966); Philip Goff,

the British Atlantic world of the eighteenth century, it is necessary to contend with the profound cultural force that was George Whitefield.

And contend we must, for the Grand Itinerant was as enigmatic as he was ubiquitous. Whitefield possessed a chameleon-like adaptability resulting in an elusive and evolving ecclesiastical identity with empire-wide influence. He was at once an establishment priest in England, a radical itinerant in America, and a moderate Calvinist in Scotland. By day he preached to tens of thousands in large open fields and when the sun went down he gave evening lectures in the parlor rooms of London's gentry. If a study of Whitefield must work out the complex puzzles presented by his peripatetic life, there is also the prospect of rich insights to be gleaned from a globetrotting celebrity who held the attention of British subjects everywhere captive. In fact, his ability to constantly reinvent himself had roots in his theological convictions about the new birth but also bore social and political implications for reimagining British imperial as well as American colonial identity.

This gift for refashioning himself can shed light on the overall trajectory of his life in the evolving context of imperial state formation throughout the eighteenth century. In the beginning of his American career, Whitefield was a British tourist and emissary who soon learned the limits of revivalistic, evangelical religion in a rapidly expanding British Atlantic world. Interpreting the Great Awakening as a social and political event, and not merely a religious one, this study will follow the long trajectory of the Grand Itinerant's life beyond the height of revival in order to trace the turn from a process of Anglicization to Americanization in the eighteenth century.[7] Whitefield started his ministry as a proponent of the virtues he believed British Protestantism had to offer colonists in

---

"Revivals and Revolution: Historiographic Turns since Alan Heimert's Religion and the American Mind," *Church History* 67, no. 4 (1998): 695–721; Patricia U. Bonomi, *Under the Cope of Heaven: Religion, Society and Politics in Colonial America* (Oxford: Oxford University Press, 2003).

7. The most helpful works on Anglicization and Briticization include: Joyce E. Chaplin, "The British Atlantic," in *The Oxford Handbook of the Atlantic World, 1450–1850*, ed. Nicholas Canny and Philip Morgan (Oxford: Oxford University Press, 2011), esp. 226–27; Patrick Griffin, *America's Revolution* (New York: Oxford University Press, 2013); Brendan McConville, *The King's Three Faces: The Rise & Fall of Royal America, 1688–1776* (Chapel Hill: University of North Carolina Press, 2006); John M. Murrin, "A Roof without Walls: The Dilemma of American National Identity," in *Beyond Confederation: Origins of the Constitution and American National Identity*, ed. Richard R. Beeman, Stephen Botein, and Edward C. Carter (Chapel Hill: University of North Carolina Press, 1987).

their settling of North America. Toward that end, he relished his role as an exporter of English metropolitan culture. By the end of his career, however, his political activism went beyond his earlier religious dissent. He became an ardent advocate for America and embraced the merits of provincial culture and activism in the context of an expanding empire.

Because the religious and imperial dimensions of Whitefield's Atlantic itinerancy illuminate each other, recognizing his religious innovations is as important as understanding his geo-political context. As Whitefield charged into the public sphere, reluctantly at first but more enthusiastically with time, his orientation bore a distinct neo-Puritan stamp. Historians have noted the paradoxical tension inherent in a Puritan worldview that is torn between impulses toward both engagement and alientation—on the one hand grasping the world by its horns and on the other hand seeking to get as far away from its polluting influences as possible.[8] Whitefield's mediation of this tension, based on his updating of Puritan theology for a changing world, represents an essential development of the eighteenth century. Although Whitefield "unleashed the sectarian impulse" in Puritanism, it is also true that, later in life, he tried to contain that very impulse. And so Whitefield continued the "long argument" of the seventeenth century by attempting to find a middle way within the Puritan solution for being in but not of the world.[9]

Although Whitefield represents continuity with the Puritans, his innovations provoked ruptures as well. It is a mistake to think that he merely course-corrected Anglican deviations and tilted the church back toward bedrock Reformation values. In fact, Whitefield might have had more in common with Anne Hutchinson than John Winthrop. His theology of regeneration, moreover, which undergirded his preaching of the new birth, benefited from the received wisdom of Lockean principles of government and the changed dynamics of the British world after the Revolution of 1688. In other words, Whitefield's theology

8. Edmund S. Morgan, *The Puritan Dilemma: The Story of John Winthrop* (Boston: Little, Brown and Company, 1958); Stephen Foster, *The Long Argument: English Puritanism and the Shaping of New England Culture, 1570–1700* (Chapel Hill: University of North Carolina Press, 1991).

9. In his final chapter, Foster focuses on Whitefield as the culminating personality and force to the long Puritan argument. I am in agreement with Foster that Whitefield, at some level, ruptured the tension that the Puritans laboriously preserved; but I would aver that he also maintained the tension in his own distinctly eighteenth-century fashion. Foster, *The Long Argument*, 286–318.

represented not merely a repackaging of Puritan content but emerged from the crucible of seventeenth- and eighteenth-century political philosophy. His contribution to this debate consisted of much more than simplification, or doctrine "newly condensed in content and tricked out in images unusual in sermons," as one historian put it.[10] Whitefield represented the vanguard of transition from Puritan to evangelical religion in a time of numerous other British cultural transformations.

In a period so characterized by upheaval, the Great Awakening came and went but Whitefield lingered long after the revivals' climactic period in the British Empire. While many prominent New Light leaders either died or faded from the limelight by mid-century, Whitefield continued to crisscross the Atlantic world into the early period of revolutionary rumblings. In his later years, he focused much of his attention on expanding the already extensive web of connections he had built during the awakenings. By dint of personality as well as an ambitious travel itinerary that gave him an air of omnipresence, Whitefield provided one of the most enduring connective sinews for what one historian has called "the transatlantic community of saints" into the latter half of the eighteenth century.[11] Aristocratic sponsors welcomed him into elite, cosmopolitan circles and a long list of evangelical ministers kept up active correspondence from the London metropole and its nearby boroughs. His reach stretched further still as Whitefield also sought out far-flung outposts of the British Empire as fertile soil for his gospel labors, overseeing an orphanage in the hinterlands of Georgia and field-and-street preaching in Edinburgh into the final years of his life. Whitefield seemed to be everywhere in the British world, and until his death in 1770 he wielded enough influence to intimidate Anglican archbishops and draw out rapt crowds numbering in the thousands.[12]

10. Foster, *The Long Argument*, 296.

11. Susan A. O'Brien, "A Transatlantic Community of Saints: The Great Awakening and the First Evangelical Network, 1735–1755," *The American Historical Review* 91, no. 4 (1986): 811–32.

12. For studies on Whitefield's international influence, see David Ceri Jones, *A Glorious Work in the World: Welsh Methodism and the International Evangelical Revival, 1735–1750* (Cardiff: University of Wales Press, 2004); Harry S. Stout, *The Divine Dramatist: George Whitefield and the Rise of Modern Evangelicalism* (Grand Rapids: Eerdmans, 1991); D. Bruce Hindmarsh, *The Evangelical Conversion Narrative: Spiritual Autobiography in Early Modern England* (New York: Oxford University Press, 2005). For a study that views Whitefield's disturbances from the establishment side, see Robert G. Ingram,

By examining a world in which Whitefield continued to exert considerable (even if significantly tamed) influence, this study will point to the significance of not only the Great Awakening's initial disruptions but also its long-term trajectory as contributing to an increasingly diffuse British imperial culture.[13] Specifically, the work of consolidating Awakening gains entailed for Whitefield the development of associational life and the establishment of educational institutions. Though he never eschewed the central thrust of revival religion, the activist preacher also saw the need for broader engagement with culture. The radical revival-monger turned reflective and conciliatory in his later years. More than pious humility, however, lay behind his efforts to bury the hatchet with past rivals. Increasingly prone to sickness and unable to maintain his physical stamina and the superhuman schedule of preaching three or four times a day on the revival circuit, Whitefield innovated in the face of numerous obstacles to his ministry in the last two decades of his life.

The missionary who began his American career as the founder of an orphanage ended his life campaigning to turn that institution into a college. The publicist-preacher, always thinking about the next big event, was prescient enough to know that while New England retained its cultural significance for a season, new centers were developing along other peripheral regions of the empire. His appreciation of Puritan history would have reminded him that Massachusetts had once been a dot on the periphery too. The hinterlands of Georgia proved an alluring location to a strategist like Whitefield because his early life had taught him the possibility of greatness rising from humble origins. His theology gave him a millennial perspective that looked forward to a climactic

---

Religion, Reform and Modernity in the Eighteenth Century: Thomas Secker and the Church of England (Woodbridge: Boydell Press, 2007).

13. Some general histories that describe eighteenth-century British developments include: Peter J. Marshall, ed., *The Oxford History of the British Empire*, vol. 2: *The Eighteenth Century* (Oxford: Oxford University Press, 1998); Nicholas Canny and Philip Morgan, *The Oxford Handbook of the Atlantic World: 1450–1850* (Oxford: Oxford University Press, 2011); Paul Langford, *A Polite and Commercial People: England, 1727–1783* (New York: Oxford University Press, 1989); Ned Landsman, *From Colonials to Provincials: American Thought and Culture, 1680–1760* (Ithaca: Cornell University Press, 2000); Linda Colley, *Britons: Forging the Nation, 1707–1837* (New Haven: Yale University Press, 1992). Works that treat the margins of empire are also significant for my study: James Livesey, *Civil Society and Empire: Ireland and Scotland in the Eighteenth-Century Atlantic World* (New Haven: Yale University Press, 2009); John Clive and Bernard Bailyn, "England's Cultural Provinces: Scotland and America," *The William and Mary Quarterly* 11, no. 2 (1954): 200–213.

eschaton. And his imperial outlook helped him to see Georgia not as marginal nowhere but as strategic outpost. On this fertile soil of possibilities, Whitefield landed as an audacious religious, social, and political entrepreneur unafraid to experiment. For these reasons, the thirteenth colony, as the site of British expansionist schemes, plays a larger role in this study than in any previous work on Whitefield. Placing the history of the Great Awakening into the longer arc of Whitefield's life illuminates processes of change under way in the British Atlantic world during the eighteenth century. We will see the ways in which the adherents of revival religion, when faced with the peril of reifying revivalism, turned to the appropriation of cultural values. In this story, Whitefield started out a nonconformist religious leader but, despite his best intentions, conformed to the ineluctable power of imperial identity.

When we consider the malleability of Whitefield's evangelical pragmatism alongside his Puritan roots, colonial sympathies, and British patriotism, a new, more complex picture emerges. A study of the imperial Whitefield will illustrate how the tenets of evangelical revival and British expansion became increasingly entwined over the course of the eighteenth century. This book will outline that process of cultural change, embodied in the development of Whitefield's public ministry, in two successive stages that describe a movement from encounters to entanglements. Chapters 1 and 2 treat the initial encounters, which were characterized by the allurement for Whitefield of the promise of British state formation. We will see how the missionary preacher recognized the strategic position of the Georgia colony in the southern frontier of a burgeoning British Empire and ordered his revival strategy around this imperial reality. Chapter 3 describes the longer arc of revival religion, which displayed not only powerful heights but also contained the inevitable decline of religious enthusiasm. We will examine how the relentless ebb and flow of revivalistic religion spurred Whitefield's transformation from idealistic promoter of British culture to pragmatic entrepreneur in the American colonies. In the second half of the book, the vexed struggle of Whitefield's imperial cultural engagement surfaces as the key motif. Chapter 4 presents the preacher's forays into slavery and chapter 5 explores his involvement in war propaganda; both provide evidence of revival religion's absorption into the cultural vortex of empire. Chapter 6 looks at how Whitefield's colonial institution building represented belated, and largely unsuccessful, efforts to separate the wheat of evangelical religion from the tares of imperial am-

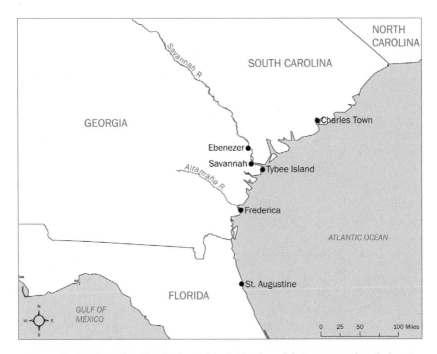

Map 1. The Southern frontier during Whitefield's first visit (courtesy of Rachel Lee)

bition. In summary, this study traces a movement from the awakening of religious fervor to the accommodation of imperial cultural factors.

The story of the Great Awakening cannot be understood apart from the particular context in which the movement for evangelical renewal not only took life but also underwent change. In this process, a constellation of religious, cultural, and political factors contributed to emerging British and American Protestant notions of selfhood and nationhood. If it is true that British imperial culture "was a classic example of an identity that was originally an ideology," as one historian has observed, then this book seeks to cast the life of Whitefield as an embodiment of that formative process in action.[14] Indeed, the best explanation for the long trajectory of the Great Awakening can be found in the dynamic movement from enthusiastic revivals to reified revivalism by way of broader cultural developments that sought to tame a chaotic and sprawling empire.

14. David Armitage, *The Ideological Origins of the British Empire* (Cambridge: Cambridge University Press, 2000), 198.

PART 1

Encounters

CHAPTER 1

A British Explorer

George Whitefield came to Georgia as much a British visitor as a Protestant missionary. A complex mix of motivations attended Atlantic crossings in the eighteenth century and Whitefield, who arrived in May 1738, was subject to the same factors as anyone else. The prospect of a fresh beginning, the allure of untold riches, and the conceit of imperial destiny emboldened adventurous spirits to brave the sea voyage. In an era of widespread expansionist ambitions, the young Whitefield harbored more than evangelistic hopes when he traveled to America in 1738. If his childhood in a Gloucester inn—not far from the port city of Bristol—predisposed him to wanderlust, his Oxford education reinforced an Anglo-centric view of the world that stoked ambitions of carrying British Protestant civilization to remote parts of the world. Situating Whitefield's decision to go to America in the middle of longstanding popular British fascination with the growing edges of empire reveals a key facet of his mission to Georgia. It is therefore important to place the fact of imperial ambitions alongside the Grand Itinerant's revival aspirations in order to yield new insights into the development of evangelicalism. Indeed at the earliest stages of evangelical Protestantism, a vital connection existed between the cause of empire and religion. By uncovering the ways in which Whitefield appropriated cultural trends like Protestant polemics, commercial trade, maritime mobility, and the celebration of individual liberty, this chapter argues that the religious activism of early evangelicals was indebted to a matrix of British imperial factors.[1]

1. For key features of the invention of Britishness in the eighteenth century, see

Seen in this light, Whitefield was not only an evangelist of Protestant renewal but also a British explorer in America.[2] And in a sense this book is a study of the complicated process of forming British national identity in an age of imperial expansion, with a focus on the evangelical Protestant awakenings in North America as one peculiar expression of translating Britishness into a new context. Remembering Whitefield's British identity and casting his life against the backdrop of a larger process of Anglicization help us to see the religious dimensions of imperial ideology and its corresponding impact on religious renewal. A corollary contention is that seeing Whitefield exclusively, or even primarily, as an evangelical religious leader is not enough. Building on important works that have established the signal importance of Whitefield as a revival figure, this study seeks to bring the religious historiography of Whitefield into conversation with broader themes in British Atlantic history.[3]

A period of religious pluralization and growing individualism, the

---

Colley, *Britons*. One effort to problematize Colley's argument and to grapple with the complex contours of the process she describes—for instance the contradictions between empire and liberty—can be found in Armitage, *The Ideological Origins of the British Empire*. This process of translating Britishness into a new context we see in Whitefield and the evangelical revivals is related to, though also distinct from, the process described in Nicholas Canny, *Making Ireland British, 1580–1650* (New York: Oxford University Press, 2003). As provinces of a burgeoning empire, Ireland and the American colonies possessed similar traits, such as a cycle of resistance, accommodation, and integration (uneven at each stage and not necessarily in any uniform order), in which both indigenous peoples and transplanted British subjects participated.

2. There are many works that support the former claim and few that support the latter. Attestations to the central, catalytic role of Whitefield in the evangelical revivals include works like: Stout, *The Divine Dramatist*; Kidd, *The Great Awakening*. For studies in a similar vein with emphasis on Whitefield's commercial strategies, see Frank Lambert, *"Pedlar in Divinity": George Whitefield and the Transatlantic Revivals, 1737–1770* (Princeton: Princeton University Press, 1994); Frank Lambert, *Inventing the "Great Awakening"* (Princeton: Princeton University Press, 1999). For studies that examine the combined force of his religious and political rhetoric, see Jerome Dean Mahaffey, *Preaching Politics: The Religious Rhetoric of George Whitefield and the Founding of a New Nation* (Waco: Baylor University Press, 2007); Jerome Dean Mahaffey, *The Accidental Revolutionary: George Whitefield and the Creation of America* (Waco: Baylor University Press, 2011). For an interpretation of Whitefield's preaching as social protest, see Nash, *The Urban Crucible*.

3. Hence, works in British imperial history and the New British history contribute significantly to this study. See especially Armitage, *The Ideological Origins of the British Empire*; Colley, *Britons*; J. G. A. Pocock, "British History: A Plea for a New Subject," *The Journal of Modern History* 47, no. 4 (1975): 601–21.

first half of the eighteenth century was also a time of imperial state formation and rising nationalism.[4] It was in such a milieu that Whitefield rallied a sprawling, ambiguously defined empire and spurred the Anglicization of the American colonies by preaching a Protestant message that bore a distinct British stamp.[5] His contributions to the cause of the British Empire is a dimension of Whitefield's life and career that historians have overlooked in the rush to explain his revival triumphs. Yet it is difficult to understand the magnitude of that success apart from his contributions to a gathering Britishness—not in lieu of, but in addition to his unmatched gifts in preaching and publicizing. The project of Anglicization and the concomitant call to evangelization were enmeshed in the person and ministry of Whitefield.[6] In recognition of Whitefield's cultural significance, one historian called him a "fashionable import."[7] He was that and much more. A detailed account will show that he was a calculating exporter of British culture who served as a conduit for dynamic cultural exchange in both directions.

4. Pocock describes a "shift toward privatization" as occurring during the transition from an agrarian to a commercial culture in which money displaced relationships as the currency of social order: J. G. A. Pocock, *The Machiavellian Moment: Florentine Political Thought and the Atlantic Republican Tradition* (Princeton: Princeton University Press, 1975), 436. This transition also accompanied a turn toward greater choice and specialization, of the kind that Whitefield so well espoused in his call to personal new birth. A helpful global history that describes well the imperial world into which Whitefield was born can be found in Alison Games, *The Web of Empire: English Cosmopolitans in an Age of Expansion, 1560–1660* (New York: Oxford University Press, 2008). Games's book argues for a broad shift in British activities abroad from commerce to colonization, though she may offer too strict a dichotomy between the two. Whitefield and the evangelical revivals serve to complicate the picture that emerged after the period of Games's book by their exploits across an Atlantic world that was more connected and entangled than merely conquered or settled. To put it another way, both commerce and settlement—in particular the centrifugal force of global expansion and the centripetal pressure of Anglicizing consolidation—were part of the eighteenth century. Linda Colley has likewise argued, "Britishness was constructed and contested after 1707 in response to overseas developments." Colley, *Britons*, xv.

5. For a precise description of the nuanced differences between "English" (Anglicization) and "British" (Britishness), see Chaplin, "The British Atlantic," esp. 226–27. For the purposes of my analysis here, I treat the two terms as synonymous since Whitefield generally equated them in his own usage.

6. For the argument that "British expansion embodied features tied to its Protestant character," see Carla Pestana, *Protestant Empire: Religion and the Making of the British Atlantic World* (Philadelphia: University of Pennsylvania Press, 2009), 14.

7. Lambert, *Inventing the "Great Awakening,"* 92.

By taking the cultural context of Whitefield's revival ministry seriously, this chapter sets the stage for understanding his extensive itinerant career as an illustrative study of the mid-eighteenth-century British Empire. With Georgia, the southern frontier of empire, as the focal point, it becomes easier to see how the interests of Protestant revivalism and British imperialism represented two sides of the same ideological coin. More specifically, they were the twin targets of Whitefield's intensely focused evangelical ambition, such that his efforts to preach for religious revival were at the same time a project of British cultural exportation. The evidence will show that, alongside his role as a revival preacher who traveled the length of the empire for the sake of the gospel, Whitefield also acted as an agent of Britishness.

In order to frame the imperial context for the rest of the book, this chapter focuses on Georgia as (1) the southern frontier of empire and (2) the site of Whitefield's southern strategy. Because of the seemingly counter-intuitive choice of Georgia as the base for his transatlantic ministry, the chapter opens with a background survey of the thirteenth colony in order to elucidate the significance of its location on the southernmost edge of empire. Delving into the early history of Georgia as the southern frontier of empire will set the stage for Whitefield's lifelong work in linking the thirteenth colony to its imperial center. For this reason, the chapter follows up the history of Georgia with a biographical sketch of Whitefield that highlights his participation in the Atlantic world stage as a British subject. In particular, we will see how his background primed him for action on the front lines of empire in Georgia. Once we have established his early preference for the American South, we will be in a better position to identify the reciprocal influence of the era's territorial expansion and religious innovations. A study of the imperial outlines of the revivals illuminates the influence of broader processes in British state formation on the religious life of its subjects.

The chapter concludes with reflections on several theological accents brought into clearer focus by studying Whitefield and Georgia together: his post-Puritan and anti-Catholic orientation as well as his differences with John Wesley, who spent two difficult years in Georgia prior to Whitefield's arrival. Whitefield's revivalist emphasis represented a new way of being British and Protestant that broke with past models and differentiated itself from contemporary alternatives. Along the way, we will see how the spread of British colonialism went hand-in-hand with attempts to rearticulate the significance of old religion for a changing world.

The Southern Frontier in Georgia

When rising Protestant evangelical leaders like John and Charles Wesley, and then George Whitefield three years after them, headed to Georgia, they sailed knowingly into the eye of an imperial storm. For these ambitious individuals, it was not so much the frontier wilderness as the front lines of imperial expansion that captured their imagination. Indeed, the colony of Georgia from its earliest years represented a galvanizing cause for British subjects on both sides of the Atlantic. South Carolina needed a buffer from Spanish Florida. Early explorations mistakenly identified silk and wine as lucrative commodities ideally suited to the Georgia climate with ready buyers in London markets. Philanthropists saw a veritable Garden of Eden in the Georgia environment, where the poor could have a new start. And, not least, fifty years after the establishment of the previous colony in Pennsylvania, the British public was itching for another colonial enterprise. In these ways, geopolitical tensions, social and economic opportunities, philanthropic aspirations, and imperial expediency converged to offer an enticing opportunity for entrepreneurs of every stripe, including the religious. A survey of early Georgia history therefore sets the stage for explaining Whitefield's attraction to the colonial South as part of his larger strategy.

The region of America that became the colony of Georgia in 1732 had been through a tumultuous history of imperial claims and native resistance ever since Ponce de Leon's arrival from Spain in 1513. In the early eighteenth century, tensions mounted with the expansion of British settlements in Carolina and opposing Spanish fortifications in Florida. As a result, multiple skirmishes broke out over what came to be called "the debatable land" in between.[8] 1715 was a cataclysmic year as South Carolina suffered over two hundred fatalities at the hands of the

8. Herbert Eugene Bolton and Mary Ross, *The Debatable Land* (Berkeley: University of California Press, 1925); John Tate Lanning, *The Diplomatic History of Georgia: A Study of the Epoch of Jenkins' Ear* (Chapel Hill: The University of North Carolina Press, 1936); A. A. Ettinger, *James Edward Oglethorpe, Imperial Idealist* (Hamden: Archon Books, 1968).

Yamasee Indians who were leagued with the French and Spanish.[9] Two years later the Lord Proprietors of South Carolina were more than happy to approve Sir Robert Montgomery's petition to establish a military colony in the land between South Carolina and Florida. Naming the region "Margravate of Azilia," Sir Robert sought public support for his work in London by publishing a promotional booklet in 1717 entitled *A Discourse Concerning the Design'd Establishment of a New Colony to the South of Carolina, in the Most Delightful Country of the Universe.* He followed up that effort with *A Description of the Golden Islands,* which appeared in 1720.[10] Despite lush descriptions and grandiose intentions, however, he was unable to secure the requisite number of settlers. His grant expired, the southern borders of South Carolina remained exposed, and opportunities for trade and commerce were left untapped. Not to be deterred by the failure of Azilia, Jean Pierre Purry, a Swiss merchant, in 1724 proposed a British settlement in the same region. Financial constraints also doomed Purry's efforts. In the meantime, due in part to the burden of mounting military defenses in this contested region of the empire, the South Carolina proprietors relinquished their land to the English crown and it became a royal colony in 1729.

Although these various efforts failed to produce their intended outcome, one byproduct of their persistence was the growing awareness among the British public of the pressing need for new settlements in the southern edge of British America. According to one historical account, James Oglethorpe's 1733 arrival in Georgia "symbolized not only the beginning of a new colony but also the culmination of Carolina expansion ideas during the preceding quarter century."[11] In the mind of the British public, this endeavor by Oglethorpe would have been viewed

9. Eric Hinderaker and Peter C. Mancall, *At the Edge of Empire: The Backcountry in British North America* (Baltimore: Johns Hopkins University Press, 2003).

10. Kenneth Coleman, "The Founding of Georgia," in *Forty Years of Diversity: Essays on Colonial Georgia*, ed. Harvey Jackson and Phinzy Spalding (Athens: University of Georgia Press, 1984), 5.

11. Kenneth Coleman pointed out the significance of the frequency of efforts to establish a colony south of Carolina as revealing an empire-wide focus on the southern frontier. He lamented that "no one has heretofore shown in detail that most of the ideas put forth by Oglethorpe and his fellow Georgia Trustees had been suggested several times before the founding of the colony and were current in the colonial circles of London after 1720." Kenneth Coleman, "The Southern Frontier: Georgia's Founding and the Expansion of South Carolina," *Georgia Historical Quarterly* 56, no. 2 (1972): 163–74.

as only the latest extension of earlier attempts. Thus, more than the extracurricular interest of a few idealistic entrepreneurs, the Georgia project as a whole represented *the* signal cause of imperial development in the early eighteenth century. If colonies like Virginia, Massachusetts, and Pennsylvania typified British focus in North America during the seventeenth century, the southern frontier rekindled the thrill of exploration and the promise of colonization in the British expansionist imagination of a new era. The numerous aborted efforts to establish a colony there revealed the difficulties of colonizing America but also the appeal of such an enterprise. The elusiveness of the goal served to reinforce public appetite for a successful venture, laying the groundwork for public opinion to rally around the next protagonist bold enough to undertake the formidable cause.

What followed has not always been clear. The long history of pre-Georgia is complicated by a divergence of historical interpretations and offers an apt reminder of the multiple dimensions of imperial developments. Clarifying the military and philanthropic dimensions of Georgia, and its strategic position for British interests, is important for understanding Whitefield's early attraction to this region. Yet many historians of Georgia have insisted on a sharp dichotomy between military expansion and philanthropic compassion, leading to falsely monolithic impressions of the thirteenth British American colony. For instance, when Jefferson Randolph Anderson argued that "the chief and controlling object and purpose for the founding of the colony was a military one," he also dismissed the role of social idealism at work in early Georgia. In his view, James Oglethorpe and the people he recruited knew well that "they were not entering into any unexplored Eden where . . . they might erect a Utopia away from strife and turmoil."[12] This distinction allowed Anderson to present Georgia as a unique case study, indeed "the only military colony ever sent out from Great Britain."[13] In contrast, other historical treatments have tended to accentuate the charitable nature of Georgia's founding. Ian Steele identified Georgia as a "major transatlantic charity and one that would attract John and Charles Wesley and then, in 1738, George Whitefield."[14] Such interpretive dis-

12. J. R. Anderson, "The Genesis of Georgia: An Historical Sketch," *The Georgia Historical Quarterly* 13, no. 3 (1929): 231.

13. Anderson, "The Genesis of Georgia," 232.

14. Ian K. Steele, *The English Atlantic, 1675-1740: An Exploration of Communication and Community* (New York: Oxford University Press, 1986), 263.

agreements continue to obscure the alignment of religious and political factors at play in the early history of Georgia. Allowing for the simultaneity of these factors, on the other hand, we can better understand the ways in which evangelical leaders like the Wesleys and Whitefield engaged their cultural contexts with religious aspirations. Tracing these early developments shows how a distinctly British Protestant version of religious imperialism—at once militant and philanthropic—blurred traditional boundaries in a time of spiritual upheaval and renewal.

In fact, such conflation of religious and imperial aims was so pronounced that one historian spoke of "ecclesiastical imperialism" to describe the spirit of the age.[15] Dr. Thomas Bray, an early supporter of the Georgia project, exemplified this spirit of ecclesiastical imperialism. Bray had long harbored interest in the cause of religion in America as the founder of the Society for the Propagation of the Gospel in Foreign Parts (SPG) and the Society for the Promotion of Christian Knowledge (SPCK). An influential churchman, he had also served as commissary in Maryland where he mediated the authority of the Bishop of London. In 1723 Bray formed a group called the Associates of Bray to leverage his substantial fortune toward ongoing philanthropic work after his death. His interest in prison reform brought him into contact with James Oglethorpe, who, in 1729, after valorous service in the War of Spanish Succession, was serving as chairman of a parliamentary committee inquiring into the state of British gaols. This reform work united Oglethorpe and Bray in common cause that eventually led to substantial funding by the Bray Associates toward the founding of the Georgia colony.

James Oglethorpe was not only the first chairman of the Bray Associates but also a colonel who possessed political acuity alongside philanthropic sensitivity. It was fitting that he would lead a group of twenty-one men to petition King George II for a colony in the contested land between South Carolina and Florida. In presenting the case for Georgia, Oglethorpe referred to the Greek colonial tradition and highlighted the strategy of Greek city-states that planted colonies "on the frontiers of

---

15. Verner Crane has noted: "To the 'imperialism' of the Carolinians and the Board of Trade . . . there were added the strong currents of English social reform and of that 'ecclesiastical imperialism' of which Dr. Thomas Bray had been for many years the indefatigable leader." Verner Winslow Crane, *The Southern Frontier, 1670–1732* (Ann Arbor: University of Michigan Press, 1956), 303.

their new empire [and] gave a new strength to the whole."[16] One historian has noted Oglethorpe's deft combination of "Machiavellianism with political economy" as well as his reliance on Francis Bacon's "On Plantations," which justified British settlements in Ireland.[17] In other words, Oglethorpe was quite consciously drawing upon a long history of colonial and imperial ideology when he explicitly pitched Georgia as a logical and necessary step in building the British Empire. On June 9, 1732, the Georgia Trustees received their charter; soon thereafter, efforts to gather colonists for the southern frontier gained unprecedented momentum. It helped that nearly two-thirds of the Trustees were also members of Parliament. To a large extent, the success of this latest colonial iteration was owing to the many prominent persons involved who embraced the cause of empire.

What further distinguished Oglethorpe's plans for Georgia from Sir Robert's and Purry's prior failed attempts was the articulation of religious and philanthropic concerns as justification for establishing a colony in the southern frontier. Indeed, publicity concerning a strong religious rationale helped ensure popular support for Georgia. In addition to the long-term benefits of securing the empire's periphery, there would be immediate solutions to problems faced by a broad range of persons in London, from languishing debtors and released prisoners to aspiring entrepreneurs with little room to grow in England. In Georgia they might find greener and more open pastures.

Oglethorpe arrived in America with thirty-five families on January 13, 1733, to the welcome of elated colonists in Charleston. Immediately the military man went to work setting up a military colony. After establishing a settlement in a strategically defensible position at the mouth of the Savannah River, he sent later arrivals such as the Salzburgers from Germany and Highlanders from Scotland to outlying locations—Bethlehem and New Inverness, respectively—that might serve as garrisons.[18] Not content with simply fortifying the colony, Oglethorpe began making plans for an offensive against Spanish Florida by establishing forts farther south on Frederica and St. Simons Island.

Back home in England, Oglethorpe and his associates were out of

16. Excerpt from Oglethorpe's *Account for the Designs of the Trustees for Establishing the Colony of Georgia* quoted in Robert Goon, "The Classical Tradition in Colonial Georgia," *The Georgia Historical Quarterly* 86, no. 1 (2002): 4.

17. Armitage, *The Ideological Origins of the British Empire*, 168.

18. Anderson, "The Genesis of Georgia," 264–66.

sight but not out of mind. This illustrative account appeared in the December 1, 1733, issue of *Hooker's Weekly Miscellany*:

> The Planting of Colonies is of such publick Utility, that we think we cannot do anything more acceptable, than to take Notice of all that occurs material on such Occasions. The new one in Georgia, carry'd on with so much Chearfulness and Ardour by the honourable Trustees appointed for that Purpose, claims our particular Attention.[19]

Describing the attitude of the colonists as marked by "chearfulness" evoked 2 Corinthians 9:7 and served to remind British subjects that the Georgia enterprise should be viewed as an act of pious sacrifice, an offering unto their God. Those familiar with the context of 2 Corinthians would have also heard the apostle Paul's exhortation: the person who "soweth bountifully" may "abound to every good work" (2 Cor. 9:6, 8, KJV).

Ever mindful of the London audience and the need for ongoing public support, Oglethorpe returned to England in 1734, bringing with him the Yamacraw chief Tomochichi, his wife, and other friendly natives. Oglethorpe and the Indians who accompanied him became a national sensation, feted by the King and the Archbishop of Canterbury and receiving glowing praise in the press. When out of the public spotlight, Oglethorpe was busy in the House of Commons and at the Old Palace Yard, where the Georgia Trustees conducted their business. The public tour of Tomochichi and his group had already made the case for the value of humanitarian and religious work in Georgia. By highlighting the French threat from the west, Oglethorpe secured a government grant of £25,800 for Georgia. When he returned to the colony in 1735, he had assembled a group of 257, notable among them a contingent of two hundred Salzburgers expelled from their homeland, the Prince-Archbishopric of Salzburg, by Catholic authorities. Fatefully for the story of George Whitefield, the party also included John and Charles Wesley as well as Benjamin Ingham, members of Oxford's Holy Club.[20] This group of religious reformers had already become notorious for practicing a rigorous piety that would later evolve into the form of evan-

---

19. Cited in Ettinger, *James Edward Oglethorpe*, 141.

20. The expulsion of thirty thousand Protestant Salzburgers transfixed an international audience much affected by their plight. W. R. Ward, *The Protestant Evangelical Awakening* (Cambridge: Cambridge University Press, 2002), 24, 104.

gelical Protestantism that gained much popularity throughout the Atlantic world. Oglethorpe's correspondence with the Wesleys' parents, Samuel and Susanna, helped secure the brothers' commitment to Georgia and evinced his desire for a strong religious life in the new colony.

Unsurprisingly, British activities in Georgia aroused the suspicion of Spanish diplomats in London, who raised a furor and demanded English conformity to the treaty of 1670 that limited English settlements from moving south of St. Helena Sound, South Carolina. On November 29, 1736, Oglethorpe sailed again for England in order to rally support for the Georgia cause, whereupon he made appearances before Parliament and the King. Parrying the diplomatic moves of Don Tomas Geraldino, Spain's ambassador in London, and outmaneuvering the pacifistic prime minister, Sir Robert Walpole, Oglethorpe made the case for Georgia's defense as a matter of urgent security.[21] At the beginning of 1737, he put forward a bold proposal in Parliament for financial investment to back the military mandate he still awaited, requesting £30,000 when he only hoped for £20,000. In August 1737, he was appointed as Brigadier General of His Majesty's forces in South Carolina and Georgia with generous funding to back his mandate, giving him sweeping authority in a strategic corner of the British Empire.[22] Over the course of the next year he worked to recruit additional men and gather munitions needed to mount a military offensive against fort St. Augustine in Florida. On the first of July 1738, Oglethorpe set sail to return to Georgia with a force seven hundred strong.

Thanks to the industry of men like Bray and Oglethorpe, Georgia "assumed a paramount place in European diplomacy" and commanded the attention not only of diplomats but ordinary British subjects in the course of the 1730s.[23] In fact, the southern frontier of mainland North America was—due to imperial holdings in the West Indies—also the geographical center of British territories in that region.[24] The philanthropic vision for Georgia attracted "merchant and minister, visionary

21. Ettinger, *James Edward Oglethorpe*, 184–206; Lanning, *The Diplomatic History of Georgia*, 85–123.

22. Thomas Spalding, *Life of Oglethorpe*, in *Collections of the Georgia Historical Society* (Savannah, 1840), 1:260.

23. Lanning, *The Diplomatic History of Georgia*, 1.

24. British maps of the New World from the early eighteenth century typically placed the region around Georgia at the cartographical center by necessity, due to New England to the north and the West Indies to the south.

and imperialist, middle class and nobility" with the result that "the Trustees were flooded with contributions."[25] The colonial enterprise became yet another site for releasing pent-up desires to improve British culture, and rising prosperity fueled optimism about the entire venture. According to historian Jack Greene, economic, social, cultural, and religious opportunities coalesced, so that "Georgia was to be not just a model colony but a model society for Britain."[26] The Trustees aimed for nothing less than Utopia, an aspiration with practical outworkings on the ground that included limited land tenure and the prohibition of slavery. Through such spartan land and labor policies, the Trustees sought to create a new colony that valued hard work unencumbered by inherited status. In so doing, they issued "both a reaffirmation of old values and a repudiation of the baser tendencies then rampant in British life."[27]

In light of these factors, it is difficult to overestimate the enthusiasm of the British public's response to the Georgia effort that resulted from a two-pronged appeal to imperial and philanthropic sentiments. The Trustees of Georgia fanned the flames of euphoria in the early 1730s by hiring publicists to write about their cause across the empire. Their pamphlets stirred such a fevered pitch of enthusiasm that a highly selective winnowing process turned many applicants away. One historian of Georgia has remarked, "All England was now aroused to the importance of Georgia, and the fervor spread to the British possessions throughout the world."[28]

Phillip Thicknesse, a young servant of the influential Savannah storekeeper, Thomas Causton, described his initial conception of the move to Georgia as "setting out to begin the forming of a new world." Never mind that a world already existed, and that to so many this so-called "new" world was anything but new.[29] His striking language re-

---

25. Kenneth Coleman, *A History of Georgia* (Athens: University of Georgia Press, 1977), 17.

26. Jack P. Greene, "Travails of an Infant Colony," in Jackson and Spalding, *Forty Years of Diversity*, 284.

27. Greene, "Travails of an Infant Colony," 284.

28. E. Merton Coulter, *Georgia: A Short History* (Chapel Hill: University of North Carolina Press, 1960), 20.

29. As one historian has argued, when Europeans came to America, "they meant to create a new world, not leave intact the one they found there." Colin G. Calloway, *New Worlds for All: Indians, Europeans, and the Remaking of Early America* (Baltimore: Johns Hopkins University Press, 2013), 9.

vealed the ambitious self-perception of British expansion as not merely discovering a new world but forging, even creating, a world of new possibilities. So taken was he with the prospect of a new beginning in Georgia that he could not imagine doing anything else with his life: "I felt a delight and a faith not to be removed, nor could at that time any offer, however advantageous in appearance, have diverted me from adding one to the number of the foolish Georgia emigrants."[30] Adumbrations of future struggle aside, Thicknesse's raw enthusiasm points to the ambitious vision that Georgia represented to many Britons. Fueling this excitement was a well-orchestrated scheme of promotional literature. "No other American colony, surely, had so good a press, or so musical a chorus," according to Verner Crane.[31] Religious motivations mingled symbiotically with political, social, and economic concerns, leading to "more than a hundred clergymen and churches set to raising money" for Georgia so that "almost a religious crusade developed."[32] As the money and applicants poured in, "the Trustees set up a sifting process more exacting and rigid than was ever used in securing settlers for any other American colony."[33]

In this context, the rhetoric of the Trustees struggled to keep pace with the enthusiasm their project received. They rose to the occasion with sometimes overwrought descriptions, such as when they claimed their territory lay in the same latitude as the Garden of Eden. They may have remembered a similar observation by Sir Robert that Georgia "lies in the same Latitude with Palestine Herself," the promised land of the Old Testament. The alliance of political, social, and religious vision proved effective; while biblical references helped highlight matters of imperial expediency, there were also propitious religious opportunities on offer. If Georgia was necessary for defending the most hotly contested area of empire, with the French in New Orleans and the Spanish in St. Augustine, it also provided the ideal site for a holy experiment and a fresh outpouring of divine blessing.

As it turned out, the long prelude to the Georgia colony's founding had tested but also intensified its idealistic vision, providing a platform on which someone like Whitefield could hope to build. In

30. Edward J. Cashin, *Setting Out to Begin a New World: Colonial Georgia; A Documentary History* (Savannah: Library of Georgia, 1995), 71.
31. Ettinger, *James Edward Oglethorpe*, 122.
32. Coulter, *Georgia*, 20.
33. Coulter, *Georgia*, 23.

fact, if Georgia was, as Paul Langford wrote, "the brain-child of a group of philanthropic enthusiasts for colonization, who indulged in a potent mixture of patriotism and piety," Whitefield was the ideal candidate to provide spiritual nurture for sustaining the long-term vision.[34] The settlers who came to Georgia ranged from the poor to the middle class who had fallen on hard times. They also came with soaring ambitions to construct "a future guidepost for colonial America."[35] In these ways, Georgia provided an amenable setting for Whitefield's emerging ministry—post-Puritan with sympathies for religious reform yet aggressively Protestant, and by extension anti-Catholic, with the kind of political and polemical features primed for imperial appropriation.

At the same time Oglethorpe was working the corridors of White-hall, Whitefield was preparing to leave for his first tour of America with Georgia as his destination. It was notably a time when the colony's focus was shifting from religious reform to military defense.[36] Since the contrast between such categories was rarely felt in stark terms on the ground, it may be more accurate to say that Whitefield's work in Georgia began during a heightened mood of ecclesiastical imperialism. According to Langford, supporters of the British Empire "fearlessly replanted the education, supervision, and welfare of the lower class to fit it for such a society, [assuming] that British power would maintain [its] international competitiveness."[37] This same group of optimists, among whom we can include Whitefield, also "made due allowance for the provision of godly discipline and pious benevolence in a commercial age."[38] Where a commercial middle class thrived as never before, care for the poor was a way of simultaneously fulfilling religious duty and investing in the cause of a Protestant empire.

34. Langford, *A Polite and Commercial People*, 172.

35. Coleman, "The Southern Frontier," 24.

36. Historian Amos Ettinger divided Oglethorpe's colonial career into three phases: a period of administration and social amelioration (1733–1736), support of religious life in the colony (1736–1738), and imperial defense (1738–late 1740s). Ettinger, *James Edward Oglethorpe*, 129–254. Two striking observations might be gleaned here. First, Oglethorpe's American career embodied distinctly social, religious, and imperial factors. Second, Whitefield's American career began in the period of transition between the second and third phases (namely religious and imperial) of Oglethorpe's work in Georgia.

37. Langford, *A Polite and Commercial People*, 4.

38. Langford, *A Polite and Commercial People*, 4.

Remembering the monumental scale of the greatest philanthropic experiment of the age can deepen our understanding of the catalyzing forces behind early missionary efforts in Georgia.[39] Rather than a form of pietistic flight from the world, it is conceivable that missionaries who traveled to the Georgia wilderness saw themselves engaged in a task of profound cultural engagement. They were throwing themselves headlong into trailblazing philanthropic work that would benefit the whole empire. To live in Georgia was not to sequester oneself in a remote part of the world; it was a means of relocating to what one person called "a sort of cross-roads of the world."[40] With a population that soon consisted of "Piedmontese, Swiss, Salzburgers, Moravians, Germans, Jews, Scotch Highlanders, Welsh, and English," the young colony "had as cosmopolitan a population as could be found in America."[41] Of all places in a rapidly growing empire, Georgia would have appeared to the Wesley brothers and George Whitefield a site well-suited to experimental religion precisely because the project involved building a new society with the enthusiastic backing of London in a key strategic location.

Due to the extended history and widespread publicity surrounding the Georgia project, when missionaries like the Wesley brothers and Benjamin Ingham embarked for the American South in 1736—and George Whitefield in 1738—there was an undeniable imperial dimension to their undertaking. They could hardly have missed the steady stream of pamphlets and newspaper stories extolling the virtues of the Georgia enterprise. They may even have known neighbors and friends who enlisted to become Georgia colonists. The heightened public awareness of this fledgling colony provided sufficient recompense and redeeming vision for these young men to leave the imperial center, giving them some hope of joining a noble and worthwhile cause. For Whitefield, focusing on Georgia paved the way toward active engagement in the empire's growing edge, where instability brought perils but fluidity also created opportunities. Georgia, in other words, represented the freest place in the empire for the work Whitefield intended to do.

---

39. Coulter, *Georgia*, 20.
40. Coulter, *Georgia*, 32.
41. Coulter, *Georgia*, 32.

The Southern Strategy of Whitefield

If it is true that motivations shaped by empire as well as religion led Whitefield to Georgia, a brief biographical survey leading up to his first American voyage will present a fuller picture. Understanding his early years can help explain his fixation on Georgia and the development of his imperial strategy as a religious itinerant. Without dismissing his spiritual convictions, we will see that attention to cultural developments contributed to the direction of his revival labors. A comparison of George Whitefield's and John Wesley's experiences in Georgia will round off this exercise. In a dramatically different storyline, Wesley left the colony so disillusioned with possibilities in America that he exhibited little interest thereafter in matters outside the British Isles. Wesley's short but tempestuous tenure in the thirteenth colony provides a helpful foil for underscoring Whitefield's imperial interests.

Whitefield's Early Life

George Whitefield was born on December 16, 1714, at the Bell Inn in Gloucester to Richard Whitefield and his wife Mary. His father died when he was two years old, and the subsequent marriage of his mother to Capel Longden opened an unhappy chapter marked by financial hardship for the family. At age fourteen Whitefield interrupted his studies at St. Mary de Crypt School to help with maintenance of the inn, where "I put on my blue apron and my snuffers, washed mops, cleaned rooms, and, in one word, became professed and common drawer for nigh a year and a half."[42] Located in southwest England, Gloucester abutted the Severn, the longest river in England, only thirty miles north-

---

42. George Whitefield, *Journals* (Meadow View: Quinta Press, 2000), 44. Quoting from Whitefield's journals involves complex interpretive issues because of their numerous editions and also because he made significant changes in a revised 1756 edition, which has become the most common version though it represents a sanitized version of his earlier, bolder self-presentation. In my citations, I rely on the edition from Quinta Press, which sought to trace the textual changes Whitefield introduced in 1756 by including both deletions and emendations. For a careful description of the publication history of Whitefield's journals, see David Ceri Jones, "'So Much Idolized by Some, and Railed At by Others': Towards Understanding George Whitefield," *Wesley and Methodist Studies* 5 (2013): 7–10.

east upstream from the port city of Bristol. In this bustling city, the inn was a place where travelers shared gossip and news from across the empire. Whitefield's mother learned from one such guest about opportunities for poor students to attend Oxford as a servitor. Thanks to this opportunity, Whitefield became a student at Pembroke College, Oxford, in the fall of 1732, where he financed his education by doing menial chores for his peers. It was not all work and drudgery, however, as he met a lifelong friend in Charles Wesley. Largely owing to this friendship, he joined the Holy Club, a group of students famous in the history of Methodism—and often derided—for the "methods" they employed to express their piety. So fervently did Whitefield embrace their regimen of self-denial and rigorous devotion that he nearly died during the Lenten season of 1735.[43] After a year recovering in Gloucester, he returned to Oxford in the spring of 1736 to complete his education. For his association with these so-called methodists, Whitefield learned the pain of social ostracism as well as habits of endurance. "Some have thrown dirt at me; others, by degrees, took away their pay from me," Whitefield wrote in his journal, all the while becoming "inured . . . to contempt."[44] Though he had no way of knowing, he could have been describing his preaching ministry a few years later.

During those heady days at Oxford, Whitefield's theological influences were wide-ranging. He mentioned in his journals a diverse set of authors from Thomas à Kempis to Juan de Castaniza to Bishop Hall. The books that most influenced him, however, were those given by his close friend Charles Wesley, which included works by the German pietist August Hermann Francke and an anonymous work revered among Oxford methodists, *The Country Parson's Advice to His Parishioners*.[45] Puritan

43. Some of his intensity may have been a consequence of needing to compensate for a sense of social inferiority. Describing Whitefield's initial sense of intimidation from the Wesleys and the Methodists, one biographer wrote: "For more than a year he intensely desired to be acquainted with them, but a sense of his pecuniary inferiority to them prevented his advances." Joseph Belcher, *George Whitefield: A Biography; With Special Reference to His Labors in America* (New York: American Tract Society, 1857), 30.

44. Whitefield, *Journals*, 45.

45. Whitefield, *Journals*, 51. Authors mentioned in Whitefield's *Journals* include: Thomas à Kempis (45, 47, 61), Castaniza's *Combat* (61), Bishop Hall's *Contemplations* (63), Burkitt's and Henry's *Expositions* (68), Alleine's *Alarm*, Richard Baxter's *Call to the Unconverted*, Janeway's *Life* (69), and William Law's *The Absolute Unlawfulness of the Stage Entertainment* (69). The use of the lower case "methodists" helps distinguish from the "Methodist" denomination that later emerged from one stream of the foregoing movement.

authors like Richard Baxter and William Burkitt and the Presbyterian Matthew Henry also made a lasting impression. Not content to regurgitate these authors, moreover, Whitefield would build on their theology to develop his own pathbreaking emphasis on spiritual rebirth. One of the most hard-hitting books for the young Whitefield, upon which he improvised to build his own distinct ministry approach, was Henry Scougal's *The Life of God in the Soul of Man*. It was a Puritan classic that pointed out the worthlessness of outward religious deeds in the absence of inward transformation. The innovation of locating soteriology in the realm of the personal, as Scougal did, emboldened Whitefield to favor individual agency over institutional authority. For Whitefield, this theological emphasis manifested in an irresistible urge to invite individual conversion to as many as would hear him on the matter. If the Holy Club was "an iron-clad regime . . . of human effort, that provided no assurance and left the all-important salvation of the soul but a distant uncertainty," Whitefield found his way to a grassroots spirituality that was more accessible to all.[46] The far-reaching aspirational quality of his ministry derived fuel from the Puritan vision of divine sovereignty but also, over time, cultural validation and empowerment on the broad canvas of a growing empire.

After graduating from Oxford in May 1736, Whitefield received his ordination as a deacon in the Church of England and began preaching to great acclaim in Bristol, London, and surrounding regions. Displaying a daring nimbleness in both doctrine and delivery, Whitefield captivated audiences with the combination of his youthful flair and oratorical force, so that "hearers seemed startled" everywhere he preached.[47] Still, he was at an early stage in his theological development and himself admitted in 1737 that, regarding the doctrine of new birth and justification by faith, "I was not so clear in it as afterwards."[48] As a result, he chastised parishioners and preachers alike, lamenting "the shell and shadow of religion" that they allowed to pass for Christian devotion. In his first published sermon, *The Nature and Necessity of Our New Birth in Christ Jesus, in Order to Salvation* (1737), he absolutized the requirement of an experiential new birth, narrowing the circle of true

46. Arnold A. Dallimore, *George Whitefield: The Life and Times of the Great Evangelist of the 18th Century Revival* (Carlisle: Banner of Truth, 1970), 1:72.

47. Whitefield, *Journals*, 92.

48. Whitefield, *Journals*, 92.

Christianity even as he broadened authentic Christian membership beyond the walls of the national church. A careful student of tradition, he nonetheless displayed a readiness to eschew any inherited constraints that did not comply with his own reading of Scripture.

Whitefield, Georgia, and Empire

Thus far we have focused on the pre-history of Georgia and the early life of George Whitefield. As it happens, the course of Whitefield's life before he left for America reveals how much he was being prepared for ministry on the frontiers of empire. In order to illuminate this point, we are now ready to take note of the significant convergence points between Whitefield as British subject and Georgia as a strategic imperial outpost.

The story of Whitefield in America begins with a geographical puzzle. For despite his ambitious agenda aimed at cultural engagement, the itinerant strangely positioned himself on the margins of empire. Although we will cover this material more fully in the next chapter, a brief snapshot of his early American travels serves to provide some framing questions. From the moment he set foot on American soil, Whitefield conspicuously avoided New England while carefully cultivating ties in the southern colonies. What drew him to the American South and why did he at first show so little interest in the North? Over the course of his first two American trips between May 1738 and January 1741, he devoted almost twenty months to his work in the colonies. Given New England's vaunted importance to religious life in America, it is astonishing that Whitefield spent barely over a month there during this period. Even that short visit did not occur until mid-September 1740 and amounted to merely one-twentieth of his time in the colonies during his first two trips. There can be little doubt that much happened during his famous September journey to key sites of revival such as Boston and Jonathan Edwards's Northampton. Indeed, his New England preaching tour has become the stuff of legend and detailed historical accounts of his fiery evangelism in New England are legion.[49] If it is legitimate to ac-

---

49. See Lambert, *Inventing the "Great Awakening,"* 111–24; Mark A. Noll, *The Rise of Evangelicalism: The Age of Edwards, Whitefield, and the Wesleys* (Downers Grove: InterVarsity Press, 2003), 13–15. Thomas Kidd provides a detailed account of White-

knowledge the significance of his brief ministry in the North, however, it is even more important to grasp his affinity for the South, to which he committed well over two-thirds of his early work in the colonies. What compelled Whitefield to pour so much of his time into Georgia? The answer lies in his awareness of imperial politics and his evolving vision of what it might mean to become a cultural force in the crowded social and political landscape of empire. The fledgling colony offered the ambitious young cleric a broad field of religious, cultural, and political experimentation. Uncovering the central place of Georgia in Whitefield's early American labors helps to reveal the imperial shape of the Great Awakening.

Before he became the catalyst of evangelical awakenings across the British Empire and chief architect of a transatlantic Protestant network, Whitefield dug his roots into southern soil in the American hinterlands, on the far fringe of empire. Neither a place of escape nor a destination of random chance, Georgia represented a strategic location where he was free to nurture a form of religion that was experimental and entrepreneurial. For such an effort, imperial expansion afforded the critical venue. If we recognize that Whitefield was not merely a product of his times but also a perceptive interpreter and aspiring shaper of the world around him, we can detect the same fault lines dividing his world into distinct regions that he apprehended. By focusing on Whitefield's wide-ranging and versatile career we can map out an imperial topography, hierarchically arranged from center to periphery. In this scheme, London takes its expected place in the center, New England occupies the middle ground, and Georgia—along with Scotland and Ireland, which Whitefield also frequently visited—represents the outer periphery.[50] Such a mental geography can help us appreciate the ease with which an itinerant like Whitefield wove in and out and across the empire's internal boundaries and also why he chose to do so. Although many aspects of Whitefield's success lay beyond his control, little was

---

field's initial trip to the southern and middle colonies in chapter 4 before providing a treatment of Whitefield's visit to New England in chapter 7, but he does not seem to detect a southern strategy or orientation in Whitefield; see Kidd, *The Great Awakening*, 40–44, 83–93.

50. My contention throughout this study is that Whitefield sensed what Bailyn and Clive have argued, namely that the cultural provinces of England provided the most fecund setting for cultural innovation. Clive and Bailyn, "England's Cultural Provinces: Scotland and America."

accidental about his selection of Georgia, in addition to London, as the base of his Atlantic operations.

As we will see, Georgia became only more important to Whitefield with the passing of time. In his early career, efforts to raise support for Bethesda Orphanage, which lay a few miles outside Savannah, provided the justification he needed for riding roughshod over parish boundaries and sparking religious awakenings and social disturbances—from Charleston and Boston to Edinburgh and Dublin. After the revivals quieted, he poured energy in his later years into establishing a college in Georgia. Though it is difficult to speculate about hopes and dreams that never materialized, it is worth noting that had Whitefield succeeded in establishing Bethesda College, it would today find its place as a peer of America's oldest universities, including Harvard, Yale, and Princeton. In fact, Bethesda would have wrested from William and Mary the distinction of being the southernmost college in colonial America. That Whitefield attempted such a feat at all shows how important it was that a little-noticed southern orientation undergirded the well-known career of this celebrity preacher.

In light of the observations above, Savannah and its outlying areas represented not only a particular site for spiritual and philanthropic work but also a key location for impacting the empire in its entirety. Whitefield lived during a time of maritime trade that extended across the globe and—by virtue of the pluralistic diversity that ensued—highlighted the need for a more coherent British identity. In this liminal context, the outward expansion and the inward consolidation of British state formation can be seen as complementary and mutually reinforcing processes. In fact, British culture had been shaped by adventures abroad that stretched both east and west. Tea, to highlight one example of a key cultural artifact, was not an English creation but an import from China, adapted and refined to British tastes.[51] Curiosity about and appropriation of the foreign became a marker of British culture precisely because Britishness was in flux and therefore negotiable.[52]

At the very moment when this international consciousness had reached its apogee, therefore, Whitefield provided a connective sinew

51. Troy Bickham, "Eating the Empire: Intersections of Food, Cookery and Imperialism in Eighteenth-Century Britain," *Past and Present* 198, no. 1 (2008): esp. 94.

52. David Hackett Fischer's presentation of folkways as persistent yet never static is helpful here. David H. Fischer, *Albion's Seed: Four British Folkways in America* (New York: Oxford University Press, 1991), 7–8.

between the old world and new. As British fashion flourished in America, the traveling preacher reminded his hearers through the Protestant message that another, more accessible, pathway existed for participating in Britishness. To the metropolitans in London, he provided a bond of unity that went deeper than the sugar and tobacco they enjoyed in their coffee houses and taverns, reminding them that they were part of something larger.[53] In this context of the exchange of British goods, Whitefield proved a theological innovator and religious entrepreneur through his preaching of the new birth, which moved beyond the prevailing national covenantalism of his day in order to call individuals to their own particular experience of salvation.[54]

To put it another way, Whitefield focused on the empire's periphery because he discerned there the most fertile ground for the development of a religious vitality that was truly Protestant, maritime, commercial, and free. These four terms, well known in recent British and Atlantic histories as comprehensive descriptors of imperial ideology, can also provide useful categories for understanding Whitefield's transatlantic ministry.[55]

First, he was a lifelong Anglican with extensive pan-Protestant connections, courting allies across the theological spectrum, from German Moravians and Pennsylvania Quakers to Scottish presbyters and English bishops. The only thing that matched his passion for Protestant unity was his virulent anti-Catholicism.

---

53. Julie Flavell's study captures the two-way exchange between London and America in this way: "If the vision and enterprise of London was transforming America, that wild hinterland was also changing London." She also describes how American exports like sugar, tobacco, and rice not only influenced the economic equation but also the cultural flavor of London. Julie Flavell, *When London Was Capital of America* (New Haven: Yale University Press, 2010), 169–70.

54. While it is generally true, as Pestana has argued, that Whitefield's emphasis on the new birth and dramatic conversion experience was consonant with "the standard sermonic theme of Reformed Christians," the intensity of his insistence on personal repentance was based on the Puritan innovation of "visible sainthood," which marked a departure from the reformers in favoring conversion over covenant. See Pestana, *Protestant Empire*, 193; Edmund S. Morgan, *Visible Saints: The History of a Puritan Idea* (New York: New York University Press, 1963). The interpretive payoff amid a complicated theological debate is that Whitefield was a disruptive theological innovator.

55. For a careful distillation of these descriptors, see Armitage, *The Ideological Origins of the British Empire*.

Second, as a tireless itinerant who took advantage of British maritime advances, Whitefield spent a great deal of time at sea aboard ships and also took a keen interest in military developments all over the empire.[56]

Third, he was an active participant in the commercial revolution, at times a prescient innovator who had an uncanny knack for being in the right place at the right time, along with the entrepreneurial astuteness to use those opportunities to his distinct advantage. His friendship with local merchants like Benjamin Franklin enabled him to gain a foothold in Philadelphia, making it possible to flank his southern strategy with reinforcements in the middle colonies.

Finally, in his multiple clashes with ecclesiastical and political authorities, Whitefield exhibited a marked preference for individual liberty over inherited traditions. For to be free was a necessary precondition of the new birth he so passionately preached. Insofar as these four characteristics revealed a view of the world grounded in an imperial outlook, Whitefield was not only a product of that empire but also one of its most outspoken heralds.

Locating his early labors in the American South not only presented imperial opportunities for Whitefield but also ecclesiastical advantages. In many ways, Whitefield's theological home should have been New England. Indebted to the orthodox theology and pietist spirituality of the Puritans, Whitefield saw his religious project as the renewal of vital Puritanism. Finding distance from Anglican establishment in England and Puritan entrenchment in the colonial North, however, proved an even more pressing strategic consideration. As a place devoid of traditional strictures, Georgia appealed to Whitefield's creative and anti-deferential mindset. There he could allow his post-Puritan proclivities to roam unfettered as he sought to build on the foundation of New England orthodoxy while incorporating new measures made available by the latest advances in commerce and communication. This sense of standing on the precipice of a new moment might explain why despite his dissenting sympathies, which would have found a more congenial environment among theological peers in New England, Whitefield by-

56. Stephen R. Berry, *A Path in the Mighty Waters: Shipboard Life and Atlantic Crossings to the New World* (New Haven: Yale University Press, 2015); George Whitefield, *A Short Address to Persons of All Denominations, Occasioned By the Alarm of an Intended Invasion* (London, 1756).

passed the north and headed south. Aware that New England's Puritan errand into the wilderness was in shambles, he appears to have been intent on initiating an altogether new errand.

Placing Whitefield in the southern context in these ways serves to highlight both the religious and imperial dimensions of his American work. Such geographical attention foregrounds the variety of roles he embraced as a revival preacher and imperial tactician. Historical studies that focus narrowly on Whitefield the preacher have overlooked the significance of his activities as a British subject, cultural architect, and institution builder. Whitefield exhibited both liberal and conservative tendencies, inventive in his proclivity for micromanaging the individual's conversion experience while retaining traditional Puritan connections in his insistence on the sovereignty of a predestinating God. With a transatlantic itinerary betraying ambitions as grand as the breadth of the British Empire, he invested much of his time clearing forests and building an orphanage in the Georgia frontier. More than the idiosyncrasies of an above-average intellect inflamed by religious passions, Whitefield's reasons for pouring so much energy into Georgia flowed from careful, indeed imperial, calculations.

Furthermore, Whitefield's willingness to break with his mentor, John Wesley, provides additional evidence of the new direction he had in mind as he visited Georgia. Before controversy famously erupted between Wesley and Whitefield over free will and predestination, Whitefield began to carve out a markedly different path from Wesley. Evidence from his early days in America further reveals the broader imperial and transatlantic scope of his ambition that led to divergent paths between the two leading evangelicals of their day.

Though the decline of the Puritan movement did not happen overnight, "the defeat of Puritanism and the disarray of Calvinism" is a well-known feature of the long seventeenth century. "What concerned American Protestants, a century after the first planting of Massachusetts Bay, was the sterility—not of colonial soil—but of its spiritual life."[57] By the 1730s, New England's guiding vision of covenant, the confidence of being a chosen people, and the hope of creating a new, godlier society had floundered. The compromise, or innovation, of the halfway covenant

57. See Alan Heimert and Perry Miller, *The Great Awakening: Documents Illustrating the Crisis and Its Consequences* (Indianapolis: Bobbs-Merrill, 1967), xvii; Foster, *The Long Argument*, 290.

in the latter part of the seventeenth century proved inadequate to right the ship in the second generation of the Puritan enterprise in America.[58] Episodic and isolated renewals at the turn of the century were insufficient to the task of restoring a full-orbed Puritan vision. The Protestant project was both in a state of disrepair and poised for dramatic innovation when Whitefield entered the American scene in 1738. The decline of Puritan vitality in New England, the destabilizing plurality and proliferation of religious sects in the middle colonies, and the uncertainties of established Anglicanism in the Chesapeake reflected the difficulties facing a contested British culture transplanted to North American soil.[59]

Nevertheless, where many saw dire challenges, Whitefield sensed emerging opportunities. As far as he was concerned, the time was ripe and the stage ready for significant change. For Whitefield the circumstances called for a geographical shift as much as theological and spiritual renewal.[60] So it was that a hundred years after the great migration of Anglican Dissenters to New England, he sparked a new movement of religious innovation across the Atlantic into America by starting in the South. He began, however, with inchoate notions and half-baked inklings. Halting steps as a visitor in a foreign land helped Whitefield form his impressions and, only later, cast a vision.

58. Morgan, *Visible Saints*. See also Lambert, *"Pedlar in Divinity,"* 24.

59. For a summary of Puritan declension in New England, see Mark A. Noll, *America's God: From Jonathan Edwards to Abraham Lincoln* (New York: Oxford University Press, 2002). For a sobering critique of how ideals of toleration gave way to fear and atrocities in Pennsylvania, see Peter Rhoads Silver, *Our Savage Neighbors: How Indian War Transformed Early America* (New York: W. W. Norton, 2008). For division and volatility in Virginia, see Rhys Isaac, *The Transformation of Virginia, 1740–1790* (Chapel Hill: University of North Carolina Press, 1999). A challenge to Isaac's argument can be found in Lauren F. Winner, *A Cheerful and Comfortable Faith: Anglican Religious Practice in the Elite Households of Eighteenth-Century Virginia* (New Haven: Yale University Press, 2010).

60. In his treatment of the transition from Puritan to evangelical Christianity, Mark Noll links the final displacement of Puritan piety to the ecclesiology of Jonathan Edwards, which in his estimation shifted "emphasis on covenant away from the complex nexus of person, church, and society to a simpler bond between the converted individual and the church." Noll, *America's God*, 45. My study presents two observations based on this argument, having to do with Whitefield's personal contribution as well as his place in the broader movement. First, no one embodied this theological shift more than George Whitefield through his preaching for individual conversion. Second, the disintegration of the Puritan canopy was a long time coming, culminating with Edwards's dismissal in 1750, as Noll argues, but beginning already in the late 1730s with Whitefield's revival preaching tours around the empire.

While he admired his Puritan forebears and sought to restore their vision of vital religion, Whitefield steered clear of New England, the then crumbling center of Puritanism. New England was too territorial, and too ecclesiastically crowded, to allow sufficient breathing room for someone like Whitefield with his creative ambitions. His decision not to go first to New England, however, took place against the backdrop of a tumultuous landscape.

It was during this same period, throughout the vast expanse of the Atlantic world, that numerous subjects of the king sought to retain a sense of connectedness to their British culture even as they scattered across the burgeoning empire. Thus, many historians have tried to make sense of the eighteenth century as a period of both sprawling empire and coalescing British identity.[61] It was during the early eighteenth century that families like that of John Black experienced new levels of mobility and scattered across the Atlantic world, marked by "the peculiarity and particularity of a family that rarely met in the same place."[62] In their case, economic opportunities resulted in a family dispersed throughout England, Scotland, Ireland, Portugal, France, and even the Caribbean. Members of the Black family "clearly identified themselves as British" but also longed for markers that reinforced their identity as Britons.[63]

Subjects of the king derived a sense of national identity, a distinct Britishness, not from their ties to physical territory but from a constellation of political, commercial, and religious associations. This self-conceptualization was in a state of flux due to imperial expansion and in need of clearer articulation. It was during this time that Commodore George Anson made his famed voyage around the world, even if it was "in origin an old-fashioned buccaneering expedition," expressing well the spirit of adventure felt by many Britons. Anson represented some of the wanderlust and bold exploration that characterized the era in which Whitefield made his own Atlantic crossings—thirteen over the

61. David Armitage, "Greater Britain: A Useful Category of Historical Analysis?," *American Historical Review* 104, no. 2 (1999); Jack P. Greene, "Empire and Identity from the Glorious Revolution to the American Revolution," in Marshall, *The Oxford History of the British Empire*, vol. 2; Livesey, *Civil Society and Empire*; Kathleen Wilson, *A New Imperial History: Culture, Identity, and Modernity in Britain and the Empire, 1660–1840* (New York: Cambridge University Press, 2004).
62. Livesey, *Civil Society and Empire*, 133.
63. Livesey, *Civil Society and Empire*, 135.

course of his lifetime.[64] In Georgia, Whitefield, as one among a throng of imperial explorers, found freedom from the fetters of tradition and sought fallow soil for his own groundbreaking work.

The polyglot nature of colonial societies outside New England also appealed to Whitefield, whose own articulation of the Christian message veered from conventional practice and sought to transcend provincial borders. In the view of disgruntled and restless young evangelicals, orthodoxy of the past generation had surrendered too much to Socinianism, Arianism, and deism. Publications like Matthew Tindal's deistic *Christianity as old as the Creation* (1730) and Thomas Woolston's positivistic *Six Discourses on Miracles* (1727–1730) assailed such dearly held doctrines as the pre-existence of Christ, original sin, and the historicity of miracles in the Bible. In response to this steady stream of what they deemed dangerous heterodoxy, the Protestant evangelical revivals of the early eighteenth century represented "a revolt of the young against the irresponsibility of their elders."[65] It was a perilous undertaking, as Jonathan Edwards would discover a decade after the great revival of 1740 when he attempted to reverse some of the innovations made by his grandfather, Solomon Stoddard, at his church in Northampton, Massachusetts. When Edwards moved to require full profession of converting faith prior to receiving admittance to the Lord's Table, he found himself embroiled in a conflict that resulted in dismissal from a parish he had served for more than twenty years.[66] Edwards's difficult experience suggests why Whitefield sought a base of operations far from the entrenched authority of those very elders whom he wanted to challenge.

As much as evangelicalism during this period represented a desire to return to the familiar tenets of traditional faith, the outlook of young evangelicals like Whitefield also sought creative adaptation to the present. On the one hand, Whitefieldian revivalists longed for a renewal of historic orthodoxy. Yet, they displayed theological nimbleness that increasingly privileged the experience and judgment of individuals in a context of market expansion and devolving social hierarchies. That is to say, although evangelicals saw themselves in competition with a range of Enlightenment principles throughout the eighteenth century, they

64. Langford, *A Polite and Commercial People*, 174.

65. Langford, *A Polite and Commercial People*, 238. See also ch. 3 in Noll, *America's God*.

66. George Marsden, *Jonathan Edwards: A Life* (New Haven: Yale University Press, 2003), 341–56.

also found themselves caught up in the shifting cultural waters, sharing a common iconoclastic spirit, or "the rejection of scholasticism, or inherited wisdom, as the basis of knowledge."[67] Impatient with the constraints of traditionalism, Whitefield sought to find room for an improvisational spirituality. In this respect, he typified the early modern impulse to embrace a commonsense pathway to truth. It is hard to deny that Whitefield for all his claims to orthodox faith was a pioneer of experimental religion. Beyond the dangers of free-ranging itinerancy disrupting parish boundaries and the established social order, there were more substantive, if subtler, changes afoot—such as the segregation of "the experience of conversion from the life of faith."[68] Whitefield was a catalyst of change during an era undergoing myriad transformations.

Seeing Whitefield as a transitional figure in this way helps us perceive the changes he inaugurated. "The twenty-five-year-old Whitefield, cocksure and anything but knowledgeable, set the actual terms of the debate over the New England way," wrote Stephen Foster at the end of his book examining the long seventeenth century of Puritan influence. This backhanded compliment, echoing the prevailing view of Whitefield as a lightweight thinker with oversized zeal, nevertheless recognized that Whitefield, for all his early foibles, initiated and frequently exacerbated longstanding debates with deep historical roots.[69] Foster pointed out the ways in which Whitefield "finally unleashed the sectarian impulses" long brewing "within the Puritan movement in America."[70] In so doing, Whitefield unwittingly abetted the process that "fatally rupture[d] the Puritan movement," which was already a "long time dying."[71] Using Whitefield to provide a dramatic bookend to his work on English Puritanism in New England, Foster's influential work offered penetrating insights into sharp discontinuities between the seventeenth and eighteenth centuries. He neglected, however, to provide for Whitefield the long view that he has so helpfully developed (and defended) for English Puritanism in New England culture.

One unfortunate consequence of Foster's otherwise helpful analysis was that he ripped Whitefield out of his southern context. This is

67. Landsman, *From Colonials to Provincials*, 6.
68. Landsman, *From Colonials to Provincials*, 6. Landsman does not make the link to Whitefield, but this was clearly, at least in part, a Whitefieldian contribution.
69. Foster, *The Long Argument*, 295.
70. Foster, *The Long Argument*, 303.
71. Foster, *The Long Argument*, 290.

a mistake that many other historians have made in their treatment of Whitefield. Yet any understanding of the meaning of his life and career for the Atlantic world of the eighteenth century must bear in mind where and how the Grand Itinerant started his ministry in America.[72] It was not a matter of mere circumstance that he began his American labors in Georgia, a place to which he would return time and again until the end of his life. He dwelled on Georgia in his letters, in his preaching, and in his ceaseless fundraising for Bethesda Orphanage. He came back often to Georgia to refresh his spirit and refocus his mind, Bethesda being one of the few places where he could find rest and repose. Toward the end of his life, Whitefield, erstwhile critic of "the establishment," would spend a great amount of time and energy trying to build a college, an eminently establishment-like institution, in Georgia. In this way, his work in the thirteenth colony—and not New England—can serve as the key to Whitefield's transatlantic career, unlocking hidden trajectories strewn across his peripatetic life.

By the early eighteenth century, idealistic visions of creating an improved, more virtuous British society in New England had given way to sober assessments of religious decline and economic recession. Hope drifted south as urban centers like Philadelphia and New York grew in the middle colonies, tobacco production flourished in the Chesapeake, and rice and cotton reaped large profits in South Carolina. Fresh efforts concentrating on Georgia during this time merely continued the trend of new ventures pushing against existing boundaries. In other words, there were good reasons for Whitefield to set his sights on the American South.

Wesley in America

As yet another way to think about the evangelical spirit and empire, it may be helpful to leave Whitefield for a moment and take a slight chronological detour to consider a close contemporary. A snapshot of John Wesley's turbulent tenure in Georgia can help us appreciate Whitefield's contrasting, and enduring, success there. Wesley arrived in Georgia in February 1736, two years before Whitefield, and promptly made himself a thorn in the sides of many colonists through his sanc-

72. Kidd, *The Great Awakening*, 43–44, 50–54.

timonious dealings. In one notorious incident, the souring of his relationship with Sophia Hopkey resulted in dramatic repercussions. When
William Williamson proposed to her, Wesley became a wreck, going to
her uncle "with grief and tears," pleading for intervention because he
"himself desired to marry her."[73] Unable to stop the marriage, Wesley
held a grudge against the couple. He withheld communion from her
and exacerbated matters by publishing false accusations against her
husband "of something notorious which in due time he would make
appear."[74] Thomas Causton, an influential merchant and Sophia's uncle, came to their aid by bringing a libel suit against Wesley. A grand
jury inquiry ensued, leading to Wesley's ignominious flight from the
colony by cover of night.

It is telling that the grand jury formed on the occasion of that
suit could hardly focus on the matter of the scandal, discussing at
length instead the dire straits of the colony and seizing on the opportunity to publicly air their grievances. In a document signed by
thirty-seven of Savannah's leading citizens, the grand jury took this
opportunity to register complaints with the colony's Board of Trustees, tacking on mention of the Wesley-Hopkey affair only in the last
page, as if an afterthought. Beginning with the fact that "the want of
Publick Roads in this Town and County is a great discouragement,"
they listed many other problems.[75] It may seem strange that a court
session called to discuss ecclesiastical and social conflict over regu-
lation of holy communion should devote most of its time addressing Savannah's "utmost need of a Good Wharfe and a proper Crane"
in order to accommodate the "Landing of Goods." The signatories
would have protested that their very livelihood was at stake, with religious matters and social offenses, under such severe conditions, of
only secondary importance.

There are many good explanations for John Wesley's failed tenure
as a missionary in America during 1736–1738.[76] Only some of them,

73. Allen Daniel Candler, *The Colonial Records of the State of Georgia* (Atlanta:
Franklin Printing and Publishing Company, 1904–1906), 5:61.
74. Candler, *Colonial Records*, 5:61.
75. Savannah Grand Jury, MS 690, Georgia Historical Society.
76. "I came to convert the Indians, but, oh, who will convert me?" Wesley wrote
in his journal. His famous conversion at Aldersgate would take place upon his return
to England, on May 24, 1738. This spiritual lament glossed over drastic failures in his

however, had to do with the man himself. Wesley was still a novice pastor who had yet to experience the new birth that he would soon exhort upon the masses. Nevertheless, if there were personal deficiencies, there were also external obstacles. Whereas New England represented the established religious center of British America with a storied, if also contested, hundred-year record, a new colony like Georgia seemed to offer fresh, new opportunities. Yet Georgia, established only in 1732 and settled with the outcasts of English society, proved to be inhospitable soil for Wesley's style of religion. With his Oxford Holy Club days just behind him, Wesley had come to Georgia looking to scale new spiritual heights. As it turned out, he found valleys and plains instead—including failures as a minister and numerous disputes with Georgia's colonists that led to the scandalous lawsuit and his abrupt flight from the colony. Before his heart could be "strangely" and famously warmed at Aldersgate back in England in May 1738, he had to undergo heartache in the Georgia wilderness. Though Georgia appealed to Wesley as a site for missionary work, the land proved intractable and the people inured to his ministerial labors.

In short, Wesley faced roadblocks and frustrations in Georgia because he failed to adjust expectations based on his location on the imperial map. He operated in the outer margins of empire as if he were still in the center; he related to the colonists in Georgia as if they were Londoners ensconced in the very heart of the empire. To Georgia, Wesley brought crates full of pamphlets, expecting the colonists to spend time reading and studying along with him. He gave lectures, chock full of the erudite learning he gained at Oxford, but they fell on deaf ears in a colony where people scraped by, unsure of provisions for the next day.

In contrast, Whitefield had a high degree of geographical awareness and sensitivity to imperial context. More specifically, he knew he was coming to an outpost of empire that was nevertheless deeply connected to, and with lingering fascination for, the center of that very empire. As the narration in our next chapter shows, Whitefield would approach Georgia in a sharply different manner than Wesley. He came to the colonies bearing the commercial goods of empire, convinced that the conduction of British culture was an essential part of the service he might render unto this distant settlement. From the beginning,

---

ministerial labors and numerous incidents highlighting Wesley's incompatibility with Georgia colonists.

moreover, he approached Savannah as a base for his American itinerancy. Whereas Wesley presumed life in Savannah should be like life in London and expressed disdain when his misplaced hopes were disappointed, Whitefield knew the two were nothing alike. He also held fast to the conviction, however, that with patience, effort, and the largesse of fellow imperial subjects back home, he could turn even this colonial hinterland into another British metropolis. With Calvin's Geneva, Winthrop's Massachusetts Bay Colony, and Francke's Halle as inspiring precedents, it was not unreasonable for Whitefield to believe that he could recast Savannah for the sake of a higher cause. As we have seen, Whitefield fit into Georgia as a hand in a glove, even as he set his sights on more ambitious imperial ventures.

Conclusion

When we observe how Whitefield began his work in America with the attitude of an imperial emissary as well as evangelical missionary, we can better appreciate the transformations that took place to turn him subsequently into an American icon and by the end of his years an advocate for American life and liberty. As a British visitor to America, Whitefield arrived with all the preconceptions of a highly educated Englishman but also the malleability of a foreigner in unfamiliar territory. Whitefield in 1738 was young, brash, and prone to many errors. Historians have made ample note of his record on these counts.[77] But he was also an attentive pupil—of British history, of Puritan divines, of the Wesleys (including some of their mistakes), and of colonial life in general. In other words, he read his Georgia context carefully. He paid attention to its nuances and textures. He listened to the people there and quickly won a following where John Wesley had left a mess. These were not the exploits of a mere self-centered prodigy, but a forward-looking strategist.

In a distant colonial outpost—snubbed by northern elites, overlooked by cosmopolitan Britons, and abandoned by the Wesley brothers—Whitefield found the cause of a lifetime. From the beginning,

---

77. Perhaps most memorably, Bruce Hindmarsh has written: "Placing some 600 pages of autobiographical prose on public record while still in one's twenties leaves plenty of time to repent one's mistakes. And Whitefield did come to regret much of what he had written." Hindmarsh, *The Evangelical Conversion Narrative*, 108.

Whitefield saw Georgia as fertile soil into which he could transplant British religion and culture. By the end of his life, the place would work a profoundly formative effect on him. Neglecting the southern orientation of Whitefield's work in America, therefore, obscures pivotal narrative themes not only in Whitefield's life but in British Atlantic society and culture. For all these reasons, a careful reexamination of his early career in Georgia is necessary for understanding the imperial Whitefield.

CHAPTER 2

A British Emissary

Having placed Whitefield and Georgia in their eighteenth-century context of empire, we will focus in this chapter on the details of Whitefield's early American itinerary in order to trace his development as an actor on the imperial stage. Savannah may not have been impressive in appearance, but it spurred Whitefield's imagination in ways that would direct and sustain his work for the rest of his life. It was a place where the acquisition of new territory, the evangelization of both indigenous peoples and transplanted Britons, and the drive for religious renewal coalesced in dramatic fashion. In this context, Whitefield chose Georgia well aware of its defensive position against the Spanish Catholic threat emanating from Florida. If there were perils to working on the outskirts of empire, there were also strategic advantages. Furthermore, even as Whitefield's itinerations disturbed the established order, they prompted social entrepreneurship by tapping into commercial trade networks, constructing educational institutions, and spreading the gospel of the new birth using innovative methods in communication.[1] With close attention to activities spanning his first two American trips, this chapter will reveal that whereas he had little patience for the plodding work of revitalizing old religion in New England, he quickly warmed to the prospect of establishing a new beachhead of British Protestantism in the growing edge of empire. Whitefield's early fixa-

---

1. See Lambert, *"Pedlar in Divinity"*; Edward J. Cashin, *Beloved Bethesda: A History of George Whitefield's Home for Boys, 1740–2000* (Macon: Mercer University Press, 2001); Harry S. Stout, "Religion, Communications, and the Ideological Origins of the American Revolution," *The William and Mary Quarterly: A Magazine of Early American History* 34, no. 4 (1977): 519–41.

tion on Georgia helps explain the entanglements of Protestant religion and British culture.

But there is more. Inasmuch as Whitefield was an agent of Anglicization, it was not a straightforward, unidirectional process where he brought the light of British Protestantism to the empire's outer borderlands.[2] To be sure, he functioned with a straightforward vision of missionary engagement as he visited remote lands to preach the Christian gospel. Without realizing it, however, he stepped into cross currents of cultural translation that flowed in multiple directions.[3] A study of Whitefield in America shows what was possible for those pushing against the age's inherited social boundaries at the very edge of what might be called Greater Britain; but it also reveals processes of change that the message and its messenger underwent—whether of culture or religion or politics—upon entering a new context. In the end this is a story about how Whitefield sought to renew religious life in America and experienced a transformation of his own.

Whitefield first came to America as a young and unseasoned British visitor, but what he experienced broadened his vision of a Protestant Atlantic world. We will see that he came to function not only as a Protestant missionary but also a British emissary in the course of his journeys throughout the American colonies, preaching evangelical religion while embodying the virtues of Britishness from the beginning of his ministry in America. The brevity of his first trip to the colonies can obscure the important role it played in shaping the rest of his transatlantic career. By giving due weight to his first American tour and paying attention to imperial dimensions throughout, we are able to expand our vision of Whitefield as more than just a famous revival preacher. Furthermore, we will examine how his return to London and subsequent planning for another trip to Savannah further contributed to his evolving strategy, even as his tours around the British countryside apparently delayed his return voyage. Far from distracting him from his American focus, however, the time in England solidified his intentions to labor on behalf of the entire British Empire, beginning with a foothold in the American

2. For Whitefield, "Anglicization" meant a presentation of British cultural, religious, political, and social standards as the normative rule for the enlightened, or godly, life.

3. See "The Translation Principle in Christian History," in Andrew F. Walls, *The Missionary Movement in Christian History: Studies in the Transmission of Faith* (Maryknoll: Orbis Books, 1996), 26–42.

South. The chapter concludes with a reflection on the significance of Whitefield's burgeoning imperial perspective and the evangelical predilection for political activism from its earliest stages.

Before joining Whitefield on the shores of Georgia, it is worth noting that there is a personal side to this story that reflects a larger reality about transformations in mobility and identity in the Atlantic world. The details of his early life established a different trajectory than the lives of contemporaries like John Wesley or Jonathan Edwards. In order to harness Whitefield's biography without surrendering to deterministic reductionism, this study will pay careful attention to the contingencies of the eighteenth century that also impinged on Whitefield's career. Identifying the factors in his life that contributed to his affinity for Georgia helps us see Whitefield as a person deeply affected by, and engaged with, his world—and not merely a preacher dissociated from time and place, waxing eloquent about timeless truths. Whitefield's socioeconomic provenance, his religious aspirations as well as insecurities, and his eventual impact on British Atlantic culture, all highlight the significant fact that he chose to start his American career in a remote plot of land outside Savannah, Georgia, in the spring of 1738.

Whitefield's First American Trip, May–September 1738

In May 1738, the *Whitaker* cast anchor near Tybee Island off the coast of Georgia, and Whitefield set foot in America for the first time. As workmen unloaded his cargo, the sophisticated thinking of an entrepreneurial mind was already on display. His packing list included an assortment of medicine, stationery, household tools, and a variety of clothing items—enough merchandise to stock the general store in Savannah for several months and spawn a few specialty shops as well. To be sure, Whitefield first and foremost meant to bring a message of spiritual rebirth. In addition to his spiritual mission, however, Whitefield brought British goods and culture with him. A close examination of the commercial sensibilities he evinced during his first two American visits reveals the close connections that existed among religious awakening, commercial entrepreneurship, cultural diffusion, and military imperialism. To the extent that Whitefield combined these potent forces from the beginning of his career, he helped set in motion an intermixing of religious consumerism and imperialism that long influenced the character of American religion.

The cargo Whitefield brought with him provides a glimpse into the work he intended to accomplish in America. In contrast to Wesley who packed little besides books and treatises, Whitefield came to Georgia bearing gifts from the bounty of a rich imperial metropolis. Shoes, stockings, hats, flannel waistcoats, and breeches lay in the belly of the *Whitaker* next to medicinal products such as rhubarb, senna, manna, Jesuit's bark, pearl barley, and so on. Cheese, wine, raisins, cinnamon, sugar, oatmeal, oranges, sage were packed alongside stationery such as sealing-wax, lead-pencils, and ingredients to make ink. Luke Tyerman provides a detailed list of Whitefield's cargo, concluding, "Wesley's ritualism repelled the people; Whitefield's donatives attracted them."[4] In addition to helping Whitefield gain trust and popularity, the goods he transported across the Atlantic reveal the mind of a consummate strategist at work.

Rather than a minor and incidental difference, their contrasting inventories reveal the chasm separating Wesley's and Whitefield's understanding of Christian ministry in a transatlantic context. Whitefield likely saw much of the empire through his experience of growing up in a Gloucester inn near the Severn River. From the traffic that passed through this family establishment, Whitefield gained a sense of the expansive world that existed outside his small corner in Gloucestershire. Aware that he lived and worked in an "empire of goods," the young preacher began his ministry in America by tapping into this world and deploying worldly means to religious advantage.[5] He believed in the power of commercial goods to attract the people of Georgia to the message he preached. Aware of destitute conditions in Georgia, he sought to inject the hope of imperial bounty into this colonial hinterland. Before Whitefield had established contractual agreements with Benjamin Franklin to publish and disseminate his writings (for which he is better known), in fact before he set sail for America from a bustling London port, he already had a commercial strategy sketched out in his mind.[6]

4. Luke Tyerman, *The Life of the Rev. George Whitefield, B.A., of Pembroke College, Oxford*, 2 vols. (London: Hodder and Stoughton, 1876), 1:108.

5. T. H. Breen, *The Marketplace of Revolution: How Consumer Politics Shaped American Independence* (New York: Oxford University Press, 2004).

6. Frank Lambert, "Subscribing for Profits and Piety: The Friendship of Benja-

Political realities on the ground further primed the colonists to receive a missionary hailing from the metropole. Whitefield arrived in Georgia during a period of military ascendancy against the Spanish. General Oglethorpe, the founder of the colony and its most fervent protector, had made progress securing the southern areas of Georgia against Spanish aggression in Florida. In 1736, ignoring protestations from the Spanish, he established Fort St. George at the mouth of the St. Johns River. The following year, Oglethorpe traveled to England to secure Parliamentary appropriation toward the raising of a regiment and the appointment of his ally, Samuel Horsey, as governor of South Carolina. During the summer of 1738, Oglethorpe and his men were on Jekyll Island, laying the foundations for a defense against the Spanish in Florida.

On the ecclesiastical front, John Wesley and his meddlesome ministry were a distant memory and settlers in Georgia were ready to make peace with their new minister. Revealing some surprise at these favorable early circumstances, Whitefield wrote a friend on June 10, 1738: "America is not so horrid a place as it is represented to be."[7] Already thinking about educational initiatives, Whitefield made long-term plans for "settling little schools in and about Savannah; that the rising generation may be bred up in the nurture and admonition of the Lord."[8] Whitefield harbored a grandiose vision from the start and "settling little schools" manifested his desire to make an impact on the social well-being of the colony. Rather than bifurcate religious renewal and social improvement, he saw them as two sides of the same coin. Whitefield's reports back home displayed a wide-ranging interest in diverse aspects of colonial life, including thorny economic issues. He complained in one letter about the prohibition on slavery, bemoaning that "to place people there on such a footing [without the advantage of enslaved labor], was little better than to tie their legs and bid them walk."[9] Despite

---

min Franklin and George Whitefield," *The William and Mary Quarterly* 50, no. 3 (1993): 529–54; Lambert, *"Pedlar in Divinity."*

7. Whitefield to Mr. H., June 10, 1738, in George Whitefield, *The Works of the Reverend George Whitefield M.A.*, 7 vols., ed. John Gillies (London, 1771–72), 1:44. Hereafter *Works*.

8. Whitefield to Mr. H., June 10, 1738, in *Works*, 1:44.

9. John Gillies, *Memoirs of the Life of the Reverend George Whitefield, Faithfully Selected From His Original Papers, Journals, and Letters* (London: Edward and Charles Dilly, 1772), 31.

challenges on the ground, however, Whitefield had "hopes, that, un-promising as the aspect might be, the colony might emerge in time out of its infant state."[10] It was not a far stretch for Whitefield, who had also risen from lowly ranks, to envision a future more hopeful for Georgia. "Their beginnings as yet are but small," he acknowledged, "but I cannot help thinking there are foundations being laid for great temporal and spiritual blessings in Georgia, when the inhabitants are found worthy."[11] Whitefield understood the present challenges of Georgia but also saw a promising future. In his Georgia philanthropy, he not only recognized a stepping stone to greater opportunities elsewhere; he identified Georgia itself as the future site of British greatness and bound up his own fate with the infant colony.

The same Thomas Causton who had brought suit against Wesley for slandering his niece Sophia Hopkey welcomed Whitefield to Savannah with open arms a year later. The preacher who had just taken London by storm appeared sensible of the need for polite humility in Savannah, recording in his journal: "In the afternoon, Mr. Causton sent word, that he and the magistrates would wait upon me; but I chose rather to wait upon them" (177). It was clear from the beginning that Whitefield would prove to be a different kind of minister than Wesley. He quickly comported himself in his Georgia surroundings as a visitor in need of orientation. "I have endeavoured to let my gentleness be known amongst them, because they consist of different nations and opinions; and I have striven to draw them by the cords of love, because the obedience resulting from that principle I take to be most genuine and lasting" (183). Ever the shrewd tactician, he began his American career with a listening tour.

Only a week after his arrival Whitefield sought audience with Tomo-chichi, the King of Yamacraw and a friend of General Oglethorpe. This leader of the Creek Indians had himself traveled to England and met with King George II in 1734. Whitefield's initiative toward this influential figure fit into a carefully crafted strategy. It was not all smooth sailing for Whitefield, however, as "there was nobody who could talk English, so I could only shake hands and leave him" (178). Whitefield returned four days later, only to find that Tomochichi had died. Rather

10. No date given, but likely in June 1738; Gillies, *Memoirs*, 32.
11. July 18, 1738, entry in Whitefield, *Journals*, 182. For the rest of this section, page references from this work will be given in parentheses in the text.

than sympathy, as one might expect, Whitefield's response came in the form of a harsh word: "But alas, how can a drunkard enter [heaven]!" (178). He may have been a foreigner in a new land, but he maintained the superiority of his British and Protestant judgments.

From the beginning of his time in Georgia, Whitefield looked for opportunities amid the dire, discouraging conditions. "Surely they speak not truth, who say that the Georgia people have been idle; for I never saw more laborious people than are in these villages" (177). It was during this time, in his search for encouraging "useful members of the Colony," that he articulated an early vision for the Bethesda Orphanage: "Nothing can effect this [i.e., improvements that the colony needed] but an Orphan House, which might easily be erected at Savannah, would some of those who are rich in this world's goods contribute towards it" (178). This early move was significant for Whitefield, as Georgia became not only his first missionary charge but also a foundation for future ministry. Similarly, when he appointed one of his traveling companions to be a teacher in the villages of Highgate and Hempstead, he expressed a desire that the French-speaking children there might "be naturalised to the colony till they can talk our language." He also evinced a long-term vision when he wrote of his hope that "the present [French-speaking] generation will soon wear off." With each subsequent generation, he was confident that "these children being well instructed in ours, will make them forget their own tongue." He saw ahead to a time when "at length we shall all be of one speech" (180).

In Whitefield's view, Georgia was a colony that would not only absorb and naturalize French children but also benefit from "the order and industry" of German-speaking Salzburgers who settled Ebenezer, twenty-five miles north of Savannah. The Salzburgers had migrated to Georgia in 1734, fleeing persecution by Catholic leaders in their homeland, present-day Bavaria. While they lived apart from the British colonists, they represented a vital piece of the diverse Protestant culture that comprised the thirteenth colony. For their industry and philanthropy, they became model citizens in Georgia's early years.

In telling fashion, Whitefield the missionary was most impressed by their work on the land that yielded "the best crop of any in the colony" (181). With similar concerns in view, when Whitefield preached before Georgia officials only four days earlier, he had "endeavoured with all plainness and humility to show both them and the people what they ought to do to promote their *temporal* and eternal welfare" (181; emphasis added). Not only did he want the settlers in Georgia to experience religious renewal, he also sought ways in which the people of the colony could improve their lives in general. In this way he exhibited both a spiritual and social agenda. When he returned to Savannah on July 18, he once again voiced these far-reaching hopes for the colony. About the condition of several families, he wrote, "Their beginnings as yet are but small; but I cannot help thinking there are foundations being laid for great *temporal* and spiritual blessings in Georgia, when the inhabitants are found worthy" (182; emphasis added). This vision of a thriving British society in America included the ability of the empire to assimilate strangers. When he found children in a Savannah school who, "though foreigners, answered admirably well," the experience "gave [him] great hopes that the other foreign children of the colony may also learn [the] English tongue" (187).

By the time his first American trip came to an end, Whitefield had succeeded in winning the hearts of Georgians, including members of the elite merchant class. Thomas Causton became an avid supporter of Whitefield, provided the boat for his journey out, and even went out personally to bid Whitefield farewell, likely conveying the community's hope for his speedy return.

After traveling no farther north than South Carolina, Whitefield made Charleston the last stop on his first American tour. While still absorbing all that he had encountered over the previous three months, he met with Alexander Garden of Charleston, who as commissary in that city represented the Bishop of London in South Carolina. Garden and Whitefield would later become bitter enemies but in 1738 Garden encouraged Whitefield to establish a future foothold in Georgia—an action he surely came to regret. According to Whitefield, Garden "said something . . . about the colony of Georgia, that much encouraged him, as if he thought its flourishing was not very far off; and that Charleston was fifteen times larger now, than when he (Mr. Garden) first came there."[12] The prospect of such exponential growth transfixed Whitefield. That Garden, who would become so hostile toward Whitefield during his second American visit, encouraged Whitefield at the end of his first visit provides evidence that Whitefield was in an exploratory frame of mind at this early stage, eager to listen and learn.

Georgia clearly captured the young missionary's imagination.

12. Gillies, *Memoirs*, 33.

After returning to England, Whitefield found it hard to get the colony out of his mind. When a packet of letters from his associate, James Habersham, who looked after his affairs in Savannah, brought bleak news, Whitefield expressed genuine sorrow that "the colony seems to be at a low ebb. Poor Georgia!" As it happened, this news arrived when he was facing stiff opposition back in England, and his thoughts on Georgia could have applied to his own situation: "When thou art universally despised and quite despairest of human help, then will God manifest His mighty arm in thy salvation" (226). While he was itinerating in Ireland a few months later, Georgia was still on Whitefield's mind. "America, infant Georgia, is an excellent soil for Christianity," he wrote a friend in November 1738, three months after he had departed from his Georgia friends.[13] No sooner did he land in England than he began making plans for his return trip to America.

It is important to keep in mind that Whitefield saw in the colonies not merely fertile soil for Christian ministry but a key outpost for British expansion. A few weeks after Whitefield left Georgia, Oglethorpe wrote on September 19, 1738, "The Inhabitants are extreamly cheerfull and now hope that they have seen the worst over and that being no longer troubled with alarms they may on with their Improvements." Writing approximately a year before the resumption of military conflict with Spanish Florida, Oglethorpe was referring to the calm before the storm of the War of Jenkins' Ear that broke in 1739. Despite the governor's rosy report, military scuffles persisted and Oglethorpe continued to send his soldiers on reconnaissance missions as a way of posturing against the Spanish throughout the latter period of the 1730s. He nonetheless held out hope that peace could be achieved and that prosperity might take hold. Whitefield's vision for his own American work took shape in the midst of these British military realities as he arrived in the face of specific and detailed Spanish threats from St. Augustine, Florida. Far from dissuading him, these circumstances appear to have galvanized Whitefield. During a time of rapid advances in travel and commerce, Whitefield became increasingly obsessed with the outermost margins of the empire—"in the very tail of the world," to use his words.[14] In this

13. Whitefield to Mr. —, November 16, 1738, in *Works*, 1:45.
14. Gillies, *Memoirs*, 45.

space, he apprehended numerous practical constraints but also boundless possibilities.[15]

The Development of an Imperial Strategy

With his first trip to America under his belt, Whitefield was in a position to devise an action plan for his work in the colonies. Toward that end, one of his goals as he returned to England was to be ordained a priest. But another goal was to see how much he could leverage his popularity in order to collect funds for the numerous causes he envisioned going forward in America. If his first American trip was a listening tour, the second would prove to be his dramatic debut. The return to England in December 1738, therefore, paved the way for Whitefield's sensational revival tour in the fall of the following year. With feet planted firmly on both sides of the Atlantic, so to speak, his imperial program could finally commence. In that sense, his time back in England was a key season for the development of a transatlantic strategy.

After a harrowing sea voyage and on the brink of disaster, with only "half a pint of water left," Whitefield's ship from America landed in Ireland on November 14, 1739 (201). There he witnessed poverty exceeding what he saw in the colonies, leading him to remark, "If my parishioners at Georgia complain to me of hardships, I must tell them how the Irish live" (204). Whitefield also wrote about Irish foibles such as their seeming inability to measure distance, apparently finding humor in what he saw as deficiencies: "Their innocent blunders often extort smiles from one" (204). Above all, he lamented the ignorance induced by Catholicism in those he called "the wild Irish" and had no trouble dispensing quick-fix solutions:

I can think of no likelier means to convert them from their erroneous principles, than to get the *Bible translated* into their own native language, to have it put in their houses, and *charity schools erected* for

15. In an otherwise helpful overview of the religious landscape of the American colonies in the eighteenth century, Boyd Stanley Schlenther does not even bother to mention Georgia. Schlenther does mention later in his chapter the significance of British welcome of religious refugees, such as Salzburgers in Georgia. Schlenther, "Religious Faith and Commercial Empire," in Marshall, *The Oxford History of the British Empire*, 2:128–29, 145.

their children . . . which would insensibly weaken the Romish interest. (205, emphasis added)

This statement reveals several key insights about Whitefield's understanding of his own work in Georgia. He believed that the work of a charity school went hand-in-hand with the essential Reformation task of translating the Bible into the vernacular. He saw both, furthermore, as being vital strategies in an anti-Catholic campaign. As he toiled for the Savannah charity school in close proximity to a Spanish, and therefore Catholic, Florida, it is likely that he saw parallels between the needs in Ireland and America. We might even venture to guess that Whitefield was thinking about his work in Georgia as he pleaded for laborers in Ireland, "Oh that some man, in whom is the Spirit of the Holy God, would undertake this!" (205). In fact, the comparison may have served to sharpen his sense of calling in America. For even as he lamented the lack of a dedicated Protestant minister in Ireland, he saw himself as that man for Georgia.

After several weeks of an Irish tour, which culminated in Dublin on November 30, 1738, Whitefield finally returned to England where he planned to receive his ordination and make further preparations for continuing his work in Georgia. According to one biographer, Whitefield had thought little of becoming a traveling preacher—"at the end of 1738, he had not the least idea of becoming an open-air and itinerant evangelist."[16] Instead, he was preoccupied with thoughts of returning to Georgia to work at the Savannah parish and to erect an orphanage on the outskirts of town. For that purpose, he met with the colony's Board of Trustees on December 13, 1738, to receive the call to serve as parish priest for Savannah at an annual salary of £50. Yet the Trustees, perhaps sensing that a local parish ministry was not enough to fully engage Whitefield, also on December 27 sealed "his commission to collect money for erecting an Orphan house at Savannah"—a fateful decision they would come to regret. Within a few weeks of his return to England, Whitefield had secured far more than he could have dreamed: the pastoral charge needed for priest's orders, a legitimating commission to travel at will in order to raise funds for the orphanage, five acres of land for personal use in Savannah, and as if all that were not enough he also found an apothecary to take back with him to Savannah "to serve the

---

16. Tyerman, *Life*, 1:323.

poor gratis." The Earl of Egmont, president of the Trustees, reported in his journal that Whitefield "went away thoroughly satisfied."[17]

This satisfaction, however, was short-lived. Whitefield's conduct in the months following his return to London reveals much about the evolution of his long-term vision for Georgia and his own future, as the two became increasingly intertwined. He quickly reached for greater independence in his Georgia affairs and tensions began to surface before a fortnight had passed since the congenial meeting between Whitefield and the Trustees. The missionary preacher appears to have had second thoughts, leading the Trustees to express remorse of their own. After considering a letter "wherein he varied a little from his first proposals," the Trustees deemed that "to put the entire direction and management of the Orphan house into his hands, without communicating to us his schemes, or giving us an Acct how the money collected by him is laid out, we thought to be not in our power."[18] In part, Whitefield's reconsideration of his arrangement with the Trustees arose from his extraordinary fundraising success. By the second week of January 1739, he had returned from London with his ordination in one hand and £46 in the other. To put things in perspective, in a few short days he had raised a sum nearly equal to the entire annual salary promised him by the Trustees. It did not take long for him to realize that he could do much of his Georgia work without the help, and meddling influence, of the Trustees.[19]

By April 21, 1739, Whitefield had experienced even greater, and unexpectedly tantalizing, success in fundraising. The initial £46 reached "upwards of 500£ for the Orphan house"—an astonishing sum by any account. His relations with the Georgia Trustees were further strained as, emboldened, he demanded "a Grant of 500 acres where he should choose," with the right of ownership going to his inheritors in perpetuity. What had seemed a generous gift of five acres, which the Trustees bestowed upon him only a few months prior, now appeared a mere pittance. Not one to mince words, he declared that, since he had raised this substantial amount of money, he should have the right to use it as he saw fit. He also declined to receive any salary from the Trustees, money he had been "thoroughly satisfied" to accept no less than four

17. Candler, *Colonial Records*, 5:86.
18. Candler, *Colonial Records*, 5:90.
19. Candler, *Colonial Records*, 5:95.

months ago.[20] A month later, as his fundraising climbed still higher, "upwards of 700£," so did his boldness. He went as far as to relinquish the commission the Trustees had "granted him on the 27 December 1738 to collect money for the uses of the Colony," claiming he "never made use thereof."[21] Aggrieved as they were at Whitefield's audacious efforts to outmaneuver them, the Trustees were nonetheless beholden to Whitefield's successes. They invited him to a Trustee meeting where they "delivered him his Commission to be our Parish Minister at Savannah."[22] Buoyed by his financial triumphs, Whitefield was having his cake and eating it, too. Yet even as he seemed to be overcoming his differences with the Trustees, he was also beset by a number of doctrinal and ecclesiastical controversies.

In fact, Whitefield's actions in settling his Georgia affairs can also shed light on the controversies he was creating by his increasingly bold theological positions. Just as fundraising breakthroughs stiffened his resolve in negotiations with the Trustees, so homiletical successes made him ever more daring in his theological innovations. A brief survey of Whitefield's ecclesiastical controversies dating from his return to England in November 1738 lays the groundwork for explaining the connections between his imperial experiences in Georgia and the development of his reputation as the Grand Itinerant.

Whitefield's preaching upon his return at the end of 1738 caused a sensation, and he immediately faced throngs of admirers as well as a steady stream of opposition, especially from church officials. Within two days of his arrival in London in December, five churches denied him access to their pulpits. In part, his association with the methodists as well as his fiery, combative style were to blame. Adding insult to injury, Whitefield played the trump card of raising funds to support orphans against those who accused him of violating parish boundaries, thereby painting his critics as heartless in their objections to the improvement of conditions for poor children. With churches closed to him—as a result of his own provocations—Whitefield turned to preaching outdoors. There he found spectacular success.

Perhaps just as alarming to his foes as his outdoor preaching, however, were the indoor services he held in unorthodox locations, from

20. Candler, *Colonial Records*, 5:162.
21. Candler, *Colonial Records*, 5:173.
22. Candler, *Colonial Records*, 5:174.

the parlor rooms of landed gentry to the barn gatherings of religious societies. One particular objection from a clergyman appealed to the authority of the Canons and the Act of Charles II, legislation designed to combat political rebellion. The complaint charged that Whitefield and his associates held public worship outside the space and schedule of the official church. Whitefield frequently expounded the Scriptures in a private home at nine or ten in the evening, ungodly hours when decent folks should have been home. It was also not uncommon for Whitefield to teach back-to-back lectures lasting three to four hours or to preach outside not only in country fields but at city gates and streets.[23] In this way, he appropriated public spaces for religious purposes and used his religious messages to air public complaints.

Even more disconcerting to establishment clerics than the outdoor locations, many revival-seeking individuals gathered for all-night love feasts—consisting of shared meals, prayers, songs, and testimonies— which critics derided as clandestine debaucheries posing as fervent prayer meetings. These anxious defenders of the establishment had a point. The revival gatherings served not only to encourage religious devotion but also to blur the lines governing social order. If not blatantly seditious, such meetings and the religious societies responsible for them were subversive movements that disturbed the peace of an already fragile social fabric. To the extent they brought together rich and poor, and other groups that rarely interacted on equal footing, they further exacerbated fears of the social elites who stood to gain most by preserving the status quo.

Yet opposition to Whitefield that focused on his methods was not the only source of criticism. Others responded to the ways in which the content of his message underwent change as he resumed his preaching in England. One example is Whitefield's preaching on the new birth, which evolved over time, especially in the early years of his ministry. The methodism of the Oxford Holy Club has been described as "a harsh legalism without the new birth" (24). That judgment is correct for Whitefield in the mid 1730s. But between his graduation from Oxford and departure for his first American trip, Whitefield's theology appears to

---

23. "Expounded from five till near nine, to thronged Societies. . . . About six in the evening I expounded to a Society without Lawford's Gate, and afterwards to another in Baldwin Street: both were exceedingly crowded and attentive." Whitefield, *Journals*, 241, 246.

have changed, as he developed a pronounced emphasis on the new birth. It is striking that every time he expounded the doctrine of the new birth in this early period, it was met with general acceptance and favor. In fact, he recounts no early public opposition whatsoever to this teaching in his *Journals*. Rather, his preaching—and presumably his doctrines—met with widespread approval. "Large offers were made" to Whitefield for settling down in Bristol, west of London, and admirers asked why he was so intent on going to Georgia when he would be "well provided for at home" (92).

While there is no specific mention of Whitefield preaching on the new birth during his first tour of America, there is a noticeable shift in his message upon returning to Britain. Whitefield first took up the theme of the new birth in a sermon on December 24, 1738, as he arrived back in England. This occasion is also the first record in his *Journals* of public opposition to preaching on the new birth (218). From this point on, controversy began to swirl wherever Whitefield dared to mention it. And dare he did, as Whitefield repeatedly insisted on the importance of preaching aimed at the regeneration of his hearers. The louder the opposition and criticism he faced, the more vehement he became in his exposition of this doctrine.

Though it calls for speculation, making sense of the growing resistance in England to Whitefield's new birth preaching can lead to an appreciation of how his imperial travels shaped his theological formulations. Specifically, it is reasonable to conclude that Whitefield's travels to the outer margins of empire helped him see British society unencumbered by the metropole's hierarchical ordering of society. The frontier was a place of fresh beginnings, liminal identity, and therefore ripe with opportunities for recasting inherited values. In such an open environment, Whitefield's theology of the new birth became a socially leveling doctrine. This wider dimension of imperial culture presents the most plausible explanation for why Whitefield's preaching of the new birth received little attention, let alone opposition, prior to his first American trip. His exposure to the far outpost of empire almost certainly radicalized his theology so that his preaching began to draw criticism unseen before his trip to America.

Substantive doctrinal reasons can certainly explain the fresh criticism he received; but the accents that made him theologically suspect also resulted from his growing perspective on the imperial landscape. That is to say, the timing behind his intensified message of the new birth and his initial tour of the empire was not coincidental but connected. Whitefield believed his time in the colonies provided clarity of soteriological vision. Regarding the "old doctrine about Justification by Faith only," he wrote on December 10, 1738 (shortly after his return from America), that he could "come unprejudiced, and can the *more* easily see who is right" (218, emphasis added). His use of the comparative construction assumes movement from a prior position to a newer understanding.

Whitefield continued preaching the new birth despite inciting more and more opposition. On the evening of February 9, 1739, when "near twenty friends came to visit" in order to dispute with him about regeneration, he was dismissive of their efforts. "They took care to show as much as possible, viz., that they had read the Fathers (I suppose the English translations)"—Whitefield was intent on highlighting his superior education and command of the original languages—"but at the same time, denied experience in religion" (235). In this way, he heaped scorn on their inferior intellect as well as lack of religious affections.

Historians have been quick to focus on the closure of prominent pulpits, which forced Whitefield to find his field preaching voice, leading to unexpected and phenomenal results. The conventional view goes on to conclude that his breakthroughs in outdoor preaching led his opponents to even more clamorous denunciation of his evangelistic style. Scholars have thus linked his most serious opposition to disputes over matters of style rather than substance. As a result, Whitefield's theological innovations are treated as secondary, or inconsequential, details. One historian has gone as far as to say that "after Whitefield became a confirmed Calvinist during his second American preaching tour in 1740, his theology was fixed."[24] But there is another way to see the matter. For it fits extant evidence to conclude that Whitefield's particular theological emphasis in talking about such doctrines as regeneration and the new birth—as well as his innovative way of promoting them— explained both his infamy and popularity. The former led to increasing marginalization while the latter resulted in ever-growing crowds. While evidence of these theological innovations was present before Whitefield visited America, they became more pronounced with his visits to the empire's peripheries.

The development of a theological emphasis that appeared after his

---

24. Lambert, *"Pedlar in Divinity,"* 202.

American voyage shows how the empire shaped Whitefield's religious outlook. We can detect this development in the change that marked reactions to his preaching after his return to England in December 1738. Why did people respond in a more critical manner during this time? The most plausible explanation is that Whitefield's theology of the new birth had itself undergone a change that threatened the prevailing ecclesiastical system. In other words, his preaching of the new birth grew openly hostile toward the social order. Whereas Whitefield had earlier emphasized the positive aspects of the new birth, upon his return to England in December 1738 he began to stress the negative implications of a message that prized personal volition above communal tradition.

At the risk of putting it too simply, theological formulation consists of doctrine and praxis, an exposition as well as application of religious beliefs. Before his trip to America, Whitefield mainly preached the doctrine of the new birth; after his trip, he began also to apply the doctrine he preached, working out its personal as well as social implications. More often than not, this extrapolation of the new birth amounted to a severe criticism of those who had not undergone the experience of saving faith. Especially when such charges involved his eccleisastical peers, the result was fierce pushback, including though not limited to the denial of pulpits. Fired by righteous indignation, Whitefield led the chorus of evangelicals that "sapp[ed] the theological outworks of the social order." In fact, many feared that his message encouraged "the poor and ignorant not merely to disregard their duty and the example of their betters but to social insubordination and perhaps even worse."[25] What is apparent from the foregoing examination is that Whitefield's travels around the empire abetted the development of his doctrine in a way that appeared seditious to the social and ecclesiastical establishment.

The progression outlined above takes seriously historical change over time while arguing also for the importance of theology in interpreting social and cultural phenomena. Taking note of Whitefield's theological development, especially his intensifying conviction regarding the doctrinal basis for the new birth, illuminates a relationship between imperial travels and theological positions. Regeneration, he insisted, came neither by way of inherited status nor one's own good works but through the mediated righteousness of a savior—"And who dare assert

25. Mark Smith, "The Hanoverian Parish: Towards a New Agenda," *Past & Present* 216, no. 1 (2012): 102.

that we are not justified in the sight of God merely by an act of faith in Jesus Christ, without any regard to works past, present, or to come?" (218). In contrast to the Puritans who had elucidated a complex *ordo salutis* (literally "order of salvation," which depicted a morphology of conversion with details of the long and arduous pathway to salvation), Whitefield collapsed the process into one punctiliar moment where the person's decision for Christ held ultimate significance for that person's eternal destiny.[26]

It was a message likely to appeal to people without social preferments, such as the settlers in Georgia and miners in Kingswood, of whom Whitefield wrote: "My bowels have long since yearned toward the poor colliers, who are very numerous, and as sheep having no shepherd" (241). In much the same way that his anti-Catholic reflections in Ireland shed light on Whitefield's vision behind his Georgia orphanage, his heightened stress on an egalitarian new birth that he preached to a variety of audiences—whether impoverished colliers, religious societies that blurred social hierarchy, or London's upper class—revealed Whitefield's faith in the liminal and limitless possibilities of an expanding Protestant empire.

Whitefield's message held attraction for the poor, but he was also intent on proclaiming it to the rich. As he went out of his way to prick their consciences, they could not help noticing the subversive undertones of his preaching. Though he had many aristocratic admirers, some of them also fretted from time to time over his indiscretions regarding proper social boundaries. To take one example, the Duchess of Buckingham wrote a letter to the Countess of Huntingdon expressing unease about methodist doctrines, especially as Whitefield preached them.[27] In her view, they were "most repulsive, and strongly tinctured with impertinence and disrespect towards their superiors, in perpetually *endeavouring to level all ranks*, and do away with all distinctions."[28] She even seemed to implicate the Countess for her lack of good judgment: "I cannot but wonder that your Ladyship should relish any

26. According to Stephen Marini, "Whitefield shortened the morphology of conversion, swept away the casuistry of covenantalism, and focused the issue of salvation on the moment of conversion itself." Marini, *Radical Sects of Revolutionary New England*, 13.

27. The date of the letter is not indicated, but it was sometime before March 13, 1742, when she died.

28. Tyerman, *Life*, 1:160–61; emphasis added.

sentiments so much at variance with high rank and good breeding."[29] The duchess was a shrewd and careful listener who understood the far-reaching disruptive implications of Whitefield's doctrine of the new birth for the existing social order. On the other side, Whitefield—who had been to the far edges of empire—appreciated, even aspired toward, a more malleable social hierarchy. For in addition to envisioning the assimilation of young French children in Georgia noted earlier, he apprehended there fertile ground for rearranging social norms. In this emerging view of the empire, the doctrine of the new birth empowered British colonists abroad to renegotiate the terms of their status in an expanding, and therefore shifting, social landscape.

While he was still in Georgia, on June 10, 1738, Whitefield articulated his plans for the colony in this way: "What I have most at heart, is the building of an orphan-house, which I trust will be effected at my return to England. In the mean while, I am settling little schools in and about Savannah; that the rising generation may be bred up in the nurture and admonition of the Lord."[30] Whitefield understood his primary purpose in Georgia as the establishment of schools rather than churches, something that had not occurred at all to the Wesleys during their Georgia experience prior to Whitefield's arrival. In this surprising difference, we get a glimpse into the long view with which he approached his Georgia ministry. "The seed of the glorious gospel has taken root in the American ground, and, I hope, will grow up into a great tree," Whitefield wrote a friend from Ireland in November 1738. He had completed his first trip to America, and to be sure, it was far from his last. With "infant Georgia," which he called "an excellent soil for Christianity," constantly on his mind, he proceeded to lay the foundation for a lifetime of work.[31]

As the lessons of his first American trip sank in and opposition in England grew apace, Whitefield's theological innovations and his imperial strategy continued to develop and, more significantly, converge. Whitefield's fundraising prowess and his field preaching success were linked to two distinct, even disparate, aspects of his career. Yet, it is possible to imagine that the large sums of money he raised and the

29. Aaron Crossley Seymour and Jacob Kirkman Foster, *The Life and Times of Selina: Countess of Huntingdon* (London: W. E. Painter, 1839), 27.
30. Whitefield to Mr. H., June 10, 1738, in *Works*, 1:44.
31. Whitefield to Mr. —, November 16, 1738, in *Works*, 1:45.

enormous crowds he attracted to his preaching events helped bolster his hopes for a transatlantic career. If he could continue to draw large crowds, he could continue to fund his colonial plans. To view this development from a different angle, his travels in America and his triumphs in England served to enlarge his imperial vision. In this vein, his metropolitan ministry enabled his frontier work in Georgia. Had Whitefield settled in Bristol, as so many friends and admirers pleaded, he would likely have had a very different life trajectory. More than idle conjecturing, this line of thinking highlights the fact that his travels abroad, and, in particular, his exposure to the fringe of empire in Georgia, opened up new vocational and theological possibilities for Whitefield.

An incident illustrating Whitefield's growing boldness is his public disagreement with Bishop Martin Benson of Gloucester, who had ordained him as deacon in 1736 and as priest in 1738. By the summer of 1739, the relationship had deteriorated into an epistolary shouting match, which Whitefield gladly made public. Reacting to the bishop's disapproval of his non-parochial ministry, Whitefield made the issue not about himself but about the missteps of other pastors. "But, if the commission we then receive obliges us to preach nowhere but in that parish which is committed to our care," he protested, "then all persons act contrary to their commission when they preach occasionally in any strange place." Whitefield showed open disdain because Bishop Benson's criticism threatened to shrink the imperial stage to which he was growing accustomed. So roused was he to defend his activity that he went on the offensive against the bishop himself: "and, consequently, your lordship equally offends when you preach out of your own diocese."[32] For his critics he reserved the harshest judgment, accusing them of "falling from their Articles, and not preaching the truth as it is in Jesus, that has excited the present zeal of those, whom they, in derision, call *the Methodist preachers*."[33] This abrupt turn away from the bishop who had encouraged his ministry and ordained him to the priesthood signifies a dramatic shift in Whitefield's mentality for ministry. At this early stage, invigorated by his preaching and fundraising successes, Whitefield threw caution to the wind. He drew a clear line in the sand and indicated in no uncertain terms to his bishop that noth-

32. Whitefield to the Bishop of Gloucester, July 9, 1739, Tyerman, *Life*, 1:261.
33. Whitefield to the Bishop of Gloucester, July 9, 1739, Tyerman, *Life*, 1:261.

ing would stand in the way of his itinerating across the empire, parish boundaries and priestly decorum notwithstanding.

The itinerant's pioneering work in the empire's outer edges legitimized his invasion of the empire's religious, social, and political centers. Without his plans in the American South, Whitefield would have had feeble justification for gallivanting around the West Country in England. Not only the pounds he collected for his orphan relief work but also the haughty disdain he incurred for daring to preach the new birth out of doors gave Whitefield both the vision for imperial strategy and the basic building blocks of a transatlantic stage. Whitefield's travel itinerary can appear frenetic to a casual observer, but it is possible to discern rhyme and reason to his frequent travels to and from the empire's center and periphery. Whitefield stayed longer in England, by a few months, than he had originally intended. But it was not because he was losing focus. To the contrary, he was finding a much deeper and broader foundation for his American southern strategy than he had anticipated, in London and its surrounding boroughs of all places. The longer he toured around England and the more he preached to adoring and thronging crowds, the more he wanted to return to America. For his work in England was truly only half the work he envisioned for his life.

Whitefield's Second American Trip

The tenor of Whitefield's second visit to America stands in stark contrast to his first. During the earlier journey, Whitefield went about his business as if he was on a listening tour, meeting with a variety of colonial officials, touring the territory around Savannah, and making plans for an orphanage and a parish ministry. At the conclusion of this information-gathering exercise, Whitefield praised Commissary Alexander Garden in Charleston as "a good soldier of Jesus Christ, [who] received me in a most Christian manner."[34] A little over a year later, much had changed. On March 14, 1740, Whitefield could be found in the home of his former admirer, trading loud aspersions with Garden. The encounter ended badly with Garden throwing Whitefield out. A month later, on Sunday, April 20, Whitefield cautioned a Philadelphia audience of "about fifteen thousand people" against the "false doc-

34. Whitefield, *Journals*, 188.

trines and many fundamental errors contained in the Commissary's discourse."[35]

In order to understand this dramatic change in Whitefield's relationship with Commissary Garden, we must work out what changed for Whitefield and why ecclesiastical leaders like Garden, once enthusiastic supporters, began to vigorously oppose his work. But to grasp Whitefield's commitment to the far reaches of the British Empire, we also need a clear understanding of Georgia's situation in the period between Whitefield's departure after his first visit in August 1738 and when he left America the second time in January 1741. The southern frontier of Georgia went through a severe testing with the eruption of the War of Jenkins' Ear in 1739. A conflict over English efforts to force their way into trade with Spanish colonies, this war had deleterious effects on the relationship between South Carolina and Georgia. We will briefly treat two specific matters that impinge on our understanding of Whitefield's American activities: the challenge of transatlantic communication and the rise of competition between South Carolina and Georgia.

War in the southern frontier highlighted the difficulty of maintaining clear lines of communication across an extensive empire separated by a vast ocean. The timing of Britain's declaration of war on Spain in 1739 provides an apt illustration of this problem. Based on faulty intelligence from Rhode Island on September 8, Oglethorpe commenced steps toward a formal declaration on October 3, sixteen days before the king's officials did in London on October 19.[36] In this case, the Georgians were saved from the major embarrassment of a colony declaring a war by itself without the mother country. But the mistake also illustrates the hazards of slow communication in the colonial world. Communication is always fraught with potential for misunderstanding, but this danger was exacerbated in the age of transatlantic letter writing. Amid this complex dynamic of correspondence across the Atlantic, Whitefield's contentious style was especially susceptible to snowballing disputes. If the preacher stirred controversy with the people he came into contact with in London, those not present had to reach their own conclusions using the secondhand accounts of biased reporters. When

35. Whitefield, *Journals*, 449.
36. This event is narrated in Kenneth Coleman, *Colonial Georgia: A History* (New York: Scribner, 1976), 63–65.

the issues involved theological nuance and ecclesiastical politics, the stakes were even higher.

Another development in the American South during the interval between Whitefield's first two American visits was the growing acrimony between South Carolina and Georgia as they found themselves in an uneasy alliance against the Spanish. One manifestation of this problem arose in the summer of 1740, when Oglethorpe led an offensive against St. Augustine in Florida to disastrous effect. Due to a variety of factors that ranged from logistical errors to unfavorable weather conditions, Oglethorpe experienced a humiliating setback. The fallout of this moment hurt not only his reputation but also the tenuous relationship between the two southern colonies as each assigned blame to the other. Oglethorpe sought to deflect or share some of the embarrassment. South Carolina's legislature conducted a year-long investigation and produced a report that was as prolix as it was critical of their Georgian compatriots. The strain rising from military frustrations spilled over into other arenas of colonial life, including the relationships of religious leaders.

With this background in place concerning Georgia, we are better positioned to understand what changed for Whitefield and why leading establishment clerics now came out so strongly against him. To put it simply, more than doctrinal conflicts were at stake; Whitefield provoked opposition because he aspired to change the imperial landscape in America. Central to this insight is the fact that Whitefield never lost interest in Georgia, even as he moved on to the more populous, better established northern colonies. Precisely because of his ongoing aspirations for Georgia he rankled many other colonial leaders as he made his second tour through the Atlantic seaboard. But before we come to that conflict, we must trace the course of Whitefield's preparations for his second American trip.

In the summer of 1739, as he looked forward to returning to America, Whitefield had a specific destination in mind: "I am convinced that God calls me now to Georgia, and so are our friends."[37] On board the *Elizabeth*, which was bound for Pennsylvania, he wrote to a friend in America: "My stay will be as short as possible at Philadelphia. I must not delay coming to my dear, though poor charge."[38] After disembarking in

---

37. Whitefield to —, August 3, 1739, in *Works*, 1:59.
38. Whitefield to Mr. —, August 14, 1739, in *Works*, 1:62.

Lewes, Delaware, on October 30, he went to Philadelphia and spent several weeks in the middle colonies.[39] But all the while his heart was fixed on Georgia. Despite ardent invitations from some of New England's most prominent ministers, that region would have to wait another ten months to host this young preaching sensation; he had other, more pressing matters to attend to in Savannah. For reasons that deserve closer scrutiny, Whitefield spent the early part of his second journey to America exploring and studying the South. His first trip to America had lasted three months in the summer of 1738, with the majority of that time spent in Georgia.[40] The singular preoccupation of his second trip was again Georgia. Though his time in the colonies lasted from August 1739 through January 1741, and though he reached as far north as New York in the spring of 1740, Whitefield did not set his course toward New England until September 1740. Disappointing many in the North, he chose to pass another summer in the Georgia heat.

Shortly after his arrival in the colonies, Whitefield wrote Howel Harris on November 10, 1739, from Philadelphia with spectacular details concerning his hopes for the southern colony: "I have had great intimations from above concerning Georgia. Who knows but we may have a college of pious youths at Savannah?"[41] He then went on to compare his plans for an orphan house in Georgia to the work of pietists in Germany: "Professor Franck's undertaking in Germany has been much pressed upon my heart. I really believe that my present undertaking will succeed."[42] It is surprising to see that at this early juncture in his American career, the work of revival seemed secondary to the more urgent work of establishing a sturdy institutional foundation in Georgia. Less than a month after his arrival in the middle colonies, Whitefield could think of little else besides his developing work in the South. New

---

39. Tyerman, *Life*, 1:319.

40. For one assessment that Georgia "was far too small a stage" for Whitefield, see Kidd, *The Great Awakening*, 44. Kidd bases his argument on the observation that "after three months in Georgia, he returned to England." Analysis of Whitefield's first trip to America, however, can cut in either of two directions: he spent *only* three months in Georgia, or he spent the three months of that trip *primarily* in Georgia. So great was his focus on the South at this early point that Whitefield evinced surprisingly little interest in seeing other parts of the New World. This point becomes even more pronounced when we realize how much of his second journey also focused on the South.

41. Whitefield to Howel Harris, November 10, 1739, in *Works*, 1:84.

42. Whitefield to Howel Harris, in *Works*, 1:100.

England seems hardly to have crossed his mind, except as a matter to put off. He wrote Boston's Benjamin Colman on November 16, 1739, informing him that he hoped "in about seven months . . . to see New England in my return to Europe."[43] On the same day, he wrote Jonathan Edwards, acknowledging the "great things" of God in Edwards's Northampton and his desire "to come and see them in a few months."[44] As it turned out, Colman and Edwards would have to wait nearly a year. Faced with the choice of revival work in the North or relief work in the South, Whitefield chose the latter. He knew how to juggle these various locations in his mind without losing sight of the need of the moment. Foremost were the opportunities awaiting in Georgia.

Such singleminded focus on Georgia appears even more remarkable when we understand the wide range of Whitefield's epistolary network. November 10, 1739, was a busy day for this missionary priest who had just arrived in Philadelphia, the colonies' second largest city. He mailed fifty-nine letters on that day—twenty to ministers (some of them "unconverted," many fellow revivalists), fourteen to women, several to groups and societies, one addressed to a house servant, and even one letter to a woman whose name he had forgotten.[45] We could attribute this prolific epistolary activity to a variety of factors, but high on any such list must be the strategic, forward-thinking, entrepreneurial mind of Whitefield. Having received letters from Benjamin Colman (Boston) and Jonathan Edwards (Northampton), who were themselves involved in broadcasting news of New England revivals to the broader British Atlantic world, Whitefield was determined to make his own contribution as a herald of evangelical renewal.[46] His fixation on Georgia, when viewed against this larger backdrop of a conscious transatlantic strategy of imperial and spiritual expansion, reveals the reasoning behind Whitefield's tactical preference for the empire's periphery. He was not heading to Georgia to withdraw but rather to establish a base upon which to launch forward movement.

Whitefield's delayed visit to New England, alongside his growing enthusiasm for Georgia as well as his active correspondence with ministers in other outlying regions of the empire such as Wales (Howel

43. Whitefield to Benjamin Colman, November 16, 1739, in *Works*, 1:121.
44. Whitefield to Jonathan Edwards, November 16, 1739, in *Works*, 1:121.
45. Whitefield, *Works*, 1:63–120.
46. For the importance of such epistolary networks, see O'Brien, "A Transatlantic Community of Saints."

Harris) and Scotland (Ralph Erskine), reveals a wide-ranging imperial blueprint. In fact, his tactical focus on the empire's margins can be understood only in the context of an overarching strategy. Whitefield himself was not so shortsighted as to view Savannah and Boston as binary choices; plying his trade in the South was not about meekly embracing contentment with one's lot, however small, in life. Instead, he had a much larger vision that went beyond the constituent pieces. If Savannah was too small a playing field, so were Boston and London. As we will come to see with greater clarity throughout this study, Whitefield's vision was transatlantic and international. He labored for a worldwide Protestant movement, and if riding the coattails of British imperialism helped him along in that trailblazing work, he was eager to take the journey where it took him for the moment.

So it was that before he returned to Savannah on his second American sojourn, Whitefield had already made up his mind to resign the parish there. He focused instead on the work of establishing an orphanage and intended to range from that center as far and wide as possible. He longed for flexibility as well as a broader reach: "The Orphan House I can take care of, supposing I should be kept at a distance; besides, when I have resigned the parish, I shall be more at liberty to take a tour around America, if God should ever call me to such a work."[47] Despite pious talk of waiting on God's will, reading between the lines makes it clear that Whitefield had made up his mind to broaden his field of ministry in America. He was also thinking carefully about how to prepare a geographical base from which to carry out that work. The cause of orphan relief gave him the justification he needed to go anywhere in the empire where he could hope to raise funds. Far from consigning him to obscurity in the periphery, his work in Georgia made it necessary for him to frequent the cosmopolitan centers of empire as much as he possibly could.

As he traveled about, Whitefield met Swedish, Dutch, and German Protestants from such diverse theological streams as Quaker, Moravian, and Presbyterian traditions. He met the Dutch Reformed revivalist Theodore Frelinghuysen in the Raritan Valley of New Jersey, and in nearby New Brunswick he found a kindred spirit in the Irish-born Presbyterian revivalist Gilbert Tennent. He witnessed firsthand the fruits of William Tennent's Log College, an independent Presbyterian seminary at Neshaminy, Pennsylvania, established in 1726, which educated many re-

---

47. Whitefield to Mr. Wm. D—, November 10, 1739, in *Works*, 1:109.

vival preachers and later contributed to the founding of the College of New Jersey at Princeton. As a reminder that the work of revival was far from an isolated event, he received reports of persecution from dissenting Protestants fleeing various parts of Europe. Many of these exiles became deeply involved in the colonial revivals. He found a like-minded spirit with these various Protestant groups and worked to discover common cause amid their great diversity. "I think there are no less than fifteen denominations of Christians in German Town, Pennsylvania, and yet all agree in one thing, that is, to hold Jesus Christ as their Head, and to worship Him in spirit and in truth," he remarked, clearly impressed but also bewildered by the varieties of Protestantism he encountered.[48]

Meeting so many religious refugees probably reminded Whitefield of the larger battles surrounding embattled European Protestants, so that foreign Catholic threats abroad and Jacobite rebellions closer to home loomed large.[49] By going so far to the edge of empire, Whitefield was able to see the world beyond it. Rather than shrink back in fear, he displayed eagerness to impose some semblance of order on that world. Indeed, he was convinced that he had the right theological formula for the occasion. The evangelical new birth of individual persons was not something that had to be vetted through high church structures or subject to the scrutiny of some Protestant form of the Roman Curia. As he was now preaching the doctrine, it leveled the playing field and opened up immediate access to a new Christian identity without the need of a formal procedure for christening.

In this expansive inter-denominational setting, Whitefield's response to the diversity of empire paralleled his turn to new birth preaching as a way to reverse England's spiritual decline. His ecumenism arose not from theological simplicity, as many have assumed, but rather from an ambitious imperial vision that recognized the need of a Protestant coalition arrayed against hostile Catholic forces, whether French or Spanish. His search for a common denominator was, far from a dilution of theological complexities, a way to achieve a coalition force in the face of a cacophonous plurality of Protestant perspectives. For Whitefield, the Protestant interest was the imperial agenda, and vice versa. Geor-

48. Whitefield, *Journals*, 392.
49. See Colley, *Britons*, 23–25. For the larger background of religious movements and migrations in Europe contributing to American revivalism, see W. Reginald Ward, *The Protestant Evangelical Awakening* (New York: Cambridge University Press, 1992).

gia was a place where he could both confront Spanish Catholicism and transcend New England Puritanism, thus heralding a new, eighteenth-century British imperial world that was vitally Protestant precisely because it was anti-Catholic and post-Puritan.

For this reason, despite manifold signs in November 1739 of a harvest to be gathered in major colonial cities to the north, Whitefield did not want to be detained long. As he made plans to leave Philadelphia and travel south toward Georgia, he had little patience for the crowds clamoring about him. "It grieves me to send them away with such short answers; but necessity compels me," Whitefield wrote in his journal, with a hint of annoyance at the people lining up to talk with him (393). The necessity in this case arose from the haste with which he wished to commence his journey south. Even the crowd of ten thousand that came together for a farewell sermon on November 28 did nothing to slow his rush to depart for Georgia. Along the way he turned down numerous "fresh and pressing invitations" to preach, and only after he reached South Carolina did he take time to relax and reflect (397). Upon his return south, Whitefield went as far as to muse in his journal about the possibility that God had a geographical preference: "I could not but think, that God intended, in His own time, to work a good work *in these southern parts of America*. At present they seem more dead to God, but far less prejudiced than in the northern parts" (408, emphasis added). There was some sense of strategic logic underneath Whitefield's affection for the South. He compared, even calculated, his chances of success in that region over against the North. And he put a divine stamp of approval on his own personal partiality for the "southern parts of America."

Yet even as Whitefield made this personal commitment to expand the empire, he still had much to learn about imperial realities. One important aspect of Whitefield's education about the fringes of empire resulted from his increasing experience with slavery. As he traveled south on his return to Georgia during December 1739 through the early part of January 1740, his personal encounters pushed him in two different directions. On the one hand, as an aspiring institution-builder eager to follow the lead of Francke, first-hand observation of African Americans led him to envisage a school for "negro children" that might achieve some of the same goals he entertained for Bethesda Orphanage in Georgia. Yet on the other hand, as his company moved toward Savannah, it also ran across what Whitefield described as a "nest of . . . negroes" that troubled him greatly when he "inferred that these . . . might be some of those who

lately had made an insurrection in the province" (420). Whitefield was observing the reverberations of the Stono Rebellion, which began in South
Carolina on September 9, 1739. Though the rebellion lasted only a few
days, slave uprisings destabilized the region for several years afterwards.

There were imperial dimensions to the Stono Rebellion, where one
direct cause was the promise of Spanish officials to grant freedom to
any slaves who came to St. Augustine in Florida. According to a contemporary account, attributed to Oglethorpe by some and written in
October 1739, "There was a Proclamation published at Augustine, in
which the King of Spain (then at Peace with Great Britain) promised
Protection and Freedom to all Negroes [*sic*] Slaves that would resort
thither."[50] America was teaching Whitefield about both the possibilities and dangers of a far-flung empire. The African population served
as a reminder of potential harvests but also serious pitfalls for the Protestant cause. The course he eventually set for himself as an itinerant
evangelist would be his way of taking advantage of the possibilities
and working to defuse the dangers. In chapter 4 we will see how Whitefield's accommodation to slavery represented his conformity to imperial economics. For now it is sufficient to note that Whitefield's American trips exposed him to imperial realities not present back home in
London or Bristol.

His rapid march south by land, which he preferred over the quicker
route by water, afforded other lessons as well. He recorded his dislike of
tobacco culture, for it kept people apart on large tracts of land. Neighbors
living in this dispersed manner would be less easy to "be gathered together
without much previous notice" and therefore put a damper on his well-
oiled field preaching machine (400). Further extending his criticisms of
life in the Chesapeake, he remarked that people in Maryland received too
much tobacco from the government, thus weakening their moral constitution. On the other hand, he admired the Scotch-Irish for the fact that they
"raise no tobacco, but things that are useful for common life" (425–26).
Observations like these—gleaned from travel throughout the colonies—
led him to encourage Georgians' investment in cotton, which fatefully
contributed to his eventual embrace of slave labor. He bought three hun-

50. "Account of the Negroe Insurrection in South Carolina," in *Stono: Documenting
and Interpreting a Southern Slave Revolt*, ed. Mark Michael Smith (Columbia: University
of South Carolina Press, 2005), 13. According to Peter Wood, the account was written by
Oglethorpe; the point is disputed by others. "Anatomy of a Revolt," in Smith, *Stono*, 59.

dred pounds at once when he arrived there and promised to "take all the cotton, hemp, and flax that shall be produced the following year through the whole province" (434). The eloquent preacher justified this expense as part of a comprehensive strategy of gospel proclamation, but there were clear traces of social, economic, and political motivations as well.

Back in Georgia at the beginning of 1740, Whitefield went immediately to work, breaking ground and personally laying the first brick for his orphan house. Because he understood the value of a broad base of support, he visited Oglethorpe in Frederica, where the general was busy extending the fight against the Spanish into Florida, marching on forts St. Augustine, St. Marks, and St. Francis. Whitefield's proximity here to imperial warfare is again worth noting, as well as Oglethorpe's coolness toward Whitefield and his plans for Georgia. Shortly after Whitefield's visit, the general expressed some of his concerns to the colony's Trustees. He especially took exception to what he characterized as Whitefield's coercive separation of a family, taking two teenagers to his orphan house away from an older brother clearly able to provide for his younger siblings. Oglethorpe criticized the language whereby orphans were "granted" to Whitefield and argued the point with Whitefield's associate, William Seward, saying, "It is most certain that Orphans are human creatures & neither Cattel nor any other kind of Chattels, therefore cannot be granted, but the Trust have granted the care of the helpless Orphans to Mr. Whitefield & have given him 500 Acres of Land and a power of collecting Charities as a consideration for maintaining all the Orphans who are in necessity in this Province."[51] That Oglethorpe detected hints of instrumental, cavalier, and even economically shaped motivation in Whitefield is telling. The preacher's response to the matter was terse, apparently not even taking time to respond directly to Oglethorpe and simply informing John Mellidge, the older brother, that "his brother and sister were at their proper home already, and he knew no other home they had to go to."[52] It was an example of the kind of imperious style that rankled so many opponents.

It was also during this same period after his return to Savannah that Whitefield's confrontation with Alexander Garden in Charleston took

51. James Oglethorpe Papers, MS 595, Georgia Historical Society. Also in Candler, *Colonial Records*, 1:330–32.

52. William Stephens and Allen D. Candler, *A Journal of the Proceedings in Georgia, Beginning October 20, 1737. By William Stephens, Esq; to Which is Added, a State of That Province, as Attested Upon Oath in the Court of Savannah, November 10, 1740* (Atlanta: Franklin Printing and Publishing Company, 1906), 541.

place. The commissary had heard of Whitefield's impertinence toward ecclesiastical superiors in England. One famous incident was Whitefield's
public letter of rebuttal to Bishop Benson of Gloucester, who only a few
months before the incident had ordained him. He concluded his letter
to the bishop with a categorical dismissal of any and all proscriptions on
his preaching activity: "But, my lord, if you and the rest of the bishops cast
us out, our great and common Master will take us up."[53] As Whitefield intensified his attack on the Anglican clergy he declared to be unconverted,
the force of criticisms arrayed against his itinerating activities saw a corresponding increase. Commissary Garden in South Carolina, who had once
welcomed Whitefield's activities in Georgia, wrote public letters decrying
Whitefield's seditious message in the spring of 1740. Whitefield quickly
dispatched a petulant dismissal, observing, "Both by your conversation,
sermon and letter, I perceive that you are angry over-much." When Garden
continued his attacks, Whitefield simply exhorted Garden, "be pleased to
read [my sermon] again."[54] If that should not suffice, he invited a public
debate to settle the matter: "be pleased to let the Publick know it from the
Press. And then let the World judge."[55] After a series of letters throughout
March and April in 1740, the debate ended without a clear winner, and
with losses inflicted upon the reputation of both religious leaders.[56]

In the meantime, Whitefield's relationship with the Trustees of
Georgia also continued to sour. More often than not, they considered
his communications with them "impudent."[57] On April 16, 1740, while
Whitefield took leave of his Georgia charge for a nine-week preaching
and fundraising tour of the middle colonies, the Trustees in London
called an emergency meeting to discuss how they might handle their
mutinous rector. Clearly exasperated, they resented Whitefield's threats
to make public his charges against the Trustees, including an account
of what he called their "irreligion." One Trustee gave voice to a long list
of grievances that went back to the spring of the previous year:

53. Whitefield to the Bishop of Gloucester, July 9, 1739, Tyerman, *Life*, 1:262.

54. Thomas Evans, Alexander Garden, and George Whitefield, *The Querists, the
Rev. Mr. Whitefield's Answer, the Rev. Mr. Garden's Letters* (New York: J. P. Zenger, 1740),
75. The offending sermon is the final entry in George Whitefield, *Sermons on Various
Subjects* (Philadelphia: B. Franklin, 1740).

55. Evans, Garden, and Whitefield, *The Querists*, 75.

56. A response from Whitefield and six letters from Alexander Garden are printed
in Evans, Garden, and Whitefield, *The Querists*.

57. Candler, *Colonial Records*, 3:291.

Dr Burton said it appear'd to him, that [Whitefield] was resolvd to be totally independent of every body: that he had refused a salary from the Trustees because he would be obliged to attend the duty of a Parish Minister longer than he cared for; and he never should think him honest since the time he accepted a Comission to collect money for the Religious Uses of the Colony, and after he had collected some, surrender'd that commission on pretence it was of no use to him, whereby he made himself not accountable to the Trustees for the money he collected, and refused to put the money into the Trustees hands, in order to dispose of it as he pleas'd himself.[58]

This frank denunciation of Whitefield provides a lengthy assessment by someone who enjoyed sustained, if adversarial, contact with the famous preacher. He suspected Whitefield of harboring ulterior motives and intending to use Georgia to further personal schemes that reached far beyond Georgia. Though Whitefield may have insisted on a more generous characterization of his actions, he would not have denied larger designs with empire-wide implications.

Perhaps because Whitefield thought himself engaged in genuine Christian charity, he remained blind to how a consumerism that bespoke the economic needs of the empire inflected his rhetoric. To take another example, when he returned to Philadelphia in the spring of 1740, he boasted of a conversation with an African American woman who promised her children to his school:

One, who was free, said she would give me her two children, whenever I settle my school. I believe masters and mistresses will shortly see that Christianity will not make their negroes worse slaves. I intended, had time permitted, to have settled a Society for negro men and negro women; but that must be deferred till it shall please God to bring me to Philadelphia again. (462)

Here we can see the ease with which Whitefield mingled rationalizations of slavery with subtle paternalism, viewing children as trading pieces for his gospel work. In these ways, as he laid the groundwork for broad American engagement, the preacher found himself entangled in the commercial machinations of empire that stretched far beyond evangelistic labors.

58. Candler, *Colonial Records*, 3:332–35.

After returning to Philadelphia in the spring of 1740, Whitefield might have been expected by his growing colonial audience to continue traveling north. Rather than head to New England, however, and likely to the exasperation of expectant friends like Jonathan Edwards, Benjamin Colman, and many others, Whitefield went back to Georgia and spent the summer there. It was not until September 19, 1740, nearly a year after his second arrival in North America, that he reached Boston, for his first New England visit to the largest colonial city. By the time of this visit, much belated in the minds of prominent ministers who had been sending him heartfelt invitations for years, he had spent a total of fifteen months traveling around other American colonies. Whitefield was happy to linger in the South. It was at the very edge of empire that he felt most at home and detected the greatest potential for growth. Just as surprising, he spent only a month in New England, before heading south again. To be sure, that month was one of the most notable periods in colonial religious history, with memorable sermons before huge crowds everywhere Whitefield went. But studies of this New England sojourn are numerous. What has not been studied is where this momentous northern triumph fit into his overall southern strategy.

Conclusion

Most studies of Whitefield in America begin the substantive part of their analysis in 1740 with the Grand Itinerant preaching to swooning thousands in New England. By more closely examining the earlier portions of Whitefield's American work, it becomes clear that Whitefield had an overarching American strategy based on a peculiarly British imperial, consumerist perspective, the outlines of which were present from the earliest days of his American tenure. Central to this argument is the southern orientation of that starting point, indicating Whitefield's desire to be at the growing edge of imperial expansion. When Whitefield first began surveying the territory outside Savannah in the summer of 1738, he did so with the perspective of a British subject, a Protestant minister, and an ambitious entrepreneur. Whitefield the visitor bore in his heart the tradition of English dissenting religion and on his back the cold, hard realities of religious indifference among the orthodox and proliferating disunity among sectarians. As unsettled as Georgia was at the time of Whitefield's visit, it was already a key factor in both colonial and imperial history. It is of consequence that the fires of renewal he helped spread up and down the Atlantic seaboard had their first flames in the South. To learn the full significance of his American southern strategy, we must next turn to examine how it is that Whitefield went from being a British emissary to an American icon.

CHAPTER 3

An American Icon

The second phase of Whitefield's transatlantic work from 1741 to 1752 occurred during a time of ecclesial fracturing, national insecurity, and imperial war. This period of crisis on multiple fronts was also the moment of Whitefield's greatest triumphs, with the fire of revival appearing to spread wherever he went and his fame achieving iconic status in America. His work of fundraising for Bethesda Orphanage took the celebrity preacher from the metropole to the far reaches of British territory, giving him a singularly broad view of that empire. He labored in established urban centers, from Boston to London to Edinburgh. But he also returned time and again to the periphery, from Savannah, Georgia, to other small towns in South Wales and Scotland. While Jonathan Edwards wrote treatises from his parish in Northampton, Massachusetts, to spread reports of New England revival across the Atlantic world, Whitefield crisscrossed that world spreading not only tantalizing news but also catalyzing experiences of religious awakening. With his on-the-ground reporting and rough-and-tumble style, he continually refined his skills as preacher as well as publicist, and he gained notoriety on both sides of the ocean. As a consequence, whether reviled or adored, he could not be ignored. Taking stock of his widespread influence, this chapter will trace the reciprocal influences of the geographical map and the religious message of Whitefield's itinerancy during the height of his revival career.

Imperial expansion created ruptures across the British Atlantic that Whitefield's evangelical message sought to repair under a common Protestant vision. With attention fixated on the floodtides of revival, it can be easily forgotten that the awakenings could ebb as abruptly as they flowed. The decline of revival over the course of the 1740s is significant, for as Whitefield grappled with the fleeting gains of the Awakening's fervor, he also found new opportunities for deepening religious work against the backdrop of newly erupted imperial conflicts with Britain's longstanding Catholic foes. His increasing international fame makes Whitefield, the American icon of the 1740s and early 1750s, an instructive weathervane of cultural change during this period of tumult and war.

Such a focus also has the advantage of locating the colonial Great Awakening in broader context. Previous attempts to place the awakenings in their social milieu identified religious backsliding, economic depression, and social frustration as key explanatory factors usually in only one or a few, mostly colonial, location(s).[1] While these studies have uncovered a colonial culture of restlessness as the essential soil for revival, they have downplayed the hopes for extensive cultural renewal undergirding religious revivals in this period. Whitefield's transatlantic activities point to other factors at work. Rather than isolated religious outbursts, the evangelical awakenings had a striking imperial outline. Through Whitefield, moreover, far-flung localized expressions of religious fervor combined to form an empire-wide, identity-shaping cultural phenomenon. If religious revivals during this time rose from the crucible of an expanding, sometimes faltering, empire, their corresponding impact on British imperial identity carried a distinct Protestant stamp. The evangelical message stressed personal human failings while also sanctioning military conquest and commercial expansion and prosperity. Missionary activity had long depended on new world exploration, exporting the home culture to colonial outposts. The significant change Whitefield inaugurated was the frequency with which he traveled back and forth between the imperial center and its margins. In so doing, he accelerated the pace of cultural exchange across the empire, with inward spiritual revival emerging as only the most visible outcome of his labors. Beyond trying to strengthen individual devotion, he called for a national reformation and sought to leverage his trans-

1. Richard F. Lovelace, *Dynamics of Spiritual Life* (Downers Grove: InterVarsity Press, 1979); Nash, *The Urban Crucible*; Butler, "Enthusiasm Described and Decried." More recently, we have seen scholarly treatments that have attempted a broader assessment of the revivals as representing the vital interaction of transatlantic factors; notable examples include Noll, *The Rise of Evangelicalism*; Kidd, *The Great Awakening*; Ward, *The Protestant Evangelical Awakening*.

atlantic revival coalition toward the goals of British as well as international Protestant interests.

In a setting of war and empire building, then, Whitefield expounded a doctrine of new birth that articulated possibilities for not only religious renewal but also a profound reformulation of social and cultural relationships. Indeed, commissaries in the colonies and bishops in Britain had more than doctrinal reasons to oppose Whitefield. Despite problems of his own making and crises generated by imperial expansion, Whitefield's ecumenical Protestant spirit offered a consolidating, if controversial, vision for the increasingly disparate elements of British Atlantic identity, and it did so—most worryingly for his critics—without featuring the Anglican Church. Over the course of the 1740s, Whitefield grew in his ability to manage the controversies swirling around him. He amended impulsive public statements and patched up relations with high-profile figures not only for pious personal reasons but also for the sake of unity among Protestants.

It should not be forgotten that even as ecclesiastical, doctrinal, and personal storms raged around Whitefield, war broke out on the frontiers of the empire and rebellion drew near to the heart of the nation. Imperial battles seemed to follow Whitefield everywhere he went during the 1740s. The War of Jenkins' Ear against Spain in the American South, an expedition against French Louisbourg in Canada, the Jacobite invasion and the Battle of Culloden in Scotland all occurred in or near places where Whitefield also itinerated, and in some cases they prompted his direct engagement. Because of his extensive travels, he had a proximate view of numerous imperial conflicts, leading to a wide-angle perspective that was unusual in his time for British subjects.[2] Though reluctant at first, Whitefield increasingly expressed support for Britain's military efforts, from helping raise troops to preaching victory sermons calculated to fan the flames of British exceptionalism. Another comparison at this point underscores Whitefield's effort: while his fellow evangelical John Wesley lamented the deleterious effects of war on religious revivals, Whitefield sought to leverage the conflict-driven stirrings of British nationalism toward a culture of revivalism.[3]

2. Benjamin Franklin is another eighteenth-century figure who traveled broadly and enjoyed extensive international connections, but his forays across the Atlantic began after Whitefield's and rose to a significant level in the latter half of the century.

3. Writing in 1745, as war on several fronts raged, Wesley expressed only the most gloomy thoughts on war: "Our armies broken in pieces; and thousands of our men either

For these reasons the leavening effect of imperial and military developments on Whitefield's religious message needs fresh inquiry. Consideration of Whitefield's evangelistic themes in primarily religious terms has not merely sidelined the significance of that message; turning a blind eye to the broader context of his activities has obscured our view of the Atlantic world he traversed with an intensity and impact few contemporaries could match. In what ways did his preaching conform to a celebration of British geopolitical ambitions? But just as importantly, what kind of impact did his revivalistic preaching have on inspiring new notions of what it meant to be a Briton in the mid-eighteenth century? Clarity on these matters will come from close attention to Whitefield's travels throughout the empire.

The chapter begins with a study of the imperial shape of Whitefield's new birth preaching, shifts focus to the precipitous retreat of revivals, and concludes by considering the impact of imperial wars on the inchoate culture of revivalism and evangelical identity. From the first revival sparks to its fading embers, war in the imperial outposts was the one consistent reality. At the same time that Whitefield was attempting to impose religious meaning on a sprawling empire, his travels through an Atlantic world in upheaval forced him to rethink and recalibrate the message he proclaimed. Neither scattered personal renewal nor isolated local revivals proved satisfactory for a sustained, long-term vision in light of his broad view of the empire. Where revival-centric treatments of the famous itinerant's life and ministry have reified a young and impetuous Whitefield for posterity, the odyssey of his decade-long transformation that this chapter traces reveals a more complex life attuned to the longings of an imperial age. When the hopes of new birth revivals dissipated after the initial outburst of revival enthusiasm, preachers like Whitefield improvised by creating a more explicit link between British Protestant identity, the growth of empire, and ongoing spiritual vitality. In that process, they both acknowledged the limitations of their religious agenda and redoubled their efforts toward a deeper alignment of religion and empire.

---

killed on the spot, or made prisoners in one day. Nor is this all. We have now war at our own doors; our own countrymen turning their swords against their brethren." From "A Word in Season: Or, Advice to an Englishman," in John Wesley, *The Works of the Reverend John Wesley: First American Complete and Standard Edition* (New York: J. Emory and B. Waugh, 1831), 365. See also S. W. Rankin, "Wesley and War: Guidance for Modern Day Heirs?," *Methodist Review: A Journal of Wesleyan and Methodist Studies* (2011): 101–39.

The Imperial Shape of Whitefield's New Birth Preaching

The evangelical religious awakenings that dotted the British Empire beginning in the late 1730s outlined not only a revival of Protestant religion but the contours of an imperial movement. During the height of revival, believers as well as unbelievers across the empire began attending religious services in unorthodox venues with unusual results. Some remained skeptical and mocked the enthusiasts. But many more were deeply touched by the preaching of these impassioned itinerants. Local revivals reverberated across the empire, stirring new awakenings in faraway locations. The most famous of the revivals' many traveling preachers was George Whitefield, whose destinations ranged from metropolitan centers to remote corners of British territories. Being subjects of empire was privilege enough in many minds; the Grand Itinerant came along, however, and invited Britons to lay claim to their citizenship in a heavenly kingdom as well. For colonists in the hinterlands of Georgia, Presbyterians in Scotland, ordinary denizens of an ever-expanding London, and for many more in between, this invitation proved alluring, even irresistible.

Whitefield's exposition of the doctrine of regeneration was an essential element in the message he carried throughout the empire. Significantly, this religious proclamation relied heavily on imperial opportunities newly emerging in the 1730s and 1740s. Far from a timeless and universal message, Whitefield's new birth preaching reveals the imperial shape of this controversial religious doctrine in a changing world.

At a level of sheer practicality, Whitefield's transatlantic influence would not have been possible without the growth of empire in the early eighteenth century and its sprawling trade and transportation routes. While British officials talked about a "blue water" policy that utilized an ascendant navy as well as troops on the ground, Whitefield traveled over land and sea, making thirteen Atlantic crossings and fourteen trips to Scotland, preaching hundreds of sermons, and reaching tens of thousands of people nearly every month with his message of the new birth.[4]

A detailed itinerary of a shorter period can demonstrate Whitefield's broader imperial ambitions even at this early stage of his career.

4. H. V. Boven, *War and British Society, 1688–1815* (Cambridge: Cambridge University Press, 1998).

After spending all of 1740 traveling up and down the eastern seaboard and fanning the flames of the Great Awakening in America, Whitefield returned to England in March 1741. After a six-week stopover in London, Whitefield hit the road again, preaching throughout the Bristol region in May. He returned to London, but he did not stay put for long. The next month he was on the road again, roaming east and north, from Essex to Cambridge to Suffolk then back to London.[5] At the end of July, he set his sights farther still and arrived in Edinburgh. For the next four months he would itinerate around Scotland, building bridges for a burgeoning transatlantic evangelical network. So impressed was Whitefield with the fertile soil for gospel labors he found in Scotland that he made sure to return the following year for another extended tour.

In England, Whitefield had been dogged by Arminian critics— foremost among them John Wesley, who thought his view of God's power unnecessarily denigrated humanity's free will. In Scotland, his broad agenda led him on an inevitable collision course with his Calvinist brethren in the Associate Presbytery, a schismatic group that was sharply critical of the Church of Scotland. In truth, he shared much with Ebenezer and Ralph Erskine, brothers and leaders of the sectarian Presbyterians, who had been conducting an epistolary courtship with Whitefield for several years. On his first trip to Scotland, however, Whitefield was eager to reach as wide an audience as possible, as per his custom. Not one to back down from a fight, he told the Erskine brothers that he would have no qualms about preaching in a Catholic cathedral or a Muslim mosque should the opportunity be afforded him. In response the spurned Presbyterians unleashed a torrent of public criticism against Whitefield, condemning not only his theology but also his politics. "The Declaration of the true Presbyterians within the Kingdom of Scotland, concerning Mr. George Whitefield" condemned him as "a base English impostor" whose mistaken ways would "lead the covenanted kingdom of Scotland back to Egypt and Babylon."[6] Full of anti-papal rhetoric, the writer of the pamphlet sought to fan the flames of an English-Scottish animosity. But Whitefield's evangelical vision

---

5. See Tyerman, *Life*, 1:493. See also George Whitefield, *A Continuation of the Account of the Orphan-House in Georgia, From January 1740/1 to June 1742* (Edinburgh: T. Lumisden and J. Robertson, 1742).

6. Tyerman, *Life*, 2:11.

had no room for anything that undermined the transnational empire created by the Scottish-English Union of 1707.

Ironically, this rupture over strict Presbyterianism came at the very same time as Whitefield's battles over predestination with John Wesley, his one-time mentor and friend. In this way, Whitefield courted trouble for being too Calvinistic with Wesley and invited biting criticism from the Erskines for not being Calvinistic enough. More to the point, Whitefield's trouble in both instances came from his abiding worry that theological disputes would stand in the way of a broadly evangelical Christian union. He had pleaded with Wesley to gloss over minor theological disagreements even as he resisted the pleas of his Scottish brethren in the Associate Presbytery to stand firm on minutiae of theological distinctives. What appears on the surface as theological laxity or inconsistency turns out to reveal a coherent imperial strategy.

When Whitefield returned to England in November 1741, in addition to getting married (which he went about in characteristic perfunctory fashion), he continued to work at building a Calvinistic Society.[7] In part he was casting about for ways to counter the assaults of Wesley and his Arminian allies. He was also looking to consolidate the revival gains he had catalyzed in diverse areas on both sides of the Atlantic. Whitefield was in Scotland again between June and October of 1742, in time to participate in the great revivals at Cambuslang and Kilsyth. Whitefield the Anglican fostered close partnerships with several Presbyterian colleagues in Scotland, including William McCulloch at Cambuslang and James Robe at Kilsyth. Though these ministers were themselves active evangelists, they both saw Whitefield as God's specially chosen instrument to spark revival. Ever mindful of the broader landscape of his spiritual work, Whitefield found time when he was not preaching in Scotland to write a financial report for his orphan house work in Georgia and a pamphlet defending the New England revival.[8] After he returned to England in November 1742, it would be another two years

---

7. David Ceri Jones, Boyd Stanley Schlenther, and Eryn Mant White, *The Elect Methodists: Calvinistic Methodism in England and Wales, 1735–1811* (Cardiff: University of Wales Press, 2012), 42–69. Contrary to the widespread notion that Whitefield lacked John Wesley's gifts for organization, "Whitefield, with the example and assistance of Howel Harris, put in place a highly effective organisational structure in England which mirrored that established by the Welsh Methodists." Jones, Schlenther, and White, *The Elect Methodists*, 62.

8. Whitefield, *A Continuation of the Account.*

before he returned to America. Hardly one to sit still, Whitefield spent most of these two years on the road, building his society of Calvinistic methodists and developing key relationships with ministers like Howel Harris in Wales.

If not for the growth of empire, Whitefield's ambitions would have appeared ludicrous. Because of Britain's expansive territory in the mid-eighteenth century, however, Whitefield could reasonably aspire toward a kingdom of Protestant ascendancy that stretched across the Atlantic world. Thanks to growing transatlantic ties, Whitefield stoked the flames of revival in Cambuslang and Kilsyth while writing letters of intervention to the Trustees of Georgia in London. He maintained active engagement throughout Britain's most peripheral regions. In August 1742, the preacher was in the midst of his second visit to Scotland during a remarkable period of revival. At the same time in Georgia, trouble was brewing. The headmaster and chaplain of the orphan house in Savannah had landed themselves in prison for antagonistic behavior against the parish minister. Revealing familiarity with internal colonial politics from faraway Scotland, he not only expressed the hope that Savannah officials would "let the Orphan House managers alone" but also expressed the wish that eventually "we might have our own magistrates, as the people of Ebenezer have." As if that were not enough, he requested additional land for himself as well as the right to offer land to prospective settlers. "Many have applied to me respecting their settling in Georgia," reported Whitefield without the least hint that such requests were out of the ordinary. In fact, he lamented the fact that he "could give them no encouragement." Motivated for the sake of the colony's well-being, Whitefield postured for greater power in no uncertain terms: "I wish I may be enabled to give them a great deal in the future."[9]

As a young and only recently ordained missionary, he was able to risk such overreach because of the precarious nature of the fledgling Georgia enterprise and because of his unusual success in raising money for the orphan house in Savannah. Vocal critics in Scotland found irksome the idea of Whitefield taking money from their poor to help the hard-pressed in Savannah. Such protests failed to register in Whitefield's mind because, in his view of the empire, Scotland and Georgia were one and the same to him as outlying provinces of a far-flung British world.

9. Tyerman, *Life*, 2:26.

At a time when most clergy were content with a local parish assignment, Whitefield engineered a sprawling trans-denominational and transatlantic ministry. For this reason some scholars have called Whitefield the first international celebrity. Situating his ministry in the unusually broad geographical context of empire reveals the far-reaching agenda that lay beneath his proclamation of the new birth.[10] This observation comports well with the general recognition of the early eighteenth century as a time of ebullience about empire. One historian has made the case that "even the most humble citizens were drawn into the imperial effort, however distant or immediate that effort may have seemed."[11] In a society where "a mercantilist, libertarian view of empire" was widespread, the revival preacher plied his trade with uncommon commercial savvy as he appropriated openness to individual economic activity by pleading for personal religious responses.[12]

Circulation of his writings was a key part of Whitefield's imperial strategy. His early exposure to writing for publication only served to whet his appetite for broadening his impact through the use of printed material. During a sickness-induced break from university in 1736, he wrote in his journal about the thrill of being published. "God gave me favour in the printer's sight," Whitefield gushed, "and, at my request, he put a little of [my piece] in the News for six weeks successively."[13] Despite his strong accent on providence, the words "at my request" revealed his eagerness, perhaps agitation, for publicity. This early taste of publication stayed with Whitefield. In addition to his *Journals*, Whitefield regularly published sermons, pamphlets, and letters in order to spread his fame and attract large crowds to his preaching events. His 1740 "Letter to the

10. Harry Stout, "George Whitefield in Three Countries," in *Evangelicalism: Comparative Studies of Popular Protestantism in North America, the British Isles, and Beyond, 1700–1990*, ed. Mark A. Noll, David W. Bebbington, and George A. Rawlyk (New York: Oxford University Press, 1994). See also Mahaffey, *Preaching Politics*; Mahaffey, *The Accidental Revolutionary*.

11. Kathleen Wilson, "Empire of Virtue," in *An Imperial State at War: Britain from 1689 to 1815*, ed. Lawrence Stone (London: Routledge, 1994), 129.

12. Stone, *An Imperial State at War*, 131. For Whitefield's commercial know-how, see Lambert, "Subscribing for Profits and Piety"; Lambert, *"Pedlar in Divinity"*; Lambert, *Inventing the "Great Awakening."* For individual response, see Whitefield's sermons "On Regeneration" and "True Marks of the New Birth."

13. Whitefield, *Journals*, 69. Whitefield would strike these words from the 1756 revised edition of his *Journals*, likely in response to the torrent of criticism he received for portraying himself in a divinely favored, self-aggrandizing style.

Inhabitants of Maryland, Virginia, North and South-Carolina, concerning their Negroes" is remarkable not only for its content but also for its intended audience—nearly one-third of the American colonies! In part, his confidence came from the high sales of his writings. Benjamin Franklin "told me he has taken above two hundred subscriptions for printing my Sermons and Journals. Another printer told me he might have sold a thousand Sermons, if he had them; I therefore gave two extempore discourses to be published."[14] With such fervent interest and the power of the press at his disposal, it was not a stretch for the preacher to imagine a broad influence that spanned the colonies.

Whitefield made strategic links with partners who could extend his reach as far as possible. William Seward, who functioned as Whitefield's public relations manager, testified to the strategic thinking that went into Whitefield's movement across the Atlantic world. Seward kept himself busy at Whitefield's side, writing letters in one day "to Savannah, Charles Town, and Frederica, Virginia, Cape Fear, New Brunswick, and New York."[15] On the same day, he also "wrote paragraphs for the News, where our Brother *was* to preach and *had* preached."[16] In this way, Whitefield and his associates carefully cultivated the public persona responsible for catalyzing revivals across the British Empire.

The public relations machine had its intended effect. "He has put a new Face upon Religion, my Letters inform me, in some populous Cities and Parts of our neighbouring Continent," declared the Charleston pastor, Josiah Smith, on March 26, 1740, alluding to an inter-colonial communication network focused on Whitefield. He strikingly attributed Whitefield with making sermons a "vendible Commodity."[17] That Smith, who was from Charleston, made these claims in a sermon he published in Boston was no less extraordinary. As leading Boston clergymen Benjamin Colman and William Cooper wrote in the preface, such words about a fellow preacher in the course of a sermon were "very unusual, or, perhaps, altogether new," and yet they were warranted in the extraordinary season Whitefield had initiated.[18]

14. Whitefield, *Journals*, 395.

15. William Seward, *Journal of a Voyage from Savannah to Philadelphia, and from Philadelphia to England* (London, 1741), 10.

16. Seward, *Journal of a Voyage*, 10; emphasis added.

17. Josiah Smith, *The Character, Preaching, &c. Of the Rev. Mr. George Whitefield* (Boston: Rogers for Edwards and Foster, 1740), 16.

18. Smith, *The Character, Preaching, &c.*, i.

With his fame growing, the itinerant's feel for imperial connections extended beyond the spiritual to the material. Not only did Whitefield bring English goods to win the good will of the colonists in Georgia on his first American trip, but on his second trip he brought similar products to sell in Philadelphia. Beginning in November 1739, Whitefield posted regular notices in *The Pennsylvania Gazette*, advertising items ranging from candlesticks to pistol powder to sewing silk.[19] No doubt leaning on help from his publisher friend Benjamin Franklin, Whitefield also bolstered his influence by notices such as this one, which appeared in the aforementioned issue of the *Gazette*:

> Last Week the Rev. Mr Whitefield landed from London at Lewes-Town in Sussex County, where he preached; and arrived in this City on Friday Night; on Sunday, and every Day since he has preach'd in the Church: And on Monday he designs (God willing) to set out for New-York, and return hither the Week after, and then proceed by Land thro' Maryland, Virginia and Carolina to Georgia.

Through the report of inter-colonial travels like this one, readers in Philadelphia could imagine a colonial society knit together by Whitefield's itinerant ministry. That such a report was followed in the next paragraph of the *Gazette* by news of military unrest indicates a high level of interest in news about the empire at large:

> We hear from Charles-town in South Carolina, that a Body of Angola Negroes rose upon the Country lately, plunder'd a Store at Stono of a Quantity of Arms and Ammunition, and murder'd 21 white People, Men, Women and Children before they were suppress'd: That 47 of the Rebels were executed, some gibbeted and the Heads of others fix'd on Poles in different Parts, for a Terror to the rest.

The editorial choice to juxtapose Whitefield's colonial itinerancy with slave insurrection in South Carolina gives us a picture of how the revival preaching of Whitefield fit into the colonial landscape. They belonged together under the broad yet specific category of imperial developments.

19. *The Pennsylvania Gazette*, November 8, 1739, and November 15, 1739.

Itinerating an Empire at War

The expansion of Britain's imperial effort resulted in nearly ceaseless military confrontations with competing nations. Sir John Seeley remarked that war was the "characteristic feature" of this period.[20] Paul Langford called the eighteenth century the "age of war."[21] H. V. Boven observed that "from 1739 the frequency of war was such that periods of peace could almost be regarded as exceptions to the wartime norm."[22]

However, studies of the Great Awakening have paid scant attention to the relationship between spiritual revival and religious, as well as imperial, warfare. If we grant that more than youthful idealism lay behind Whitefield's early interest in Georgia and acknowledge the possibility that he deployed a deliberate southern imperial strategy, then fresh lines of inquiry emerge. Despite the natural pull of New England for someone like Whitefield and the earnest invitations from Massachusetts ministers like Benjamin Colman and Jonathan Edwards as early as November 1739, Whitefield tarried. As we have already seen, rather than head north, he spent the first fifteen months of his first two American trips mostly traveling around the southern part of America. He did finally arrive in Boston in the fall of 1740 for a much celebrated visit. Before he ventured to the logical colonial venue for his ministry, however, he spent a great deal of time lingering in the South and setting up a colonial base of operations in Georgia. In these actions there are strong hints of self-consciousness about empire driving his travel plans. Far from oblivious to the Spanish threat, Whitefield well understood the strategic position of the southern frontier, implying that since "Georgia is a Frontier Colony, and stands as a Barrier to all the other English Provinces," his work on the Georgia orphanage played a key strategic role in the cause of empire.[23]

An example of Whitefield's involvement on the forefront of this colonial frontier was his experience during the War of Jenkins' Ear (1739–1748), which smoldered dangerously close to his orphanage initiative in Georgia. With bluster that bordered on recklessness, Whitefield sounded as if he welcomed Spanish invasion of Georgia. While on a preaching tour through Scotland, he wrote: "The place where [the

---

20. Boven, *War and British Society*, 1.
21. Cited in Boven, *War and British Society*, 1.
22. Boven, *War and British Society*, 3.
23. Whitefield, *A Continuation of the Account*, 21.

Spaniards] landed, is about one hundred miles to the southward of the Orphan-house: and, supposing it should be taken, I do not repent the erecting of it, because the advantages that have flowed already from it, as appears from my accounts, have abundantly answered the pains and expense it has cost." Even if the orphanage were lost at this point, Whitefield declared he was satisfied with its impact. He sounded oddly oblivious to the human costs, appearing to prioritize the successes of fundraising activities on its behalf. For the battle-hardened revivalist, the threat of Spanish soldiers on orphanage grounds paled in comparison to the benefits he had already extracted from his Georgia enterprise. His confidence also derived from a belief that Georgia was absolutely essential for the British imperial cause, so much so that "it is reasonable to believe that [all the other English provinces] will unite in its defence and protection."[24]

When he wrote these words from Scotland, Whitefield was unaware that already two months prior, the residents of his Georgia orphanage— whom he frequently referred to as his "family"—had fled before the invading Spaniards who came down "like a flood." Fearing the worst, James Habersham, Whitefield's on-site deputy, rushed to evacuate children and personnel from the orphanage and stayed behind to salvage what supplies he might. Whitefield's orphans-turned-refugees took shelter at John Bryan's plantation in South Carolina, arriving at midnight on July 10 and remaining six weeks.[25] So dire did the situation become at one point that Habersham wrote desperately to Whitefield, "I know not whether I shall be ever able to write to you again."[26] A little over a month later, a weary Habersham complained that God was "chastising us with whips" and "scouring us with scorpions." He pined for Whitefield's return—"Indeed I hope you are now in your passage to us. We cannot but expect you"—even as he held the orphanage together in Whitefield's absence.[27] Far from setting sail for America, however, Whitefield had his hands full in Britain. While Habersham was contending with whips and scorpions in Georgia, Whitefield was putting out wild fires in Wales and Scotland. In May of the following year, Whitefield was still in England, with no definitive forecast for returning to

24. Whitefield, *A Continuation of the Account*, 21.
25. Tyerman, *Life*, 2:23.
26. James Habersham to George Whitefield, July 11, 1742, in *Works*, 3:460.
27. James Habersham to George Whitefield, August 19, 1742, in *Works*, 3:463.

America. Likely to Habersham's growing exasperation, Whitefield described his plans for more "gospel-ramblings": "After I have fought the Lord's battles in Moorfields, these holidays, I think to take a tour into Cornwall and Wales, and, perhaps, to Ireland."[28]

To judge by only his travel itineraries and his deliberate choice of locations close to the centers of imperial conflict, Whitefield's goal was nothing short of a total makeover of religious life across the British Empire. Yet much more than simple travel was involved, including his relationship with religious as well as political leaders. Whitefield was an ordained Anglican priest who made alliances across the Protestant and British world, exhibiting a catholic spirit unusual for his time. Unlike Wesley, who was "almost exclusively the poor man's preacher," Whitefield also welcomed every opportunity to consort with the rich and influential.[29] Back in England, he fostered friendship with the Earl and Countess of Huntingdon, who were "constant in their attendance upon his ministry."[30] This relationship would provide numerous benefits for the remainder of his life. The countess, Selina Hastings (1707–1791), used her aristocratic privilege to support the evangelical cause. She earned the title of a "Mother in Israel" among evangelical preachers who jockeyed for position to earn her patronage.[31] Whitefield used his connection with the countess to good effect, becoming her chaplain and turning to her for support during moments of intense opposition. In addition, many dukes, duchesses, and "even royalty itself, in the persons of William Augustus . . . and his brother Frederick, Prince of Wales, helped to swell some of Whitefield's congregations."[32] Importantly for our purposes, Whitefield evinced by his relationship with aristocrats that his ministry was aimed at more than converting the masses. He was tirelessly casting about for a wider circle of influence.

Further displaying his ambitions, in Scotland Whitefield showed he was willing to risk the loss of his relationship with the Erskines for the sake of gaining a broader audience. In fact, there too he was careful to cultivate relationships with nobles and titled ladies so that he

28. George Whitefield to James Habersham, May 21, 1743, in Tyerman, *Life*, 2:60.

29. Tyerman, *Life*, 2:37.

30. Tyerman, *Life*, 2:37.

31. Boyd Stanley Schlenther, *Queen of the Methodists: The Countess of Huntingdon and the Eighteenth-Century Crisis of Faith and Society* (Durham: Durham Academic Press, 1997).

32. Tyerman, *Life*, 2:37.

could boast of "Christian intimacy with persons of distinguished rank in Scotland."[33]

In the closing months of 1742, while safely ensconced in London, "in [his] winter quarters, preparing for a fresh campaign," Whitefield surveyed the whole of British imperial territory.[34] He dispatched letters on a regular basis to Wales, Scotland, and New England. One such letter went to Boston, as he sought to comfort and strengthen his friend, Benjamin Colman, the influential Boston minister, by his impending return: "The confusion in New England has given me concern. . . . When I shall come to Boston, the Lord Jesus only knows. I believe it will not be long."[35] Six days after writing Colman, Whitefield was planning the next step of his fresh campaign for Bethesda Orphanage by writing a letter to Gotthilf August Francke at Halle, Germany. "I should be glad to know how it is with your Orphan House"—Whitefield sought to establish a connection with the pietist work in Europe—"and whether you have any commands for Georgia."[36] As busy as he was with myriad religious and political affairs in Britain, Whitefield did not lose sight of the ongoing importance of broader connections in the old as well as the new world.

The Tactical Theologian

Whitefield was an ordained Anglican priest who could make alliances with Scottish Presbyterians, New England Congregationalists, Philadelphia Quakers, and Moravian refugees in Georgia. He either had a knack for glossing over theological differences or a skill in negotiating his way through them. Historians have routinely assumed the former; this book argues the latter. Whitefield was admittedly not the most nuanced theologian, but neither was he a theological pushover. When he felt the stakes were high enough on certain doctrinal matters, he readily confronted even towering figures like John Wesley and Count Zinzendorf. With Wesley, he parried over predestination. From Zinzendorf, he was gratified to receive an "imperious censure" for teaching

---

33. Tyerman, *Life*, 2:37-39.

34. November 15 and December 18, 1742, in Tyerman, *Life*, 2:38, 45.

35. George Whitefield to Benjamin Colman, November 18, 1742, in Tyerman, *Life*, 2:39.

36. Tyerman, *Life*, 2:44.

"the abominable doctrine of reprobation."[37] And this is not to speak of several well-documented clashes with his Anglican superiors, such as Alexander Garden, the Commissary in Charleston, Edmund Gibson, the Bishop of London, and the Archbishop of Canterbury, Thomas Secker.

A letter written to Whitefield in 1741 by one of his converts is instructive for how the sermonic themes of this gifted preacher moved beyond traditional ecclesiastical boundaries. Sixty-three-year-old Thomas Webb was a church clerk and tailor by trade in Bretforton, Worcestershire, who had spent much of his life duty-bound to his parish. Webb's letter to the preacher detailed a model conversion for Whitefield, who proudly printed the entire letter in the August 14, 1739, entry of his *Journals*. Webb described what he heard from Whitefield as "a new language," confessing, "though I remembered the letter of these doctrines, yet the spiritual sense thereof I was an utter stranger to." Conscientious church clerk that he was, he "searched an old Exposition of the Catechism, the Church Articles, and Book of Homilies, which I found exactly to correspond with what I had heard you deliver."[38] This observation was in keeping with Whitefield's oft-repeated rejoinder to naysayers that he was merely preaching what Protestant orthodoxy had always taught, but had laid aside or forgotten in recent times.

To be sure, however, a forceful challenge to establishment norms permeated his sermons as well. When he preached "On Regeneration," for example, Whitefield assailed common standards of membership in the Church of England. He lambasted the folly of assuming that everyone "baptized into Christ's church" might be said "to be in Christ." He pointed to the paramount importance of "an inward change and purity of heart" accompanying outward profession. By placing the accent on a conscious inward change, Whitefield defied an important church teaching on baptism found in Article 27 of the Thirty-Nine Articles of Religion, which linked baptism with regeneration. Revival preachers worried that presuming regeneration obviated the need for spiritual alertness and discipline. As a corrective measure, Whitefield swung the pendulum in the other direction and denied any relationship between baptism and regeneration altogether. He placed the new birth decisively in the realm of individual experience apart from baptism. In so doing, Whitefield's interpretation represented a significant downgrading of

37. Tyerman, *Life*, 2:68.
38. Whitefield, *Journals*, 359.

the church's teaching on baptism—something that even his Puritan forebears had not attempted. Not content to attack Article 27, Whitefield in another sermon entitled "Marks of a True Conversion" went as far as to decry baptism as "a sorry rotten foundation."[39]

Though an ordained Anglican priest, Whitefield was reaching back to the Separatist argument of Henry Barrow, an English Puritan. Barrow, who was executed for his views in 1593, had opposed John Calvin's indiscriminate practice in Geneva of receiving "the whole state, even al the profane and ignorant people into the bozome of the Church."[40] Unlike the Separatists who abandoned the church, however, Whitefield seized the corrupt state of the church as an opportunity to fly headlong back into the church. By the mid-eighteenth century, Whitefield held that the danger of merely notional religious adherence spread by the state church had become so pervasive that it justified his evangelistic tours of parishes throughout Britain and the American colonies. Whitefield's preaching of the new birth among professing Anglicans amounted to an audacious rebuke of their parish priests, calling the bluff on what many awakeners saw as superficial religion.

He ran further afoul of the established church in his sermon *The Nature and Necessity of Our New Birth in Christ Jesus* when he described his insistence on new birth "as an infallible rule for every person of whatever denomination, age, degree or quality, to judge himself by."[41] This trans-denominational message was heard by many of his Anglican colleagues as another form of all-out assault on the Church of England. In this manner, Whitefield's fast and furious travels placed contradictory impulses on display. He was an Anglican who preached a dissenting doctrine. At the same time, he traveled the breadth of the empire and sought to unite persons of all denominations. Rather than stake his claim on a single corner of the empire, he laid claim to all of it.

A key component that tied the content of Whitefield's preaching to the shape of his travel was his ceaseless networking for causes not directly related to individual churches. These activities demonstrated that

39. George Whitefield, *Sermons of George Whitefield* (Peabody: Hendrickson, 2009), 69.

40. Morgan, *Visible Saints*, 24.

41. George Whitefield, *The Nature and Necessity of Our New Birth in Christ Jesus, in Order to Salvation* (London, 1737), 23. The sermon, later reprinted as "On Regeneration," can be found in Lee Gatiss, ed., *The Sermons of George Whitefield* (Wheaton: Crossway, 2012), 2:275–87.

his aim was more than a religion of the heart. Whitefield embodied this aspect of his religion by supporting—and at times building—numerous orphanages, schools, and other institutions for the public good. Worth noting for our purposes is the fact that Whitefield's institution building activity took place in the backwoods of Georgia, the countryside of Pennsylvania, the southern part of Bristol, and so on. So prominent was this entrepreneurial streak that Benjamin Franklin noticed and proposed they work together to build a colony in the Ohio territory.[42] Given all of his activity, it might be said that Whitefield was one of the most creative empire builders of the early modern period.

A telling incident early in his career demonstrates this preference for far-flung networking over local religious efforts. In 1738, when the Board of Trustees of the Georgia colony charged him with the parish ministry at Savannah, it was an assignment he would utterly fail to fulfill, though not for lack of earnestness. The Trustees wanted him to erect a building for the church as soon as possible. To their consternation, however, he quickly got sidetracked into other projects. One of the first things he did early in 1740 was to break ground for his orphanage in the outskirts of Savannah. Not content with this work in Georgia, he agreed to purchase five thousand acres of land in Pennsylvania in order to build what he envisioned as "a school for negroes."[43] Back in England, he purchased another five hundred acres of land in Kingswood to start a school for children of colliers. An interest in charity work and institution building outside the church had been present even while he was a student at Oxford, as evidenced by his interest in prison ministry.[44] And so while these other projects absorbed his attention, the plan for an Anglican church building in Savannah languished.[45]

Previous studies have underappreciated the significance of these early institution-building efforts scattered across the Atlantic world,

42. Benjamin Franklin to George Whitefield, July 2, 1756, in *The Papers of Benjamin Franklin*, 42 vols. to date, ed. Leonard W. Larabee et al. (New Haven: Yale University Press, 1959–), 6:468–69.

43. Seward, *Journal of a Voyage*, 80.

44. Whitefield, *Journals*, 98–100.

45. Kenneth Coleman attributes part of the reason to the lack of Trustee willingness to fund the project. This claim is discredited in notes by the Earl of Egmont: "Mr Geo. Whitefield attended, and deliver'd in an acct of the money received by him and Mr Habersham for building a Church at Savannah, and disbursements made by him on that Acct." January 23, 1744, *The Journal of the Earl of Egmont*, in Candler, *Colonial Records*, 5:714.

which testified to Whitefield's strategic emphasis in diverse areas of empire. These projects also contradict the notion of Whitefield as a young anti-institutionalist who only in his later years saw the folly of his ways. Though by no means a comprehensively articulated vision, the imperial shape of his early labors is discernible in the ways he employed new birth preaching to spark entrepreneurial activity in various parts of British territory.

A tragic aspect of Whitefield's career comes into focus when we follow his frantic institution-building activity, which had a number of regrettable developments. As we will see more fully in the next chapter, so invested did Whitefield become in the fledgling imperial project in Georgia that he changed course from his early criticism of slavery and lobbied for the introduction of slavery in the struggling colony. Nimble theological footwork that envisioned proselytizing enslaved Africans aside, this example of moral attrition serves to highlight the close competition between religious and imperial concerns in the Grand Itinerant's ministry.

The Whitefield who exploited emerging imperial possibilities for new preaching opportunities, nonetheless, did not accept every aspect of empire without criticism. While attention to the imperial context appears to have heightened his concern for the strong evangelistic focus in his preaching, his message also conveyed a compelling critique of the state of empire. A prime example is Whitefield's critique of wealth and worldly amusement amid his efforts to promote the new birth in the fiercely competitive marketplace of a growing empire. He made known to his listeners that the wealth and glamor of Charleston, bearing striking resemblance to London, grated on his pious sensibilities: "I question whether the court-end of London could exceed them in affected finery, gaiety of dress, and a deportment ill-becoming persons who have had such Divine judgments lately sent amongst them."[46] For Whitefield, the divine judgment of imperial warfare served as a reminder that Charleston was not London. Rather than repeat the mistakes of London, a city like Charleston, exposed as it was on the fringe of empire, had an opportunity—and obligation—to carve out an improved Christian identity.

In Philadelphia, Whitefield's deputy William Seward stirred controversy when he wrote in *The Pennsylvania Gazette* that "since Mr. White-

---

46. Whitefield, *Journals*, 421.

field's Preaching there, the Dancing-School and Concert-Room have been shut up, as inconsistent with the Doctrines of the Gospel."[47] As publicist for Whitefield's American tour, Seward routinely submitted his brief notices and summaries of the preaching sensation without much controversy. This time, however, a spokesman for the dancing school in Philadelphia took Seward to task for his spin on the facts. With a rejoinder in the following week's paper, he accused Seward of misrepresentation, "as tho' [Whitefield] had met with great Success among the better Sort of People in Pennsylvania, when at the same Time, to his great Mortification, he can't but be sensible that he has been neglected by them."[48] Thus a protracted battle commenced between Whitefield and some of the Philadelphia elite.

Benjamin Franklin himself joined the conflict on Whitefield's side, using the pseudonym Obadiah Plainman and objecting vigorously to the unfortunate choice of words in "the better sort." Marshaling the "New Whig" argument of authors like John Trenchard and Thomas Gordon, Franklin decried the elite condescension of wealthy Philadelphians who gathered among themselves in institutions like the dancing school.[49] In this light, it is apparent that a controversy over "innocent diversion" represented, more than fussy moralism, a critique of the wealthy elite in that city. Some might dismiss the controversy as curmudgeonly interference with harmless social entertainment. As Franklin knew, however, much more than an innocent form of amusement was at stake. The ensuing battle in the public square of colonial Philadelphia demonstrated the combustibility of Whitefield's new birth theology and its potent critique of the social order. His message not only offered spiritual hope indiscriminately to all social classes, but it did so by attempting to level the playing field for all sorts throughout British society.

47. *The Pennsylvania Gazette*, May 1, 1740. Also in Whitefield, *Journals*, 16–17.
48. *The Pennsylvania Gazette*, May 8, 1740.
49. For a fuller discussion of the embattled Habermasian "public square" in Philadelphia and of the significance of Whitefield's and Franklin's contributions, see William Pencak, "Beginning of a Beautiful Friendship: Benjamin Franklin, George Whitefield, the 'Dancing School Blockheads,' and a Defense of the 'Meaner Sort,'" *Proteus: A Journal of Ideas* 19, no. 1 (2002): 45–50.

Beyond the New Birth

So far this section has explored the content of Whitefield's new birth preaching, the imperial context in which he proclaimed that message, and the transatlantic ramifications of his empire-wide ministry. We saw the ways in which Whitefield's confrontation with historical debates over theology and ecclesiology shaped his impact in society and empire. He preached a fiery religious message, but his was also a homiletical strategy focused on the growing edges of empire and responding to the challenges of identity in a constantly expanding and contested world. The progress of empire proved difficult to manage as religious controversies, military conflicts, and scientific discoveries piled on throughout the eighteenth century. Revival religion, and more specifically the hope of new birth, became one way to articulate British identity during this period. What Susan O'Brien has called "a transatlantic community of saints" also amounted—through the efforts of itinerant preaching, letter writing, and institution building—to a reimagined empire of Protestant Britons.[50]

But to put empire at the center of Whitefield's career also enables a charting of significant changes in his religious interests. In fact, a study of Whitefield's early emphasis on the new birth prepares the way for a deeper understanding of developments in his later life. One of the untold stories of that life is the dramatic homiletical shifts that occurred in his later years. For all of his early energy advocating the new birth, Whitefield's later years witnessed much less attention to regeneration in his public ministry. At the very least, he became less vocal about the new birth. This change must be understood in terms of the life cycle of a revival, which has an inevitable end.

And so it is appropriate to conclude this section with a reflection on the devolution of Whitefield's new birth emphasis over the course of his career. His published *Journals*, which cover his life through the year 1741, contain forty-eight separate references to spiritual regeneration and the new birth. In volume one of his collected works with letters in the period 1735–1742, there are no less than sixteen references. Yet these high figures, indicative of Whitefield's preoccupation with this particular doctrine, declined dramatically in the period after the peak

---

50. O'Brien, "A Transatlantic Community of Saints." For the role of Protestantism in fashioning British identity, see also Colley, *Britons*.

of revival.[51] For instance, in the second volume of his collected works, which covers the years 1742–1753, the new birth is mentioned in only two letters written in 1749. In the third volume, containing letters from the final period of his life, 1753–1770, there is not a single mention of either regeneration or the new birth. While any attempt to extrapolate from these numbers should proceed with caution, it is nevertheless reasonable to infer that in the years following revival fervor Whitefield's other activities appear to have eclipsed new birth preaching. Having reckoned with the transitory nature of revival gains, Whitefield would turn his attention to encouraging imperial expansion, establishing networks to hold British identity together in the growing Atlantic world, and building institutions that embodied revivalistic ideals. At the very point where religious historians lose interest, Whitefield's revival theology began developing the cultural sophistication necessary to make it useful to British imperial society. For this shift to happen, the new birth's focus on personal interiority had to give way to broad-level interaction between a theology of renewal and a politics of empire.

When revival embers died down and Whitefield struggled to fan the flames of a movement beset by backsliders, his religious message evolved. Only by duly noting the emphatic focus on new birth preaching in the early phase of his ministry can we also appreciate the changes that occurred later. Though Whitefield never stopped preaching the gospel of new life, he tempered his sermons and recalibrated his strategy along the way. By the end of his life, he had become a fully invested builder of institutions, spending the last decade of his life trying to turn his orphanage in Georgia into a college and seminary of higher learning.

In an age of sweeping commercial and cultural changes, Whitefield presented old doctrines in new garb as he adapted to a period of enlightenment critique and imperial warfare. The combination of open philosophical inquiry and economic as well as political acquisitiveness created the very setting in which a post-Puritan like Whitefield could thrive.[52] As he oversaw the power of new birth preaching to disrupt the social order, to remake individuals, and to reconcile individual piety

51. This downturn also helps signal a pivot away from revival preaching to other kinds of activities and strengthens the argument made in the next section of this chapter that the revivals came to an end in the early 1740s.

52. Foster claimed that Whitefield "fatally rupture[d] the Puritan movement." Foster, *The Long Argument*, 290.

with imperial expansion, what was once a Puritan dilemma between self and society became an evangelical opportunity.[53] His success shows the ways in which religious revivalism and empire building each informed the other during the period of the First Great Awakening.

Whitefield was not merely a subject of the British king but also a product of the British Empire. Whitefieldian revival rode the coattails of imperial expansion. With his help, religious practice and meaning imbued a sprawling empire with a cogent sense of identity, or at least the possibility of one. To put it another way, the evangelical revivals may have helped anglicize British imperial outposts far more effectively than direct political pressure. Before John Wesley uttered the same saying, Whitefield declared, "The world is my parish." He might more accurately have said, "The empire is my parish." Whatever pious language Whitefield may have used to color over his frenetic activities, his actions reveal a wide-ranging ambition with pretentions for the whole empire. This section on Whitefield's preaching has sought to uncover both the religious power and historical contingency of his new birth preaching in the Atlantic world of the eighteenth century. To the decline of revival and to Whitefield's improvisational work in consolidating religious gains throughout the empire we now turn.

The Decline of Revival

The revivals, like most things in life, faded over time. Before long, Whitefield's preaching of the new birth, which once sparked the Great Awakening, gave way to the doldrums of ordinary life and institutional management. This later development is a neglected feature of the story due to the inordinate attention historians have given to the heyday of revival. Retrieving a fuller picture of the Great Awakening's history in order to capture not only its climax but also its denouement is a fruitful historical endeavor. For if a single snapshot can reveal much that is intriguing, a series of pictures encompassing a longer story offers the possibility of uncovering larger trends, especially if they represent a sustained period from a variety of angles.

By listening to diverse voices, including naysayers, evangelical supporters, and Whitefield's own perspective on the changing arc

53. See Morgan, *The Puritan Dilemma*; Foster, *The Long Argument*.

of revival, this next section documents the decline of enthusiastic religion, followed by another section that establishes a more direct alignment between the revival's winding course and British empire building. To do so is to recognize that, however lasting the effects of the Great Awakening, the sharp downturn in religious intensity that followed also merits examination. To follow the course of revival has the potential to deepen our understanding of both religious and imperial forces at work in the British Atlantic world of the mid-eighteenth century. While subsequent chapters will probe Whitefield's post-revival activities in the last two decades of his life, the remainder of this chapter will treat the period of transition in the 1740s and the immediate aftermath of the Great Awakening. As spiritual fervor waned during these years, Whitefield cast about for stronger moorings. Because he was a controversial public figure, many of his adversaries relished the crisis of religion that so quickly followed on the heels of those remarkable years of apparent revitalization. Listening closely to these critical voices will permit a clearer assessment of what happened after revival.

Whitefield's relationship to the Anglican mission of the Society for the Propagation of the Gospel (SPG), and to one SPG cleric in particular, is a good place to begin an account of the revivalist after the revival. Despite Whitefield's Anglican credentials, missionary priests of the SPG generally found him irksome. Established in 1701, the SPG arose out of the conviction that America offered not only political and commercial benefits but also obliged faithful Protestants to evangelistic witness among the natives. In contrast to Whitefield's wide-ranging itinerancy, SPG missionaries settled where they ministered. In typical fashion, William Becket heeded the call to missionary work and in 1721 settled in Lewes, Sussex County, in Delaware, where he labored faithfully into the 1740s. His letterbook chronicles a life devoted to dutiful execution of his responsibilities as a missionary priest of the Church of England. Setting down his roots in a sparsely populated region, Becket was the sole spiritual authority for several scattered villages. "I must ride generally 40 or 50 miles every week, sometimes 60–70 miles in summer, else I cannot do the duties of this County," he reported with a sense of pride to his superiors back home.[54] So arduous

---

54. *Reverend William Becket's Notices and Letters Concerning Incidents at Lewes Town, 1727–1742*, Historical Society of Pennsylvania, 128.

was this routine that "A Horse lasts me a year or 2, and a suit of cloths half a year."[55] Judging by their repetition throughout a letterbook covering several decades, his requests for additional funding to meet the expenses of this demanding environment went largely unanswered. It was thankless work in a remote parish larger than anything seen back in England.

Yet Becket appears to have made good of a difficult situation. And others provided a good report of his work, including the Deputy Governor of Pennsylvania, Patrick Gordon, who described Becket as "a man of a sober good character likewise" in charge of "The Church of Lewestown & two other Churches or Chapels."[56] The honeymoon between Becket and Gordon, however, did not last long. The governor managed to offend Becket with his meddling in ecclesiastical affairs when he gave dissenting ministers the authority to sign marriage licenses. Becket wrote to his superiors protesting this grave offense, citing that he "hath granted marriage licenses promiscuously to be lodged with us & the Presbyterian ministers, a thing never done before in this Government except only in the last year of Sr Wm Keith his immediate Predecessor when his fortune grew precarious & he was willing by any means to raise money."[57] With deep investment in the social, religious, and political life of his colony, Becket was an active public leader. As such, he was sensitive to slights against Anglicanism and protective of his standing as the parish minister and guardian of theological orthodoxy. His turf protectiveness against the governor's liberal policies reveals the complex nature of ecclesiastical politics and colonial identity during this time. On the one hand, Becket held fast to the distinctions and authority afforded him by his ordained office in the established church. He sought to do his part in upholding some semblance of order, which meant replicating the ways of Lambeth and Whitehall. On the other hand, the colonial context provided little of the familiar stability and advantage he may have expected as an Anglican priest.

55. *William Becket's Notices and Letters*, 128.

56. P. Gordon to the Lord Bishop of London, July 19, 1726, in William Stevens Perry, *Historical Collections Relating to the American Colonial Church* (Hartford: The Church Press, 1871), 2:150. Delaware was part of the Penn proprietorship from 1682 to 1776 and was under Pennsylvania's jurisdiction.

57. W. Becket to the Lord Bishop of London, March 15, 1728, in Perry, *Historical Collections*, 2:150.

In early 1738, Becket still saw the world through a British lens. He described the people of his parish as being "generally Professors of the Ch of England and . . . little inclined either to Bigotry, or Enthusiasm."[58] Though there were dissenting parties, he was not too worried about their influence. In a revealing statement, he noted, "Quakerism decays strangely, even in this Province, the Nursery of it; only for want of Opposition. The Missionaries here are generally of Opinion, That let it alone & it will die of itself. We study to be quiet & mind our own Business."[59] A year prior to Whitefield's arrival in Lewes, Becket assured himself and others that he possessed an adequate strategy for dealing with religious enthusiasm. He was in for a great surprise.

Becket appears also to have developed a severe case of wanderlust by 1738, after years of grueling and repetitive work in Lewes. An appreciation of his relative geographical immobility is helpful for understanding the intensity of his contempt for Whitefield, which was influenced to some degree by envy. He requested an exchange with the SPG's agent on Staten Island, the details of which he had worked out beforehand with the New York missionary, Brother Harris. He wrote an impassioned letter to the Society, describing the attraction of city life for a family man like himself as well as the eminent suitability of a rural parish for the aging Harris. Lewes was "generally poor" but the society's salary would "well support a single person, as [Harris] is." After years of being passed over for a raise, this was yet another attempt to let his needs be known. Besides, "as this is a very private Corner of the World, [Harris] desires to end his Days in Retirement, being now about the Age of Sixty." He also assured the society that the people of Staten Island and their governor were agreeable to the exchange and eager for his services, "more especially because they want a Man of Learning to assist in the Education of their Sons." Becket believed he could fill this void by a move to the city. The relative comfort and glamor of an urban context no doubt appealed to Becket as well, who observed that the parents of that place were "not only able but willing to be at the Expence of as good an Education as may be had for their Children." It is possible he felt that his good education and strong pastoral skills were being underutilized in Lewes and wanted the opportunities available in a

---

58. Letter dated March 29, 1738, in *William Becket's Notices and Letters*, 82.
59. *William Becket's Notices and Letters*, 82.

more densely populated setting like Staten Island. In concluding his letter, Becket appealed to the Society's concern for learning and the common good. "If the Hon Society judges that this Affair will be of any Service to Learning & Rel; as well as to My Health & Interest"—Becket's words turned almost to pleading—"I know they will grant the Prayer of my Petition."[60]

The following year, in the fall of 1739, Becket was still unhappily stationed in Lewes when the upstart itinerant preacher George Whitefield passed through his parish. In this celebrity priest, Becket perceived a rival more than an ally. He saw in Whitefield all that was wrong with religious enthusiasm and the frustrations of his own missionary work in a colonial setting. Though little is known about his time in Lewes, Whitefield began his second American tour by landing at this port town in October 1739 where he preached a few sermons before making the 120-mile trek by land to Philadelphia. Even in this short period, Whitefield managed to ruffle feathers, including Becket's. In a letter of March 18, 1740, Becket offered perfunctory thanks for the published letters and journals Whitefield had sent him and quickly moved to a scathing critique of the itinerant's ministry. Perhaps Becket sensed that the packet of books was not merely a sign of friendship but part of Whitefield's aggressive strategy of preaching and printing to reach as wide an audience as possible. Among other things, he protested Whitefield's "fathering of Adam's sin upon us . . . damning of infants . . . accusing the mercy and justice of God by absolute Predestination . . . [and] inward feelings which are no evidence to any one (besides yourself) . . . and throw[ing] about you Hell and Damnation Fire and brimstone enough to have burnt a Wooden Frame." So upset was this missionary priest of Lewes that by the end of the letter he ascribed to Whitefield "the highest impudence from a beardless Boy." (He seems to have had second thoughts about an overly acerbic tone and later crossed out "from a beardless boy" in his letterbook.)[61] Historians have recognized the powerful effects of Whitefield's approach: "In a number of complex ways, Whitefield's revival reshaped both the oral present and the printed past, and it did so on a scale hitherto undreamt of. His preaching was accompanied by printed accounts of its impact, published in both England

60. *William Becket's Notices and Letters*, 82–84.
61. *William Becket's Notices and Letters*, 103–4.

and the colonies."[62] By coordinating his preaching appearances with his published accounts, Whitefield sought to broaden his impact. Becket had no desire to aid and abet the evangelist's schemes.

Writing to Whitefield apparently put Becket in an apoplectic mood and he took a break in his letterbook to sketch out a "recipe to make a Methodist." It seems likely that he was thinking specifically of White-field as he called for "'two tablespoons of impudence' to a concoction that also included 'the tongue and teeth of a rattlesnake' along with 'the heart and gall of a Pharisee.'"[63] Becket was furious with Whitefield for consorting with the very Presbyterians he reviled and for wreaking havoc on the decades of work he had poured with great sacrifice into Lewes. In his view, the revivalist "hath done more mischief in America by reviling the Clergy, & misrepresenting Xanity than all the Dissenters put together," he wrote to his superiors the following March. Shedding greater light on Becket's situation not only helps us understand his fury but also the broader impact of Whitefield's itinerant ministry on exist-ing conditions in the American colonies.

Yet, by 1741, Whitefield's brand of religious enthusiasm had faded as suddenly as it swept the area. Although schismatic factions persisted, it appears Becket soon regained control of his parish. His church ser-vices were once again well-attended, with overflow services happening outside "under the green trees" in summertime.[64] On September 26, 1742, he wrote a routine report to his SPG superiors that likely con-tained some embellishments but also depicted the ephemeral state of Whitefieldian revival:

I have the pleasure to acqt you now, yt Enthusiasm abates, as fast as it once increased here. Mr. Whitefield & followers have recanted, some of them the most considerable in Print. And the truth is, your Mission-aries have conquer'd & convinced them, not so much by Opposition, as by Patience and by Studying to be quiet & to mind their own Business.[65]

---

62. Hugh Amory and David D. Hall, *A History of the Book in America* (New York: Cambridge University Press, 2000), 50.

63. "A Receipt to make a Methodist," March 4, 1740, in *William Becket's Notices and Letters*, 115.

64. It appears Becket was not bashful about employing some Whitefieldian tech-niques himself. Becket, letter on October 16, 1741, in *William Becket's Notices and Letters*, 127.

65. *William Becket's Notices and Letters*, 134.

Two things about his remarks are worth noting: the timing and the mode of the alleged abatement. In the fall of 1742, Whitefield was back in England embroiled in theological controversy with the Wesleys, traveling to Scotland, and laying the groundwork for the Calvinistic Methodist Association for which he would become the inaugural moderator in the following year. In other words, at the very height of the revival years, those revival gains in other parts of the empire were already vanishing. Furthermore, it is striking that Becket should point out the use of print in "recanting" the advances made by Whitefield and his followers. The very tools Whitefield so creatively used were being used against him.

Thanks to Becket's letterbook, the situation in Lewes reminds us of the limits of traveling itinerants like Whitefield who passed through towns offering a new and exhilarating message of religious vibrancy but rarely lingered long enough to see the established fruits of their labor. Through little more than "patience and by studying to be quiet," but also by the sheer weight of enduring presence, missionaries of the Anglican Church successfully resisted and in some cases quelled the revivals.

Lewes presents, moreover, a lesson in contrasts. Unlike nearby Philadelphia, Boston, or even Savannah, which held strategic value for Whitefield's burgeoning imperial work and which received his concentrated attention, there were many other places that fell by the wayside in the afterglow of revival. Inasmuch as the awakenings presented the opportunity of an inter-colonial movement, for Whitefield it was the bigger imperial picture that received his full attention. From his earliest period in America, he demonstrated this preference for a transatlantic consolidation of evangelical revivalism. Any attempt to view Whitefield's influence on only one side of the Atlantic fails because he had a markedly bilateral strategy when it came to his itinerancy and institution building activities.

Far from a lone voice in the wilderness, Becket provides evidence for the kind of vehement opposition Whitefield faced. When Whitefield returned to America in August 1744, the publication of anti-Whitefieldian literature had become a burgeoning industry. Penned by a growing coalition of parish ministers as well as college professors and presidents, the attacks on Whitefield ranged from defamation of his personal character to charges of doctrinal negligence and cultural nescience.[66] By the mid-

---

66. For examples of the opposition to Whitefield, see Charles Chauncey, *Enthusi-*

1740s, some nonconformists in New England tried to dismiss White-field's brand of revival religion by referring to it as "imported Divinity."[67] The fact that these British colonists objected to the perceived British "importation" of religion (in much the same way that Scottish Presbyte-rians had heaped scorn on Whitefield's ties to the corrupt Church of England) provides evidence of an inchoate sense of American differentness that was already forming in the early 1740s. In his peculiarly bellicose way, Whitefield labored to hold together a fragmenting British imperial identity. What appears on the one hand as a scattershot approach to his travels in preaching, emerges upon deeper inspection as an intentionally broad vision and strategy. The elusive nature of lasting and widespread revival, in other words, ought not to detract from the more focused goal of a distinctly British vision rooted in Protestant religious vitality. An appreciation of Whitefield's imperial-minded thinking provides the groundwork for apprehending the scale of not only the high aspirations but also the deep disappointments of his imperial hopes in the mid-eighteenth century. The decline of enthusiasm is just as much a part of the story of the Great Awakening and Whitefield's part as its most well-known champion.

Not only anti-revivalists but also radical revivalists hampered the revival's momentum. During Whitefield's time away from America between 1741 and 1744, there were several high-profile incidents that

---

asm described and caution'd against (1742); *The Testimony of the Pastors of the Churches in the Province of Massachusetts Bay, in New England, at their Annual Convention in Boston, May 25, 1743, against several Errors in Doctrine and Disorders in Practice, which have of late obtained in various parts of the Land* (Boston: Printed by Rogers and Fowle, for S. Eliot in Cornhill, 1743); "The Testimony and Advice of a Number of Laymen, respecting Religion and the Teachers of it. Addressed to the Pastors of New England" (Boston, September 12, 1743); "A Letter from two neighbouring Associations of Ministers in the Country, to the Associated Ministers of Boston and Charlestown, relating to the admission of Mr. Whitefield into their pulpits" (December 26, 1744); Edward Wigglesworth, D.D., and Rev. Edward Holyoke, "A Testimony from the President and Professors, Tutors, and Hebrew Instructor of Harvard College, against the Rev. Mr. George Whitefield and his Conduct" (December 28, 1744); *A Letter to the Rev. Mr. George Whitefield, by way of Reply to his Answer to the College Testimony against him and his Conduct. By Edward Wigglesworth, D. D., Professor of Divinity in said College. To which is added the Reverend President's Answer to the things charged upon him, by the said Mr. Whitefield, as Inconsistencies. Boston, New England, 1745* (Boston: T. Fleet, 1745).

67. While Kidd attributes this phrase to Thomas Foxcroft, he was actually citing the words (and evoking the caricature) deployed by Whitefield's enemies. Kidd, *The Great Awakening*, 50; Lambert, *Inventing the "Great Awakening,"* 88.

caused embarrassment to the revivalists, discrediting the awakenings in the eyes of many.[68] A notable example can be found in the life of Hugh Bryan, a wealthy planter in South Carolina who converted under Whitefield's preaching ministry in June 1740. Bryan's new religious convictions soon became a source of consternation for his neighbors in South Carolina when he combined prophetic tirades against immoral settler behavior with a paternalistic rhetoric of sympathy toward slaves. Two years later, when Bryan, who had been growing increasingly unstable, attempted to part a river by smiting it with a stick and nearly drowned while trying to cross the unresponsive river, his neighbors took full advantage of the opportunity to put him in his place.[69]

A year later, on March 6, 1743, a radical revivalist named James Davenport, whose erratic behavior had for some time worried his fellow revivalists, created a bonfire of religious protest in New London, Connecticut. At his instigation, participants hurled not only books but items of clothing they had torn away from persons in their midst. Adding insult to the injury of Davenport's bonfire, Andrew Croswell, a Harvard graduate and Connecticut pastor, called for separation from existing churches, thereby throwing down a gauntlet that would be hard to take back.[70] In his enthusiasm, Croswell began criticizing several prominent moderates—including Eleazar Wheelock, missionary and college founder in New Hampshire, and Thomas Foxcroft, a New Light pastor and defender of Whitefield in Boston. When critics accused Croswell of saying "where a Minister and his People are at Peace, Satan is at the Head of it," he denied saying it while simultaneously declaring, "There seems too much Truth in the Remark."[71] Such outbursts roused a few but proved unpalatable for most enthusiasts. In these ways, it was not only the opposition of anti-revivalists but

68. For the growing rift between moderate and radical revivalists, see Kidd, *The Great Awakening*, 65–67.

69. A detailed account is in Harvey H. Jackson, "Prophecy and Community: Hugh Bryan, George Whitefield, and the Stoney Creek Independent Presbyterian Church," *American Presbyterians* 69, no. 1 (1991): 15–17.

70. One historian has protested the lack of scholarly attention on Croswell's infamy: "Croswell was more persistent and visible, provoked more controversies, itinerated longer, and published more tracts than any other incendiary New Light, including James Davenport." Leigh Eric Schmidt, "'A Second and Glorious Reformation': The New Light Extremism of Andrew Croswell," *The William and Mary Quarterly: A Magazine of Early American History and Culture* 43, no. 2 (1986): 214.

71. Cited in Schmidt, "'A Second and Glorious Reformation,'" 222.

also the radicalism of some pro-revivalists that led to the stifling of revival fires.

Moderate critics also began to express qualms about the Awakening's tendency toward extremism. A few weeks before Whitefield landed on American soil for his third tour, Boston pro-revivalist Thomas Foxcroft penned a letter to Samuel Philips on October 10, 1744, defending the Grand Itinerant, though not without a fair amount of equivocation. He acknowledged that Whitefield "may not always have so happily expressed himself, with that nice judgment and care of exact distinction between different cases, which it were to be wished he had." As best as he could, Foxcroft attempted to salvage what was possible from the publication of Whitefield's *Journals*. He blamed "the slips of a young pen" and admitted that "he has sometimes been greatly injudicious in the Choice of his Phrases . . . spoken in terms abundantly too strong." Because of Whitefield's frequent travels, which meant he was often "writing in haste and as it were extempore," Foxcroft requested "charity which covereth a multitude of sins."[72] He might as well have issued a public apology on behalf of Whitefield.

By 1745, even the stalwart Benjamin Colman had wearied of Whitefield's antics. In a draft of a letter to Whitefield, he apologized for an earlier indiscretion, in all probability referring to some strong expression of doubt or criticism toward the itinerant: "if there was any thing too sudden, severe, suspicious or judging in mine to you, I retract & ask pardon for it."[73] Yet if Colman needed to patch up relations with Whitefield, that task was even more urgent with ministers close to home. With the revivals rapidly becoming a distant memory, Colman did not have the luxury like Whitefield of setting sail for a new destination. Instead, he had to contend with the residual effects of division and a bitter partisan spirit. He vented to Solomon Wiliams, "You will bewail the Spirit of Wrath, Bitterness, & Contention, Scorn & Division, with wch our Papers & Prints here are overflowing from week to week." He expressed relief that Whitefield himself "seems to grow more & more sensible of the Evil Spirit of Alienation and Animosity among us & the wrath of our Ministers." Such a sentiment coming from one of Whitefield's

72. Thomas Foxcroft to Samuel Philips, October 10, 1744, Gratz Collection, Historical Society of Pennsylvania.

73. Draft of letter, Benjamin Colman to George Whitefield, January 14, 1745, Benjamin Colman Papers, Massachusetts Historical Society.

staunchest allies in Boston gives some indication of the dire straits in which revivalists found themselves at this late stage of the Awakening. Notwithstanding the challenges he faced in New England, Whitefield, who had only recently returned from England, was preoccupied with thoughts of Georgia, according to a leery Colman: "He speaks of hastening toward Georgia and was hesitating last week whether directly by water." While acknowledging Whitefield's orphanage there as a worthy charitable effort, Colman also expressed doubts about its broader utility, wondering, "how the house will answer the expence in benefits to the church and state, is a matter of doubtful event in my dark mind."[74] To judge from Colman's concerns about whirling controversies and philanthropic distractions, there was a very real sense that the revival movement was coming apart at the seams.

Thus when Whitefield returned to America in the fall of 1744, there was no hero's welcome, no rabble of fawning fans. The resounding positive press he enjoyed only a few years prior had weakened to a barely perceptible whisper. To make matters worse, he suffered a serious illness during the sea voyage that left him bedridden for the first few weeks of his third American visit. During this period, much of the blame for the abatement of revival also fell on Whitefield and the publication of his *Journals*. The criticisms so stung the itinerant that in 1756 he would issue a revised version with some of the most controversial parts excised. Until then, however, Whitefield had to live with the consequences of his rash, immodest words.

In truth, the dissemination of Whitefield's *Journals* flummoxed many of his friends even as they roused the opposition. Though Whitefield insisted that they were published prematurely without his consent, he regularly sent copies to friend and foe alike on both sides of the Atlantic. Unusual for their self-conscious disclosures and self-aggrandizing details, the *Journals* left an indelible imprint on Whitefield's public image. For instance, when he drew parallels between the circumstances of his birth in an inn and Jesus's birth in a manger, he elicited ridicule rather than awe or admiration. Perhaps even more significant is the fact that the outcry against the *Journals* constrained Whitefield's writing and publishing activity for much of the rest of his career. The fact that he published so little subsequent to the *Journals* represents not only a tactical shift but a profound change in his overall approach to his trans-

74. Benjamin Colman to Solomon Williams, April 12, 1745, Gratz Collection, Historical Society of Pennsylvania.

atlantic work. Instead of aiming for large-scale impact through personal missives, he would use isolated and incremental pieces of communication. Though he never quite ceased being the inveterate self-promoter, he began much more to rally attention not around himself but rather around British imperial concerns.

Print coming from Whitefield himself was not the only evidence for the decline of revivals; the magazines that had served to promote revival were also going out of business. The *Christian History* published weekly stories about the revivals in a transatlantic market over the course of two years, from March 1743 to February 1745. As a compilation of the most riveting accounts culled from across the British Empire, the magazine sought to inform, promote, and shape the revivals. It featured some of the most prominent revivalists, such as Tennent and Whitefield, but also shared news of lesser known preachers in remote places, such as James Robe in Kilsyth, Scotland. Readers in New England learned of similar revivals affecting communities across the Atlantic. By presenting the revivals as an empire-wide phenomenon, the *Christian History* presented a new way of looking at the world, which those who experienced the revivals in turn had the opportunity to refashion.

Despite its ambitious goal of introducing a new hermeneutic of revival that helped participants reshape their world, the publication came to an abrupt end during the early part of 1745.[75] Though declining interest and plummeting sales may be the most obvious reasons, it appears that Thomas Prince Jr. also had trouble finding current stories of revival. Evincing scarcity of new materials, the last two months of the *Christian History* (in January–February 1745) presented little more than rehashed narratives of Whitefield's ministry from 1740 and 1741. In the last section of the final issue, there was the hope of new issues based on fresh stories: "it is propos'd to publish [new narratives daily expected] in intire Pieces of about three Sheets once a Quarter at 12d New Tenor; and those who would encourage their Publication are desired to send their Names to Kneeland & Green in Queen-street."[76] It appears new materials were difficult to attain. That no further issues were published is not surprising given what we know about the general lessening of

75. On "hermeneutic of revival," see Tim D. Hall, "Imagining a Transatlantic Awakening: The *Christian History* and the Hermeneutics of Revival," in *Periodical Literature in Eighteenth-Century America*, ed. Mark Kamrath and Sharon M. Harris (Knoxville: University of Tennessee Press, 2005), 29–46.

76. *Christian History*, No. 104, February 23, 1745.

revival episodes after the mid-1740s. It is reasonable to surmise that the suspension of the *Christian History* resulted from the decline of actual incidents and, therefore, a diminishing reportage of revival.

On the other side of their mountaintop experiences, Whitefield and his fellow revivalists had to contend with the challenge of maintaining a revival movement that was spread thin across the Atlantic world. Whitefield spent the first half of the decade shuttling from New England to the American South to the English countryside. He traveled both east and west of London, journeyed to Wales, and made two trips to Scotland. After a three-year tour around Britain, Whitefield returned to America in the middle of 1744 only to resume his fast-paced travels through the American colonies. It is as if he believed that by his furious pace he could keep the flame of transatlantic revivals burning all by himself.

An argument for the downward turn of the Great Awakening by the mid-1740s is persuasive in the end because its most prominent proponents said as much. Major pro-revivalists like Jonathan Edwards, Thomas Prince, and Gilbert Tennent all declared the revivals to be over in the mid-1740s. Though their precise dating varied, there was unanimity in their declaration about the end of revival. By the middle of the decade, numerous revival preachers including Edwards, Colman, and Whitefield himself were speaking and writing about the *late* great and glorious work of God, relinquishing the season of revival to the past.[77] One historian has argued that "as early as 1746, no semblance of an extensive, uniform, intercolonial revival could any longer be found."[78] In that year, Prince was found once again writing about the "Greatness of that Salvation God has given us," by which he meant not religious revival but military victory. Gilbert Tennent could pronounce in 1749 that "the Church is now in its ordinary State." In short, the late revivals appeared to have been thoroughly "conquered"—to use William Becket's words—in areas where they had only recently spread like wildfire.

---

77. Lambert, *Inventing the "Great Awakening,"* 251–53.

78. Lambert, *Inventing the "Great Awakening,"* 251–52. Lambert assigned blame for this stifling of revival to religious squabbling, in the form of Old Light critique as well as internal schisms rising out of the imprudence of ministers like Davenport and Croswell. In addition, he asserted the role of "Whitefield's own indiscretions" in contributing to the decline of revival. Others have emphasized the continuation of revival, albeit at a reduced tenor and in more localized forms; see Kidd, *The Great Awakening*; Catherine A. Brekus, *Sarah Osborn's World: The Rise of Evangelical Christianity in Early America* (New Haven: Yale University Press, 2013).

Religious Revival and Imperial War

In a century filled with war, the decade of the 1740s had more than its share of military conflicts. During the War of Austrian Succession (1740–1748) in Europe and King George's War (1744–1748) in America, Britain and France faced off in a number of battles across the Atlantic world. Compounding this picture was the War of Jenkins' Ear (1739–1748), a conflict with Spain. War came to the home front as well. With Jacobite aspirations to reclaim the British throne, Charles Edward Stuart, the Young Pretender, landed with an invading force in Scotland in 1745. His defeat and a decisive victory for Hanoverian reign at Culloden in the Scottish Highlands provided sorely needed encouragement for beleaguered Britons across the Atlantic world.

Meanwhile, back in America, Colonel William Pepperell called on his preacher friend Whitefield to help raise troops for the expedition against French Cape Breton in present-day Canada. Though Whitefield balked at first, he later confided in a letter that "Providence seemed to force me into it."[79] After sleeping on the matter, he issued the motto, "Nil desperandum Christo duce" (no need to fear with Christ as leader) and preached on the importance of national duty at such a critical juncture.[80] Whitefield mingled political and spiritual efforts in order to bolster both and in the process cast his lot with the empire. The eventual capture of Louisbourg, capital of the French colony of Île-Royal, further helped rally British patriotism among provincials in America. Amid the tumult and triumph, Whitefield got his first taste of mixing war with religion. It would certainly not be his last.

In fact, the relationship between imperial war and revival religion became increasingly complicated in the aftermath of the Great Awakening. One common view has been that worries over an impending war superseded the religious concerns that had helped to enflame revival.[81]

---

79. Letter dated Boston, July 29, 1745, in Tyerman, *Life*, 2:150.

80. Translation: "Nothing is hopeless where Christ leads." In recounting this moment, Tyerman notes: "To say the least, this is a curious episode in English history,—Whitefield, the despised Methodist preacher, associated with one of England's conquests,—a conquest so important, that King George II raised Colonel Pepperell to the dignity of a baronet of Great Britain; and London and other places went mad with joy." Tyerman, *Life*, 2:151–52.

81. Scholars like Frank Lambert posited a causal link between the declining interest in religion and a corresponding rise in public attention on war (in addition

Far from seeing war as a distraction to religious concerns, however, Whitefield capitalized on the conditions of fear and uncertainty produced by war to reassert his religious message. Furthermore, he saw the opportunity for war and religion to be allied around the shared cause of British Protestantism. In a 1747 letter to Wesley, he credited military threats with extraordinary yields in religious awakening: "I rejoice to find that the Rebellion has been over-ruled for the awakening of many souls. Our Lord generally builds His temple in troublesome times."[82] Whitefield came to see that, rather than displacing religious revivals, the imperial wars were a means of catalyzing a new wave of revivals.

In contrast, Wesley was convinced that where the tide of war dominated, the flood of revival must correspondingly fade.[83] Along these lines, the methodist leader lamented, "wherever war breaks out, God is forgotten, if He be not set at open defiance. What a glorious work of God was at Cambuslang and Kilsyth from 1740 to 1744! But the war that followed tore it all up by the roots and left scarce any trace of it behind."[84] On the other hand, revivalists like Samuel Davies and George Whitefield "were expressing with much less reservation the necessity" of war.[85] Indeed, there were moments when Whitefield, in direct contradiction to Wesley, equated the cause of religion with that of the British Empire. In this view, military skirmishes with Catholic and heathen forces on the outskirts of colonial settlements did not supplant revivals as the object of evangelical passion; they supplied new fuel for religious fervor.

---

to connecting the decline of religion to internal controversies; see note 78 above). He therefore put part of the blame for revival's demise on war as well as religious controversies and infighting. See Lambert, *Inventing the "Great Awakening,"* 252–53. Jerome Mahaffey emphasized the influence of conspiratorial suspicions that endangered methodists' public standing in turning their evangelical concerns toward politics. He made the case that, in an age of intrigue when "spies and plots were everywhere," "Whitefield understood the severity of the charges [of treason]." Mahaffey, *The Accidental Revolutionary*, 77–78. My study takes a different approach. Whereas Lambert builds on the presumed incompatibility of war and religion and Mahaffey detects political maneuvering in the face of military danger and social instability, I argue that Whitefield sought to imbue imperial war with religious meaning.

82. George Whitefield to John Wesley, September 11, 1747, in Tyerman, *Life*, 2:176.

83. This is basically the view of Frank Lambert. See notes 78 and 81 above.

84. John Wesley to Thomas Rankin, May 19, 1775, in John Wesley, *The Works of the Rev. John Wesley: With the Last Corrections of the Author* (London: Wesleyan Conference Office, 1872), 12:326–27. Cited in Noll, *The Rise of Evangelicalism*, 259.

85. Noll, *The Rise of Evangelicalism*, 260.

What Wesley described as two antithetical forces were viewed as mutually reinforcing, allied influences by ministers such as Whitefield, Davies, and Thomas Prince, a Boston minister and popularizer of revival news. Prince's "The Salvation of God in 1746" and Whitefield's Philadelphia sermon, "Britain's Mercies, Britain's Duties" (also preached in 1746), provide compelling evidence for this evangelical conflation of war and religion. To celebrate news of British victory in Culloden and Louisbourg in 1746, evangelical ministers preached sermons attributing victory to God's providential care. While such sermons might provide evidence that war had pushed revival aside as the focal point of New Light ministers, there is another possible interpretation. Rather than causing religious concerns to fade, war provided another venue for promoting religious vitality and highlighting the outpouring of God's Spirit into the lives of British subjects. Without denying the fact of revival's decline, it is possible to understand the revivalists' use of war as a means of maintaining, or salvaging, revival gains.

Thomas Prince reflected this way of thinking when he criticized those who viewed war through a non-providential lens: "In short, they act too much like Atheists who view these Things as a meer Piece of News, or the meer Operations of created Causes, to please their vain Curiosity, and don't religiously behold them as the Works of God in Providence: And they don't act like Christians who don't in the Exercise of Faith behold them as the Providential Works of our exalted Saviour in the Rule of the World."[86] Rather than allow war to usurp the place of religion, Prince called for a religious interpretation of the military events overtaking his world. Though Prince and Whitefield proclaimed the same basic message, a close reading of both sermons serves the purpose of demonstrating that Whitefield's wartime rhetoric outlined a broader Protestant evangelical message tying the future of revival with that of empire.

This linkage of war and religion explains the long history lesson Prince provided throughout his thanksgiving sermon, where he recounted the tumultuous history of Catholic antagonism that characterized much of the previous century. In that recitation, he began with Charles I's marriage to a "Spanish Papist" in 1623, brought the story

86. Thomas Prince, *A Sermon Delivered At the South Church in Boston, August 14, 1746, Being the Day of General Thanksgiving for the Great Deliverance of the British Nations By the Glorious and Happy Victory Near Culloden* (Boston, 1746), 7.

to a crescendo with the revolution of 1688, and reminded hearers of the recent French invasion of English soil in the winter of 1745. The consistent thread throughout this rehearsal of history was the threat to the "Protestant Interest" posed by the forces of Catholic tyranny. At stake, in Prince's view, was the very survival of British Protestant culture. Should the unthinkable happen and a Jacobite insurrection prove successful, "it is to be feared that upon their Army's seizing London, He or his Regent would apprehend it necessary to employ his Popish barbarous Highlanders and other numerous Papists thro' the Nation, at once to massacre all the chief Friends of the Hanover Succession, if not of the Protestant Party in the City and Kingdom." As Prince saw it, the consequences of Catholic victory over Protestant Britain would be catastrophic, for "As in such a horrible Scene as this, the City of London wou'd run down with Blood; so all the immense Treasures of the Protestants therein wou'd be suddenly seized." The destruction levied would not be limited to the mother country, as "Cruel Papists would quickly fill the British Colonies, seize our Estates, abuse our Wives and Daughters, and barbarously murder us." Geo-political implications would reverberate to the rest of Europe as well, and even "Holland wou'd be suddenly overwhelmed by them, and the reformed Interest in other Parts of Europe soon follow the fate of Great Britain."[87]

With a heightened sense of what was at stake during the mid-1740s in the aftermath of revival, we can better appreciate the highly aspirational character of Whitefield's 1746 thanksgiving sermon preached in Philadelphia. On August 24 Whitefield preached one of his most famous sermons; he spoke to an audience in Philadelphia, but his thoughts were with events near Inverness in the Scottish Highlands. Good news of national salvation spread throughout the empire with the defeat of Bonnie Prince Charlie's forces at the Battle of Culloden. In part to quell suspicions of Methodist disloyalty to the crown, but also in order to resuscitate a waning revival, Whitefield spoke of "Britain's Mercies and Britain's Duty" in a sermon that expounded a dual theme, describing the unmerited favor of divine rescue (mercies) and emphasizing the need for renewed religious attentiveness (duty).[88]

87. Thomas Prince, *A Sermon Delivered At the South Church in Boston*, 13–18.
88. George Whitefield, *Britain's Mercies and Britain's Duty* (Boston: S. Kneeland and T. Green, 1746).

Whitefield took pains to connect Britain's salvation with America's well-being. He proclaimed, "if the Lord had not been on our side, Great Britain, not to say America, would, in a few weeks or months have been an Akeldama, a field of blood [Acts 1:19]." By evoking the site of Judas Iscariot's death, Whitefield warned his audience against both spiritual perfidy and political treason. The consequences he warned of, moreover, would be far-reaching, leading to economic, social, and military calamities. In the course of his sermon, he hypothesized "that the sinking of the national debt," the "rending away the funded property of the people," and "the dissolution of the present happy union between the two kingdoms" would all have been the "immediate consequences of [the Young Pretender's] success."[89]

The sermon presented more than high-sounding triumphalism. Whitefield took the opportunity to point out grave failures on the part of his Christian audience. He contrasted the mercy of God and the stubbornness of the people, lamenting "that as God has not dealt so bountifully with any people as with us, so no nation under heaven has dealt more ungratefully with him."[90] To make his point, Whitefield issued some of the harshest words found in any of his sermons, combining lament with accusation: "We have played the harlot against God, both in regard to principles and practices." After quoting a litany of prophetic verses, he declared, "We have crucified the Son of God afresh and put him to an open shame."[91]

One can only imagine how his words affected the mood of his hearers, but we can be sure about their intended effect. Though lacking poetic subtlety, Whitefield sought to lead hearers to dramatic heights as well as desperate lows. A walloping barrage of condemnations followed a glorious crescendo of triumph. In the middle of 1746, Whitefield knew exactly what he was doing. He endeavored to reap spiritual benefit out of imperial events. Citing the victory at Culloden, he pleaded with his hearers, "But, O let our rejoicing be in the Lord and run in a religious channel."[92] He called on the colonists in Philadelphia to stand in contrast to "those ungrateful Israelites, who are branded in the book of God," and to live instead in a manner worthy of the mercies bestowed

89. Whitefield, *Britain's Mercies*, 10.
90. Whitefield, *Britain's Mercies*, 12.
91. Whitefield, *Britain's Mercies*, 12.
92. Whitefield, *Britain's Mercies*, 15.

upon them. He wanted nothing less than "a national Reformation," lest they be struck with the blows of "other arrows in [God's] quiver."[93] Whitefield's jeremiad was not perfunctory, but rather filled with pathos and marked by a sense of urgency. He exhibited keen political and religious sensibilities about the times in which he lived.

The prophetic, even apocalyptic, tone of both Prince and Whitefield, with their dire warnings of local as well as international consequences, provides an apt reminder of the religious dimension of imperial wars. The transatlantic revival networks, developed only shortly before, meant that French incursions into Canada, Spanish fortifications in Florida, and Jacobite insurrection against Scotland all held spiritual significance. There was the potential for a domino effect that could send an international Protestant edifice careening out of control. In this way, the imperial wars were not a distraction or a displacement of the religious stirrings of the Great Awakening. If anything might be said of the connection between war and revival, it may be that imperial battles upped the ante for religion. Despite their volatile nature, with capacity for rapid decline as much as sudden upsurge, the awakenings also provided a common, empire-wide frame of reference for experiential religion.

Conclusion

For religious enthusiasts swept off their feet by the awakenings, subsequent years required coming to grips with a multitude of post-revival disappointments in order to forge a new way forward. This process was not merely one of consolation but also one of consolidation and damage containment. It did not happen in a vacuum but rather in the thicket of a social and political milieu in flux. Though the Great Awakening has been amply documented in primary sources, studies have largely neglected the years that followed revival. Four decades ago, Nathan Hatch criticized the lack of serious inquiry into what happened after the height of the revivals: "while recent scholarship has focused on the exultant hopes that characterized the Awakening, it has conspicuously avoided the same careful analysis of New Light thought in the years of the revival's demise."[94] Hatch's book

93. Whitefield, *Britain's Mercies*, 21.
94. Nathan O. Hatch, *The Sacred Cause of Liberty: Republican Thought and the Mil-*

focused on the convergence of religious and revolutionary ideologies, but his backgrounding of the story in the revivals took seriously the abiding influences, however scattered, of revival experiences. In discussing the different explanatory courses various pastors and theologians took, Hatch described the fertile soil of a new "civil millennialism" that presented an amalgamation of the theological with the political. Without necessarily acceding to a cynical view of Whitefield's tactical shifts, it is possible at the very least to notice the famous preacher's growing attention to geopolitical developments, especially as they impinged on the religious liberty and outlook of Britons. As we will see in the next chapter, Whitefield began in the 1750s to scan the horizon with an increasingly watchful eye for imperial warfare and especially Catholic incursions.

Some historians have pointed to Whitefield's perseverance in itinerant preaching as a sign of revival's persistence: "While other itinerant preachers settled down to tend local parishes, Whitefield continued to travel and preach to vast crowds as if the revival was still going. As far as Whitefield was concerned, the revival never really ended."[95] This characterization is not entirely accurate, however, as a closer examination of Whitefield's efforts in the last two decades of his life will demonstrate. Not only did Whitefield draw smaller crowds, he faced stiffening, at times violent, resistance to his preaching. Confronted with these changing realities, the stubborn preacher began employing new tactics. Whether he was riding on the coattails of British imperialism or fighting on the frontiers of British liberty, one thing is clear: Whitefield exhibited no qualms about mixing religion and politics in order to counter the decline of revival fervor.

In part this admixture of religion and empire proved so alluring because each needed the other. More to the point, religion was not the

---

lennium in Revolutionary New England (New Haven: Yale University Press, 1977), 27. Similarly, William H. Kenney III argued that after 1744 Whitefield was able to marshal widespread personal support only when he joined in the invective against the arbitrary power and Catholicism of France: "The uniformly feared French and Indian threat continued to be Whitefield's only avenue to his former following." Cited in Hatch, *Sacred Cause of Liberty*, 32.

95. Mahaffey, *Preaching Politics*, 147. Mahaffey goes on to observe a tendency to combine religious and military/political purposes: "After 1745 Whitefield viewed his evolving enterprise as having a twofold function: first was his well-known mission to preach the gospel wherever he could find an audience, but second, he felt a call to protect Protestant freedoms as well as British civil liberties."

only force needing a jump start; imperial politics had much to gain from the support of religious rhetoric. Notwithstanding the fast pace of territorial expansion during this period, British ascendancy remained contested and uneven. One historian attempted to debunk notions of the relative stability of British political life during the reign of George II, detecting instead cracks in the facade: "It is possible to argue . . . that the surface calm of political life for much of the final years of George II's reign is potentially very misleading. One of the most important themes in political life in this period was a sense of mounting vulnerability to French international ambition and military power."[96] Another historian described a pervasive British Protestant worry over "the prospect in the first half of the eighteenth century of a Catholic monarchy being restored in Britain by force, together with recurrent wars with Catholic states."[97] Not only was there "a vast superstructure of prejudice" against all things Catholic and foreign, there was also a crying need to fill in the meaning of British identity with content more substantial than what mere English bluster had to offer.[98]

External threats dovetailed with internal weaknesses, much more visible in hindsight but no less influential on British imperial life in the mid-eighteenth century. Because George II was born before the Glorious Revolution, he may have been conscious of a more tenuous hold on the crown. If British weakness indeed rose "from a failure of nerve and from a lack of dynastic confidence and continuity," as one historian has noted, the mismatch created by imperial growth and dynastic insecurity amounted to a serious vulnerability. Compounding these issues were "the pressures and politics of space," as the growing royal family spread out through London in rival centers like Leicester House and Carlton House due to the cramped quarters of the court.[99] The royal family's politics of space, one might well imagine, paralleled the larger dynamic of territorial expansion that attended imperial growth. Protestant dissidents, methodists, and evangelicals, as they came to be called, were also scattering at this time of increasing political and geographical outreach. That their religious hopes mixed with imperial realities on the ground and overseas does not come as a surprise.

96. Mahaffey, *Preaching Politics*, 147.
97. Colley, *Britons*, 25.
98. Colley, *Britons*, 36.
99. Colley, *Britons*, 198–99.

Against the backdrop of a congested metropole, a capacious periphery gave Whitefield and his boundless energy plenty of room to maneuver. Calling Whitefield "an international phenomenon," Harry Stout observed that "London was the center of commerce and exporter of culture throughout the British Empire" from where he launched his international revival movement.[100] Whitefield's frequent travels throughout England, Scotland, and the North American colonies enabled the famous preacher to weave together a network of likeminded religious persons. In this scheme, his itinerancy stands out as a vital point of connection for regions otherwise riddled by persistent differences. The tension becomes even more interesting when we view Whitefield's preaching routes as a means of exploring and reinforcing the bounds of imperial identity in a way that united religious and political perspectives. As he mediated these cultural and geographical boundaries, the evangelical leader found himself increasingly entangled in the worldly affairs of the British Empire, including moral quagmires that compromised his religious calling.

100. Harry Stout, "George Whitefield in Three Countries" in Noll, Bebbington, and Rawlyk, *Evangelicalism*, 58–59. Stout presents a more disjointed view (i.e., his language of "three [distinct] countries") of the pan-Protestant British national identity than Colley, but both help us to see the liminal and emerging nature of British identity.

PART 2

Entanglements

CHAPTER 4

Whitefield and Slavery

The middle of the eighteenth century was also the midpoint of White-field's public ministry, an appropriate time for both reflection and re-calibration. In fact, a close study of Whitefield's life and work in the 1750s reveals a conscious shift.[1] We can observe him adjusting to a post-revival phase as well as to an expanding yet contested imperial landscape. An acquaintance who "did not approve of his former pro-ceedings, or many of his present ones" was also able to write about some changes he perceived in the bombastic preacher as early as 1748. Remarking on Whitefield's plans for revising his *Journal*, James Stone-house observed that he "is a very different man to what he was; as your Ld may see by his Letter, wch was sent to me, & wch he intends as the Preface to the new Edition of his journal." Stonehouse went on to offer details on the extent of Whitefield's change: "he proposes to erase many things that have given offense, & to make a public Recantation of all his Enthusiastic expressions: nor dost he ever more intend to enter so far again into the depths of Calvinism."[2] Without overstating the change

---

1. Frank Lambert has noted the change in Whitefield beginning with his fourth trip (1751–1752) to America this way: "When Whitefield embarked for Georgia aboard the Antelope in 1751, he was a different person from the young minister who had first sailed for America in 1737. . . . In his last four colonial visits, Whitefield's persona was that of evangelical statesman as opposed to partisan warrior." Lambert, *"Pedlar in Divinity,"* 199.

2. Extract of a letter to "My Lord" [Lavington] from "Dr. S. of N." [James Stone-house] concerning George Whitefield, his changing views, and the new edition of his journal. October 1748. In the hand of Lavington. The Papers of George Lavington, Secker 8, f. 46, Lambeth Palace Library.

Whitefield underwent—Stonehouse noted that his writings were still "rigid, Turbulent, confus'd & abusive"—what cannot be denied is the advent of a new direction based on hard-earned wisdom from the awakenings and their aftermath.

Whereas he had spent the previous two decades importing British Protestant faith and culture to America, in the course of the 1750s he embraced a different vocational trajectory. The alteration is clear in the doubts he expressed about revival's long-term prospects to a friend: "It tries me to hear that religion is at so low an ebb amongst You. Strange That we should grow older & yet grow worse, Receive more from Xt & yet do less for Him."[3] These pensive words came at a time when he was experiencing renewed hope in other areas of his life, for instance jubilation at the possibility of using enslaved labor to support his enterprise in Georgia. Most strikingly, during this period he became more than a participant in empire who freely made use of Atlantic trade routes and communication tools when expedient. Instead, his life began to more fully embody imperial culture and values—less countercultural post-Puritan and more imperial, if still evangelical, statesman. The previous chapter argued for the end of a general revival season by the middle of the eighteenth century.[4] This chapter examines Whitefield's activities in the years that followed, after the height of revival fervor, in order to understand the changes gripping British Atlantic culture and the ways they influenced his life. Although historians have never treated the last half of Whitefield's public life as thoroughly as the first half, pursuing his importance for religion in the Atlantic world as a whole will show those latter years were just as important as the former.

3. Whitefield to William Bradford on February 24, 1750, American Philosophical Society.

4. To be sure, isolated and persistent episodes of revivals continued to reverberate into the latter half of the century. Some scholars have argued that there is no divide between the Great Awakening and the Second Great Awakening, conflating two epochal moments into one. For instance, Thomas Kidd has argued, "There was simply no clear break between the First and Second Great Awakenings." Kidd, *The Great Awakening*, 321. One way to read the seemingly conflicting reports is to acknowledge that a kind of low-grade revivalism continued well into the nineteenth century after the burst of concentrated revivals in the early 1740s.

Table 1. A Chronology of Whitefield and Slavery

January 9, 1735	Prohibition of slavery in Georgia
December 9, 1738	Malcontents petition Trustees to legalize slavery (117 sign)
April 1740	Whitefield purchases five thousand acres of land in Pennsylvania to build a "school for ne-groes" and writes to a friend of his intention to purchase "young ones"
April 17, 1740	Whitefield publishes *To the Inhabitants of Maryland, Virginia, North and South-Carolina, concerning their Negroes*
April 1742	Thomas Stephens publishes *The Hard Case of the Distressed People of Georgia*
May 1742	Thomas Stephens appears before Parliament, Whitefield accompanies Stephens
Spring 1747	Whitefield purchases 640 acres of land toward a plantation in South Carolina along with slaves; writes letter complaining of the slavery prohibition in Georgia
May 19, 1749	Trustees petition king to repeal prohibition of slavery
October 26, 1749	Trustees' petition approved
January 1, 1751	Slavery becomes legal in Georgia
1751–1753	Whitefield purchases Ephratah Plantation in Georgia along with enslaved laborers

The exigencies of Whitefield's numerous religious and philan-thropic initiatives across the empire did not fade away when the re-vivals waned. To be sure, market demand for his published writings, clamor for his public appearances, and pledges for financial gifts all declined precipitously in the latter part of the 1740s. As a result, White-field had to find alternative sources of support.[5] Once the catalyst of widespread transatlantic revivals, he became by necessity the organizer of a far-flung evangelical network with numerous constituent pieces

---

5. The decline of the sale of religious titles provides clear evidence of a shift in public consumption. For a description of this downward trend from majority of sales in 1739 to 20 percent by the 1760s, see Lambert, *"Pedlar in Divinity,"* 201.

that were not easily corralled into a coherent movement. In ways he did not anticipate, Whitefield reaped what he had sown as he took stock of the short-lived religious boom he had largely orchestrated. To put it another way, the agent of Anglicization in the colonies was himself becoming Americanized as he traveled across the Atlantic.[6] Over two decades of traveling around and obsessing over colonial religious life had left their mark on Whitefield as his religious concerns made room for social, economic, and political realities. Life as an imperial subject meant that even the Grand Itinerant had to adjust to the changing currents of the time.

More specifically, during these middle years of his public career, the revival preacher waded deeper into the marketplace of empire and theater of war. As Whitefield struggled to maintain relevance and influence, he sought additional means of reinvigorating his work across the Atlantic world. So when faced with the legalization of slavery in Georgia and the start of the Seven Years' War in North America, Whitefield's

6. In his last chapter entitled "The Americanization of Whitefield," Frank Lambert argues for a "direct link between the Great Awakening and the American Revolution." Lambert, *"Pedlar in Divinity,"* 198. In contrast, my analysis focuses on the changes in Whitefield himself and not so much the patriotic uses to which he was put during the revolutionary era. Consequently, my study conceives of "Americanization" as a process in which new cross-cultural encounters led to symbiotic exchange, resulting in profound alterations to both sides. A work along these lines that received wide acclaim when it first appeared yet received little scholarly engagement is James Axtell, *The Invasion Within: The Contest of Cultures in Colonial North America* (New York: Oxford University Press, 1985). Though quite different in their methods as well as the stories they tell, Rachel Wheeler picked up where Axtell left off, over two decades later. See Rachel M. Wheeler, *To Live upon Hope: Mohicans and Missionaries in the Eighteenth-Century Northeast* (Ithaca: Cornell University Press, 2008). Both works represent meaningful efforts to place Christian missionary efforts in the larger context of the British Empire. A teleology of British triumph limited Axtell's choices to resistance and accommodation in the British-Indian encounter. Wheeler moved past Axtell's two-pronged fork in the road by positing the third way of a genuine Mohican conversion that received Christianity without compromising indigenous integrity or agency. My work seeks to investigate the other side of the European–American encounter, investigating ways in which Whitefield's own social, cultural, and religious views were changed by his travels around the empire. By evaluating the changes in Whitefield's message and strategy through the lens of symbiotic adaptation, beyond a false dichotomy between resistance and accommodation, I argue that the world that made George Whitefield was itself undergoing profound changes, which reverberated into his life and ministry. To quote Wheeler: "Cultural encounter transformed not only the missionized but also the missionaries." Wheeler, *To Live upon Hope*, 226.

response went beyond the merely spiritual concerns of a minister. By resisting the temptation to spiritualize Whitefield's interests in slavery and war, we will see the extent to which the drive for profit and the allure of politics worked alongside his religious zeal, thus coloring his transatlantic activities in the 1750s. The renowned preacher found himself increasingly preoccupied as a plantation owner and patriotic writer, becoming ever more immersed in the empire. In other words, Whitefield's continued success lay not only in preaching but in his ability to engage the emerging trends of a society and culture in flux.

Digging into these thornier aspects of Whitefield's later career presents opportunities for detecting transformations in his transatlantic work, which in turn can shed light on the relationship between empire and religion. Inasmuch as Whitefield's commercial astuteness enhanced his religious message, so too did his spiritual aspirations push him into the competition of the open market. Not only the hope of converting and civilizing lost souls, but also his desire for profit—and the stability that profit would bring to his Georgia undertaking—nudged Whitefield into slave ownership. Like any entrepreneur, he was willing to take the risks because he saw the potential rewards. In an age of reason and refinement, Whitefield's earlier, singular focus on the new birth gave way to active participation in an empire of trade and commerce. His forays into plantation management reveal a Whitefield in transition from his Puritan moorings toward a distinctively new evangelical mood.[7]

In short, this chapter will explore Whitefield's entanglements in slave ownership in order to assess his struggles to maintain Protestant vitality amid shifting cultural challenges. Appreciating the ways in which his activities were subject to the vicissitudes of Britain's expansionist schemes can show the interconnectedness of economic forces, political developments, and religious life in the mid-eighteenth century. Crucial to this endeavor will be an evaluation of the ways in which Whitefield struggled to maintain a vision of empire that was theological at heart in spite of distractions created by larger processes of imperial state formation.

7. For an in-depth study of this transition from the seventeenth-century Puritan suspicion to the eighteenth-century evangelical embrace of commerce, see Mark Valeri, *Heavenly Merchandize: How Religion Shaped Commerce in Puritan America* (Princeton: Princeton University Press, 2010).

Slavery in Georgia

The legalization of slavery in 1751 changed the course of Georgia's history. Almost overnight, a colony that had been losing settlers and limping along economically witnessed the heartening sight of settlers migrating into its lands. The increasing availability of labor reinvigorated economic output as the number of enslaved African Americans increased over tenfold during a twenty-year period resulting in 10,625 total slaves in Georgia by 1770.[8] Thanks to the growing labor force, Savannah's rice exportation catapulted from 2,299 barrels in 1755 to 22,129 in 1770—a growth figure roughly parallel to the rate of increase in slave labor.[9] Restrictions on land grants, so long decried for limiting lots to 50 acres per male head (and 500 acres for those who purchased with their own money) since the beginning of the colony, were also relaxed in 1751. At the news that they could purchase as much land and as many slaves as they could afford, wealthier settlers began pouring into Georgia—in effect pushing out yeoman farmers and extinguishing the Trustees' hopes of an idealized agrarian society.

Amid the merchants, landlords, and royal officials who benefited from the economic reform and subsequent boom of the 1750s was also George Whitefield.[10] With over a decade personally invested in the colony by this time, he was as eager as anybody to reap the fruits of Georgia's loosening economic policies. And while he had from the beginning advocated for slavery in Georgia, there was a definitive shift in his position during the course of the 1740s. In a 1740 public letter to the inhabitants of Maryland, Virginia, and North and South Carolina, he had equivocated on the crucial point: "Whether it be lawful for Chris-

8. Julia Floyd Smith, *Slavery and Rice Culture in Low Country Georgia, 1750–1860* (Knoxville: University of Tennessee Press, 1985), 22.

9. Smith, *Slavery and Rice Culture*, 213.

10. Julia Floyd Smith has written about the making of a Georgian aristocracy, to which Whitefield was vitally connected if not an actual member: "The tidewater experiment in rice planting and the liberal land policy evinced during the twenty-four years of royal government created a society of exclusive slaveholding planters in coastal Georgia, not unlike the society along the coast of South Carolina. These Georgia aristocrats, representing a small minority of the white population, attained wealth in land and slaves because of the benefits accruing to them from imperial policy." Smith, *Slavery and Rice Culture*, 28. Thomas Kidd has acknowledged that by his involvement in slavery "Whitefield contributed to evangelical Christians' troubling record on race relations and ethnic inequality." Kidd, *George Whitefield*, 261.

tians to buy slaves, *I shall not take upon me to determine.*"[11] Over a decade later in March 1751, he was expressing an altogether different conviction: "As for the lawfulness of keeping slaves, *I have no doubt,* since I hear of some that were bought with Abraham's money, and some that were born in his house."[12] In the years leading up to 1751, Whitefield went from hesitating about the scriptural justification for slavery to articulating a strong theological endorsement, even presenting an array of biblical proof texts to bolster his position. This remarkable change in Whitefield's stance on slavery is the focus of this chapter.

The problem of slavery reveals much about the long trajectory of evangelical revivalism as a movement. More precisely, the famous revivalist's involvement in slavery presents an opportunity to understand both evangelical engagement with the emerging world of market exchange and responses to the diminishing returns of revival enthusiasm. Yet interpretive difficulties must be overcome, such as the all too apparent contradiction between his vocal concern for human souls and the harrowing lived experience of enslaved persons. Simple moral evaluations remain woefully inadequate, whether to exonerate him as a person of his times or to excuse him on grounds of naive or overly optimistic idealism.

Historians have grappled with Whitefield's relationship with slavery in a variety of ways, excoriating him for uncritical scriptural interpretation or implicating him in the origins of slaveholder paternalism in antebellum America.[13] Here we build on these previous efforts by focusing on the economic and social possibilities opened by imperial expansion. More specifically, the focus is on Whitefield as an influential actor in Georgia's tumultuous colonial life. Despite his frantic pace of travel to the hotspots of transatlantic revival, he maintained deep ties to frontier life in Georgia. As a person very much embedded in the local politics and economics of Savannah, the missionary priest was always

---

11. *A Letter to the Inhabitants of Maryland, Virginia, North and South-Carolina,* in George Whitefield, *Three Letters from the Reverend Mr. G. Whitefield* (Philadelphia, 1740), 13; emphasis added.

12. Whitefield to Mr. B—, March 22, 1751, in *Works,* 2:408; emphasis added. Kidd, *George Whitefield,* 255.

13. For an example of the former, see Lambert, *"Pedlar in Divinity."* For an example of the latter, see Allan Gallay, "The Origins of Slaveholders' Paternalism: George Whitefield, the Bryan Family, and the Great Awakening in the South," *The Journal of Southern History* 53, no. 3 (1987): 369-94.

committed to more than the religious and philanthropic work for which he is most often remembered.

The following pages offer a narrative of the conflicts over slavery in Georgia from 1735, when the Negro Act explicitly banned slavery, to 1751, when the sales of enslaved persons began flooding the markets and plantations of Georgia. An analysis of Whitefield's participation in this process along with his evolving position on slavery follows, detailing his numerous land purchases, political protests, and aggressive orphanage recruitment as steps integral to his eventual embrace of slave ownership. The chapter concludes with an interpretative reflection on Whitefield's position on slavery at the middle point of his career that explains much about his direction after the fires of revival cooled. Throughout we will see a movement toward the deployment of slavery for consolidating revival gains and contributing to an increasingly militant imperial ideology. This examination will show that Whitefield's disappointment at the harvest of the awakenings sowed the seeds for his deepening involvement in slavery. It is a story of how his reaction to religious and theological crisis paved the way for political, social, and economic developments of grave moral consequence.

The Malcontents in Georgia

In order to understand Whitefield's evolving position on slavery, it will be necessary to grasp the general course of Georgia's history. That history is clearer when we outline what the Trustees envisioned for the colony and then examine why their efforts generated such strong protests from settlers actually living in the colony. When, in turn, we look at Whitefield's relationship to the protests, we gain fresh insight into why he would eventually come out as such a strong proponent of slavery. General questions of morality, or of evangelical biblical interpretation, were not unimportant for Whitefield's stance. But his part in the history of Georgia was just as significant. A side-by-side comparison of the Georgia Malcontents and George Whitefield's efforts to legalize slavery in Georgia shows that both were animated by concerns for British liberty as well as commercial profit. To understand Whitefield's position on slavery, therefore, a brief survey of Trustee rule and colonial dissent in early Georgia is in order.

From the beginning, the proprietary colony of Georgia was the product of both an economic and imperial strategy. The Trustees quickly discovered the extent to which these two aspects of the colonial enterprise conflicted, as their work included not merely underwriting the venture but also governing a distant settlement. In an early effort to exert control, a committee appointed by the Trustees proposed three laws on January 9, 1735—prohibiting slavery, outlawing the use of rum and other strong drink, and regulating the Indian trade. With these decrees, the Trustees started on a collision course with settlers living on the ground in Georgia. For it was impossible that the Trustees could be as responsive to the needs of the fast-changing scenery of frontier life as a local governing body. The Trustee policy on slavery, in particular, supplies a prime example of the growing challenges facing British state formation. Paradoxically, but also reflecting a pattern common in imperial history, their location in London elevated their sense of empowerment to rule from afar while at the same time putting them at a disadvantage for the practicalities of governing Georgia.[14] Ensconced in their metropolitan seats of privilege, the Trustees initially conceived the ban on slavery as a matter of military strategy, minimizing any possibility of slave insurrection and foreign intrusion. They subsequently failed to accommodate to changing imperial, and especially economic, realities. When the need arose for a nimble response to the growing involvement of settlers in the Atlantic world of trade, the Trustees' response (or lack of one) deeply troubled Georgians. After all, the Trustees had never expressed the prohibition as an immutable or universal principle. Far from advancing moral qualms about slavery, some of the Trustees owned slaves in other parts of the empire. In fact, General James Oglethorpe, the esteemed servant of the Trustees, operated a plantation in nearby South Carolina with numerous Negro slaves—a path Whitefield himself would follow.

As a chiefly practical matter in the early days of the Georgia settlement, the reasons cited against slavery ranged from fear of inducing laziness in white settlers who acquired them to jealousy in those who could not afford additional laborers to the ease with which silk (unlike rice) could be cultivated such that "Women and Children might be of as much Use in as Negroes."[15] Yet since it was the southernmost British

14. For a fuller description of state formation as the "struggle to come up with ways of governing space and bringing diverse peoples within the state," see Griffin, *America's Revolution*, esp. 39–41.

15. *An Account, Shewing the Progress of the Colony of Georgia in America, From Its First Establishment: Published Per Order of the Honorable the Trustees* (Jonas Green, at his printing-office, in Annapolis, 1741). Also in Trevor R. Reese, *The Clamorous Malcon-*

territory in North America, Georgia's economic prospects were closely tied to, or subsumed under, its priorities as a military outpost. Indeed, the logic behind the land and labor policy of the Trustees owed mainly to the needs of a colony set up to provide a buffer between Spanish Florida and South Carolina. By playing their part in the imperial project, the Trustees aspired to gain greater prominence in their affairs at home. The British subjects who made Georgia home naturally came to view matters from a different vantage point. It was not long before the interests of the Trustees and the aspirations of ordinary Georgians had little to do with each other.

Increasingly the Trustees' primary interest was in a colony that would serve their cause at home by helping to accumulate wealth and enhance influence. It was the age-old dynamic of imperial primacy over the outlying provinces. For a thriving colony with its own landed gentry presented little benefit to the Trust in London. On the other hand, a colony of middling farmers dependent on the largesse of benefactors in England could provide a source of lucrative trade, bolster their status as philanthropists, and trumpet their zeal as devoted subjects of the king. For good measure, the notion of an imperial buffer against Catholic Spain and its holdings in Florida generated additional positives for their public reputation. Toward that end, in order to populate the colony with as many yeoman soldiers as reasonable, the Trust limited land grants to fifty acres. The intent was to "prevent an Accumulation of several Lots into one Hand, lest the Garrison should be lessened."[16] Since the Spanish had already lured many African slaves away from South Carolina with promises of freedom, the Trustees believed the presence of slaves in Georgia would only further endanger the safety of British colonists with the specter of sedition. Both militarily and economically, slavery made no sense from the vantage point of the London-based Georgia Trustees.

On the ground in Georgia, however, the plan of the Trustees made little sense. Historians have identified a number of different sources

tents: Criticisms & Defenses of the Colony of Georgia, 1741–1743 (Savannah: The Beehive Press, 1973), 190–92.

16. *An Account, Shewing the Progress of the Colony of Georgia in America, From Its First Establishment: Published Per Order of the Honorable the Trustees.* Also in Reese, *The Clamorous Malcontents*, 186. Reese presents this pamphlet as the authoritative version of the Trustees' defense, which "all historians of early Georgia have used . . . as the most reliable contemporary account available." Reese, *The Clamorous Malcontents*, xiv.

that fed the tributaries of discontent. The Malcontents, pejoratively labeled by the Trustees, were a diverse group.[17] Though comprised mainly of lowland Scots and English settlers, they represented a wide economic spectrum.[18] There were wealthy "adventurers," charity settlers, a small number of indentured servants, and even a few intrepid employees of the Trustees. In contrast, highland Scots in Darien and German Salzburgers in Ebenezer remained loyal to the Trustees and wrote counter-arguments against the Malcontents. Historians believe these latter refugees, unlikely to self-identify as British, were bound by a debt of gratitude to the Trustees as their benefactors.[19] William Stephens, writing as secretary to the Trustees, noted racial tensions that resulted over the slavery issue: "The Trustees' German Servants in general behave well, and are industrious . . . but this exposes them to the Envy and Hatred of our Negro-Mongers."[20]

In contrast, the wealthy adventurers who paid their own way to the colony looking to make a profit became increasingly bold as they dissented against the Georgia proprietors.[21] Since they were not "maintained at the Expense of the Publick" and instead driven by their commercial interests, they were at greater liberty to air their grievances.[22] Known also as the St. Andrews Club, after the patron saint of Scotland, they shared more than common economic interests. It was a moniker

17. In attempting a definition, Betty Wood at first applies a highly technical requirement: "an individual who actively opposed the Trustees' scheme by signing one or more of the following documents: the three major petitions sent from Georgia in 1738 and 1740, and Thomas Stephens' Commission as 'Agent for the Malcontents,' drawn up in October, 1741." Betty Wood, "A Note on the Georgia Malcontents," *The Georgia Historical Quarterly* 63, no. 2 (1979): 264. Only a few pages later, she appears to regret this strict definition, claiming, "The malcontents were not a monolithic, unchanging group," and going as far as to assert that the group was "quite fluid in terms of its personnel." Wood, "A Note on the Georgia Malcontents," 273.

18. According to Wood, "Almost ninety percent of the 212 malcontents [who signed a formal petition] can be positively identified as English or Lowland Scots in origin." Wood, "A Note on the Georgia Malcontents," 271.

19. Wood, "A Note on the Georgia Malcontents," 271.

20. William Stephens, *A State of the Province of Georgia: Attested Upon Oath in the Court of Savannah, November 10, 1740* (London, 1752), 27.

21. Milton Ready, "The Georgia Trustees and the Malcontents: The Politics of Philanthropy," *The Georgia Historical Quarterly* 60, no. 3 (1976): 265.

22. Reese, *The Clamorous Malcontents*, viii; *An Account, Shewing the Progress of the Colony of Georgia in America, From Its First Establishment: Published Per Order of the Honorable the Trustees*, 188.

that most certainly pointed out their Scottish origins in a derogatory sense. They met regularly at Jenkins's tavern in Savannah for social and cultural as much as political reasons. One of the leading Malcontents, Patrick Tailfer, was a well-to-do medical doctor who had little use for the land he received from the Trustees because it was so far from Savannah. Probably for this reason he harbored greater resentments toward the limitations imposed on his economic activity. In spite of the odds stacked against him, he built a successful medical practice in Savannah and married the sister of Robert Williams, a prominent Savannah merchant. David Douglas was another merchant and close associate of Tailfer. He owned property and likely had some contact with Whitefield as the landlord of temporary building space for the preacher's Bethesda Orphanage.

While the Malcontents' national provenance never became an explicit issue in the controversies, the fact that they were not English (despite being British subjects of the king) contributed to a heightened sense of marginalization and sensitivity to slights. Since the Act of Union in 1707 had brought England and Scotland together under one British kingdom, the lowland Scots would have felt more entitled to their British rights—given the proximity of their native land to England—than highland Scots in Darien or German refugees in Ebenezer. In many of their petitions to the Trustees, the Malcontents appealed to their rights as subjects of the British king. Despite being a cosmopolitan colony with a pan-European population, Georgia remained at its heart, especially in its most influential settlements and seats of authority, an English colony and therefore exacerbated the internal tensions that existed within a relatively young British kingdom that was also growing rapidly as an overseas empire.[23]

Although the Scots may have been at the epicenter of protest, they were far from alone. Widespread displeasure among Georgia's English settlers grew from their sense that the Trustees were infringing on cherished political rights as well as frustrating their economic prospects. And so in addition to the lowland Scots adventurers, there were what one historian has called "constitutional" Malcontents. We should be cautious about too sharply demarcating these two groups, but a delineation can be helpful insofar as we are able to see sev-

23. See John Pitts Corry, "Racial Elements in Colonial Georgia," *The Georgia Historical Quarterly* 20, no. 1 (1936): especially 30–31.

eral distinct groups bound by a common concern for liberty as well as profit in Georgia's marketplace.[24] While Patrick Tailfer led the Malcontents who found themselves on the outer margins of English Georgia, Thomas Stephens arose from within the inner circle of the Trustees. Thomas was the son of William Stephens, Secretary of the Colony and one of the most trusted servants of the Trust. Arriving on December 21, 1737, as his father's assistant, Thomas provided valuable help to his father at the beginning of their tenure. As he toiled over the land with little noticeable improvement, however, it did not take long for Thomas to become disillusioned with the state of the colony.[25]

The younger Stephens wrote several treatises detailing what he deemed the foolhardy policy of the Trustees.[26] In *The Hard Case of the Distressed People of Georgia* (1742), he lamented that "after *Nine Years* Experiments, 'tis evident, that the most zealous industrious Planter is incapable of making out a Livelihood by the Return of his Labour and Expense, *this Scheme being utterly impracticable* upon the Footing it has been attempted."[27] Signing the pamphlet as "Agent for the People of Georgia," Thomas considered it his mission in life to help the distressed colonists. Although he was certainly concerned about the economic outlook of the colony, Thomas's distinctive contribution to the Malcontent cause was the elaboration of a constitutional argument for liberty. One outworking of his logic is the vehemence with which he attacked not only the Trustees' unjust laws but also their failure to create a legislature or a legislative code in Georgia. In a 1743 pamphlet,

24. In contrasting the "constitutional" Malcontents with those who were Scots "adventurers," Milton Ready goes too far when he asserts that they were "motivated not by a desire for personal gain but rather by a wish to reform the existing Trust system." To impugn the motives of one group while valorizing the other group introduces an unrealistic standard of unadulterated virtue. At the same time, the distinction between the lowland Scots and the English is a helpful one. Ready, "Georgia Trustees and the Malcontents," 273.

25. For a detailed account of the contentious father-son relationship between William Stephens and Thomas Stephens, see Julie Anne Sweet, "William Stephens versus Thomas Stephens: A Family Feud in Colonial Georgia," *The Georgia Historical Quarterly* 92, no. 1 (2008): 1–36.

26. Thomas Stephens, *The Hard Case of the Distressed People of Georgia* (London, 1742); Thomas Stephens, *A Brief Account of the Causes That Have Retarded the Progress of the Colony of Georgia in America* (London, 1743).

27. Stephens, *Hard Case*, 260; emphasis in original.

he cited the lack of legislative structures as tantamount to withholding English rights from Georgia settlers:

> although the Trustees were apply'd to by the People, for a Body of Laws for the Government of the Colony . . . yet they never received, or heard of any other Laws except the Salique Law, one for the Prohibition of Negroes, and a third, prohibiting the Use and Importation of spirituous Liquors; any one of which was sufficient to prevent, or defeat the Settlement of a Colony in their Situation.[28]

To be sure, the Trust did issue numerous resolutions and guidelines, taking every opportunity to remind settlers of their continuing authority over the colony. According to Stephens, however, withholding a "body of laws" was equivalent to depriving the settlers of the "Rights and Liberties of English Subjects."[29] As his argument went, "It seems a little odd, that *three* Laws should be form'd, that had a visible Tendency to distress the Colony, and *not one* fairly calculated for its Increase and Encouragement."[30] In the same vein, Stephens suspected the Trustees of not creating a representative system of government in the colony because of their own despotic hold on power. At least one modern historian agrees with Thomas Stephens: "The strangest feature of the Trustees' government was the absence of a legislature." More than dereliction of duty, it was an active form of malfeasance, as he went on to conclude, "This inflexibility plus the failure to allow the colonists to participate in the government was the Trustees' greatest political failure."[31]

If the Trustees were intent on consolidating power, the Malcontents were motivated at least in part by what they considered a struggle for liberty in the face of arbitrary authority. It was only natural that the Georgians should find themselves at cross purposes with the Trustees as they pursued their own welfare in the colony. In this strained relationship, the slavery question became a touchstone issue. When Oglethorpe and his forces successfully repelled the Spanish, war in the southern frontier effectively came to an end in 1742. Besides, "If [slaves] are as well and better treated in Georgia than they can be there

28. Stephens, *Brief Account*, 280–81.
29. Stephens, *Brief Account*, 278.
30. Stephens, *Brief Account*, 281; emphasis in original.
31. Coleman, *Colonial Georgia*, 102, 110.

[in Florida], where is the Temptation?" Increasingly, as the danger of slaves escaping to St. Augustine faded, the irksome realization dawned upon Georgia's settlers that their most menacing competition lay to the north. Indeed, many Georgians marveled that the Trustees should so easily hand over the competitive advantage to South Carolinians—"our Neighbors having such an Advantage, as the Privilege of Negroes, can always under-sell us in any Manufacture or Produce."[32] As Stephens made clear, settlers in Georgia became more and more cognizant of their own interests, which went beyond the Trustees' goal of setting up a defensive barrier to preserve the wealth and ease of their rivals in South Carolina and proprietors in London. If the Trustees' arguments against slavery were pragmatic rather than moral or theological, the colonists agitating for slave labor also focused on the economic payoffs.

Owing to his prominent family connections, Thomas Stephens appeared before Parliament in 1742 and 1743 to represent the Malcontents' cause. The Trustees had too many friends in the House of Commons, however, for the young Stephens to carry the day. In defying his father and the powerful Trustees, he only succeeded in putting his own personal fate at significant peril. He was publicly reprimanded by the House of Commons and fortunate to escape imprisonment for libel against the Trustees. It is easy to see why historians generally credit Thomas with having "a genuine concern for the future of Georgia."[33] Maligned by the Trustees and their influential allies in London and disowned by his father, Thomas eventually left Georgia and settled in South Carolina, following a host of other Malcontents who had gone before him. Given the troubles Stephens endured for his support of the Malcontents' cause and the very little reward he received, there is good reason to presume a sincere motivation for the good of the colony. A sense of outrage over the Trustees' infractions against the liberties of the colonists seems to have loomed large in his mind. One historian, however, goes too far when she posits, "If any one person can be credited with responsibility for the introduction of black slavery in Georgia then Thomas Stephens . . . was the man."[34] Though not at all a distinction to be coveted, the actual evidence is much greater

---

32. Stephens, *Hard Case*, 2.

33. Betty Wood, "Thomas Stephens and the Introduction of Black Slavery in Georgia," *The Georgia Historical Quarterly* 58, no. 1 (1974): 38.

34. Wood, "Thomas Stephens," 24.

for George Whitefield. At the very least, it is not convincing to assign credit to Stephens for the legalization of slavery in 1751 that occurred some seven years after he disappeared from the scene. Whitefield held a consistent pro-slavery position that only became more ardent over the course of the 1740s.

Whitefield's Discontent in Georgia

Juxtaposing our survey of the Malcontents in Georgia with Whitefield's own pro-slavery activism not only addresses a historiographical lacuna but also sheds light on the religious dimension of British imperial developments in the mid-eighteenth century. Although Whitefield is rarely associated with the Malcontents, they were allies in Georgia's pro-slavery movement.[35] During the same period when the Malcontents were agitating against the Trustees, Whitefield too found himself in an embattled relationship with the Georgia proprietors in London for a variety of reasons that paralleled the Malcontent cause, ranging from struggles over British liberty to economic ambitions to the slavery issue. Unlike most Malcontents who, despairing of change or improvement, moved out of Georgia, Whitefield stayed the course to reap some measure of vindication. Far from exculpating Whitefield's involvement in slavery, this line of reasoning helps us to understand how the missionary pastor might have constructed intellectual and theological justifications for actions that were also stirred by mercantile and pragmatic designs. It was not a far leap to go from attending to the need for spiritual renewal to assisting settlers through their physical privations. If his preaching of the new birth democratized religious initiative by placing matters of eternal destiny in the hands of individuals, his pursuit of economic freedom and profit similarly insisted on the right of personal agency. Whitefield saw his labors as being "of vast Service to this Northern Part of the Colony," even if it was "greatly detrimental to [his] own private Interest."[36] As he told John Wesley, while the colony languished, the orphanage shone as one of its few beacons of hope: "Notwithstand-

35. Whitefield is absent in the best historical treatments of the Malcontents, such as Wood, "A Note on the Georgia Malcontents"; Ready, "Georgia Trustees and the Malcontents."

36. George Whitefield, *A Brief Account of the Rise, Progress, and Present Situation of the Orphan-House in Georgia* (1746), 62–64.

ing the declining state of Georgia, the Orphan House is in a better situation than ever; and, in a year or two, I trust, it will support itself."[37]

Despite allegations of wanderlust and a chronic inability to stay in one place, Whitefield tied his own interests to the long-term prosperity of the colonial enterprise in Georgia. So far did he become embroiled in this project that he sided with the Malcontents in principle. When Thomas Stephens learned that Whitefield was "for allowing Negroes in the Colony, & if examined would declare his opinion that way," he arranged to have the cleric appear before the House of Commons at the time of his own ill-fated appearance in the spring of 1742. In the end, Whitefield was prevented from testifying because "many exprest their dislike at examining an Enthusiastical Mad Man as they call'd him, & thought it demean'd the dignity of the house."[38] Despite obstructions to his official testimony, his willingness to go before Parliament to argue for slavery in Georgia constitutes in itself a forceful statement. Time and again Whitefield spoke of his strong desire to see slaves in Georgia. Not only was this yet one more example of his inveterate opposition to arbitrary authority, it was also evidence of his economic pragmatism and political prescience.

As further demonstration of Whitefield's ability to distinguish between matters of moral integrity and economic exigency, he complained almost as much about the prohibition on rum as he did about the ban on slavery. For all his preaching about a regenerated life, Whitefield was a realist who recognized well the constraints with which he needed to work. The prohibition of rum and slaves in Georgia dismayed Whitefield enough that during his first trip to America in the summer of 1738 he criticized the scheme as "absolutely impracticable in so hot a country abroad."[39] Along with the restrictive land policy of the Trustees, these limitations seemed to him "little better than to tie their legs and bid them walk."[40]

The activism of James Habersham, a follower of Whitefield who accompanied him during the preacher's first American trip and settled permanently in Georgia, can help shed further light on Whitefield's role in advocating for slavery in the colony.[41] Habersham

37. George Whitefield to John Wesley, October 14, 1746, in Tyerman, *Life*, 2:165.
38. Candler, *Colonial Records*, 5:480.
39. Gillies, *Memoirs*, 32.
40. Gillies, *Memoirs*; Tyerman, *Life*, 1:141.
41. Habersham arrived in Georgia only six months after William and Thomas

initially went to Georgia with Whitefield as a missionary and then stayed to become superintendent of the Bethesda Orphanage. While his mentor traveled around the Atlantic world, Habersham became a leading Georgia planter and merchant. Beginning in the 1750s, he wielded political influence as secretary of Georgia and later as president of the Council. Throughout, he maintained close ties with his friend, Whitefield. As the itinerant's spiritual disciple and business representative, Habersham would not have staked out a position that was contrary to Whitefield's wishes. As early as June 26, 1740, he was telling the Earl of Egmont that "he believed the Colony could not possibly go on without [slaves]."[42] It was at Habersham's urging that Whitefield in 1747 purchased a plantation in South Carolina where he could employ slaves. And it was Habersham's letter to the Trustees in 1748, effectively an economic development plan for the colony, that played a significant role in convincing the Trustees to relent from their long-held position.[43] All of these things Habersham did as a friend and associate of Whitefield.

Although Whitefield and Habersham never formally joined the Malcontents, they rallied in common cause with them. In fact, one need not delve deep into the records of the Georgia Trustees to see that Whitefield was as much a thorn in their side as the most vocal Malcontents. The unlikely alliance befuddled Whitefield's biographer, Luke Tyerman, who remarked regarding the Malcontents' 1736 petition: "Not only in one, but in all these respects, Whitefield, oddly enough, sympathised with the malcontent inhabitants of Georgia."[44] Despite the fact that his advocacy for the introduction of slavery was a significant feature of his life and ministry during the late 1730s and throughout the 1740s, Whitefield receives little to no attention in the story of Malcontents and their conflict with the Trustees. Yet Whitefield and Habersham were among the most persistent critics of the Trustees' no-slavery policy. In contrast to most Malcontents who abandoned Georgia, Whitefield and

---

Stephens and patiently built a life for himself, eventually becoming secretary of the colony then later president. During the 1740s, he served as the headmaster of Whitefield's orphanage and became the revival preacher's most trusted spokesperson. For more, see Frank Lambert, *James Habersham: Loyalty, Politics, and Commerce in Colonial Georgia* (Athens: University of Georgia Press, 2005).

42. Candler, *Colonial Records*, 5:376.
43. Lambert, *James Habersham*, 74–80.
44. Tyerman, *Life*, 1:141.

Habersham never let up on their quest to see the introduction of en-slaved labor in Georgia. If any one person does indeed deserve blame for the introduction of slavery in Georgia, it may actually be George Whitefield.

Slaves, Schools, and the Search for a Viable Strategy

In the midst of his frenetic transatlantic itinerary, Whitefield some-how found time to make numerous land investments in multiple colo-nies with the intention of building schools, to lodge vehement protest against the Trustees' land and labor policies in Georgia, and to stir con-troversy with strong-arm tactics in bringing children into his Savannah orphanage. When these activities are set alongside his evolving view on slavery, we can detect the development of an ambition, both religious and economic, that spanned the empire. The public letter we will exam-ine in this section shows Whitefield working all of the angles mentioned above. At the height of his revival activities, Whitefield the preacher was also thinking like an imperial investor and looking for a way to combine his religious purposes with the cause of an expanding empire.

Whitefield's audacious missive, "To the Inhabitants of Maryland, Virginia, North and South Carolina, concerning their Negroes," first published on April 17, 1740, in *The Pennsylvania Gazette*, is filled with harsh words upbraiding slaveholders for their mistreatment of slaves. It is also filled with a copious amount of hedging and prevarication. Far from the expression of a proto-abolitionist sentiment that it is some-times taken to be, the letter carved out the moral and theological space needed for Whitefield to work out his own beliefs over the course of the coming decade.[45] Composed in the midst of his second American tour, it showcases the itinerant's inchoate, yet fast-growing, awareness of the American landscape and his struggles to form a long-term strategy.

With his strategy in flux, Whitefield's letter enabled him to gauge the reach of his influence during the heyday of revival. He was sure to

45. Whitefield, *A Letter to the Inhabitants of Maryland, Virginia, North and South-Carolina*, in Whitefield, *Three Letters*, 13–16; Tyerman, *Life*, 1:353. The Quaker aboli-tionist Anthony Benezet quotes from this letter of Whitefield in a letter to the Countess of Huntingdon on May 20, 1774, citing it as an example par excellence of Christian virtue; see John R. Tyson and Boyd Schlenther, *In the Midst of Early Methodism: Lady Huntingdon and Her Correspondence* (Lanham: Scarecrow Press, 2006), 227–29.

receive a wide array of responses from numerous corners of his broad constituency by broaching a subject as complex as slavery. If he had premonitions of requiring slave labor on his own growing land investments throughout the colonies, feedback on the letter would give him a sense of the moral boundaries and economic realities he was up against.

To begin the letter, Whitefield the pastor sounded a grand prophetic note, overflowing with compassion for fellow human beings. "God has a Quarrel with you for your Abuse of and Cruelty to the poor Negroes," he declared in his opening paragraph. The pathos of his conviction was unmistakable as he wrote, "my Blood has frequently almost run cold within me, to consider how many of your Slaves had neither convenient Food to eat or proper Raiment to put on."[46] Intent on displaying a tender reaction to the brutal treatment of enslaved persons, he did not hesitate to take his protest to the court of public opinion. That he set aside time to write such an open letter illustrates his awareness of a literate audience interested in his opinion. The letter also evinces deep awareness of his own public persona and the need to manage that image for the sake of his larger aims.

In the course of the letter, there was a distinct shift in tone as Whitefield turned pragmatic, even sympathetic toward the slave owners, perhaps rushing to find relief for the tension he had wound up: "Your present and past bad Usage of them, however ill-designed, may thus far do them good, as to break their Wills, increase the Sense of their natural Misery, and consequently better dispose their Minds to accept the Redemption wrought out for them, by the Death and Obedience of Jesus Christ."[47] Having excoriated them publicly, he gave the slaveowners a way out, a chance to save face. Upon closer scrutiny, it is possible to see Whitefield visibly oscillating between two positions despite the surface rhetoric of assured confidence. He recoiled at the horrors of slavery but also recognized the necessity of slave labor for the colonial cause in the South and even pointed out the possibility of redeeming virtues. He had, after all, seen enough to surmise that slavery might provide a much-needed boost to his own Georgia enterprise.

Owing to his internal struggles with the institution of slavery, Whitefield tried alternative means of securing labor and raising profits to support his religious aims before himself turning to slave ownership. Such

46. Whitefield, *Three Letters*, 13.
47. Whitefield, *Three Letters*, 15.

considerations were likely part of the picture when in the spring of 1740 he purchased a large plot of land in the backwoods of Pennsylvania to establish a "school for negroes." He had already demanded five hundred acres of land in Georgia, an amount ordinarily reserved for wealthy adventurers who paid their own way to the colony. In April 1740, he purchased a much larger amount of land in Pennsylvania. William Seward, Whitefield's close friend and publicist with substantial wealth of his own, had just parted from Whitefield in May 1740 and was on his way from Philadelphia to London when he wrote to the Trustees of Georgia, informing them that he "had assisted Mr. Whitefield to take up 5000 Acres of Land in Pensilvania in order to erect a Negroe-School." As if he could not disassociate the two issues, in the same sentence he criticized the prohibition of slavery in Georgia: "I did not doubt, but if the Obstacles, which now hindered, were removed, and the Colony put upon an equal footing with the other Provinces, many Persons would take over their Families and Fortunes, which till then they would not do."[48] Seward clearly had slavery in mind at the top of his list when he mentioned "obstacles" to the prosperity of Georgia. By their close proximity in his letter to the Trustees, it appears that the issue of a "school for negroes" in a remote part of Pennsylvania was tied to the urgent need of slave labor in Georgia.

The sheer magnitude of this Pennsylvania purchase requires further thought. To be sure, the disjunction of space needed for an academic institution and the staggering space of five thousand acres can only mean that Whitefield and Seward had other purposes in mind for the land in addition to the education of displaced Africans. The preacher said as much when he wrote to a friend in London that he had "actually taken up 5000 Acres of very good Land, in order to erect a School for the Education and Maintenance of all such Negroes, whether young or old, that shall be sent unto me—Young ones *I intend to buy*, and do not despair of seeing a Room full of that despised Generation in a short Time making Melody with Grace in their Hearts unto the Lord."[49]

He glossed over the intention to buy slaves by claiming to have their physical and spiritual welfare foremost in his mind. In fact, as we will soon see with Whitefield in Bethesda, there was great potential for com-

48. Seward, *Journal of a Voyage*, 52–53.
49. George Whitefield, "A Letter from the Reverend Mr. George Whitefield to a Friend in London, Dated at New-Brunswick in New Jersey, April 27, 1740" (London, 1740); emphasis added.

bining the industriousness of students and the possibility of a profit-making industry. Under the guise of a school, Whitefield was building a massive plantation and purchasing slaves to make the investment profitable. To judge from William Seward's words in 1740, Whitefield was perhaps more interested in these Pennsylvania efforts, given their rich prospects, than in his beloved Bethesda in Georgia: "Many desire to go to Georgia, and some I believe Mr. Whitefield will take, but most of them he puts off, designing to employ them in the Negroe School, or settle them in Societies in Philadelphia."[50] There is credible evidence, therefore, that the establishment of schools was one way of getting around the hard restrictions against slavery in Georgia.

In May 1740, the same month that Seward was writing about a school in the hinterlands of Pennsylvania, Whitefield was also formulating a plan for a "school for negroes" closer to the urban center of Philadelphia. Although he had to shelve those ambitions for the moment, two months later in July the idea still lingered in his mind, with the addition of possible new ventures closer to his Georgia headquarters: "Had I time and proper schoolmasters, I might immediately erect a negro school in South Carolina, as well as in Pennsylvania."[51] To summarize, in addition to his orphanage in Georgia, Whitefield also had his sights on two additional schools in Pennsylvania (one rural, one urban) and a fourth in South Carolina. Though he lacked time and personnel for such undertakings, there is also mounting evidence that he was casting about for a more robust financial base for his American operations and that schools presented the possibility of serving a dual, spiritual and economic, purpose. Even as he itinerated for more converts throughout the colonies, Whitefield was also devising a strategy for acquiring more capital and laborers to support the cause of revival.

School Master in Savannah

From his earliest days in America, Whitefield fixed on a simple solution for making his Bethesda Orphanage economically viable: the labor supply of his orphans.[52] These able-bodied children, who were benefi-

---

50. Seward, *Journal of a Voyage*, 11.
51. Whitefield, *Journals*, 462, 487.
52. Frank Lambert writes that Whitefield and his associate James Habersham

ciaries of his charity, would take part in building and maintaining the institution. They would serve not only as objects of compassion but as workers for the larger cause of Protestant renewal across the Atlantic world. Toward this end, he prescribed a daily regimen for the children at Bethesda that would not only strengthen their spiritual discipline but also provide economical labor. "Not a moment of innocent recreation tho necessary to the health & strengthening of growing children is allow'd in the whole day," was the Earl of Egmont's criticism of Whitefield's daily schedule for the pupils at Bethesda.[53] The earl, as a visitor, quibbled with the excess of prayer and singing of psalms and hymns. What he missed, however, was the plan to put the orphans to work. Whitefield prescribed a meticulous daily schedule that began with a morning bell at five o'clock in the morning. He then appointed hours in the morning and in the afternoon for "their respective Employs, as carding, spinning, picking Cotton or Wool, sewing, knitting."[54] With the children's lives strictly regulated, Whitefield boasted that "tho' we are about seventy in Family, yet we hear no more Noise than if it was a private House."[55] One historian has noted the economic dimension of Whitefield's orphanage in this way: "Bethesda might well be called the artisan nursery of the colony, because its children were all taught trades."[56] This use of orphan labor takes on greater significance as we trace Whitefield's evolving position on slavery and the questionable means by which he attempted to increase the number of orphans at Bethesda.

Whitefield's efforts to recruit orphans and students for his school in Savannah served a purpose that went beyond charity work. If slave labor was outlawed in Georgia, the children provided another way of securing a steady flow of economic output. Before pursuing slaves as an option, Whitefield explored the possibility of using the children he already possessed to fulfill the same purpose. He soon discovered, how-

---

identified "two types of dependent labor: indentured servants and orphans." Lambert, *James Habersham*, 46.

53. *Journal of the Earl of Egmont*, in Candler, *Colonial Records*, 5:359.

54. George Whitefield, "The Manner of the Children Spending their Time at the Orphan-House in Georgia," 2. Appended to "A Letter from the Reverend Mr. George Whitefield to a Friend in London, dated at New-Brunswick in New Jersey, April 27, 1740."

55. Whitefield, "The Manner of the Children Spending their Time," 3.

56. Coleman, *Colonial Georgia*, 141.

ever, that many of the orphans at Bethesda were too young to work and that there was a finite, limited supply of them. He therefore went out of his way to corral youth who had no need of his assistance.

In other words, he went after prospective "orphans" aggressively, in some cases where there was no apparent need for his philanthropy or intervention. In several controversial and high-profile situations, he separated individuals from siblings and guardians, insisting on the authority granted to him by the Trustees. At a meeting of the magistrates in the home of William Stephens on February 9, 1739, Henry Parker protested the injustice of Whitefield taking an orphan from him. Strikingly, he framed his complaint as the loss of an economic investment. The boy in question, Tondee, was a "Lad of fifteen or sixteen Years of Age" and "he thought it would be a great Hardship to have that Boy taken from him, now he is grown capable of doing him some service, after living so long with him when he could do him none." How Whitefield responded to Parker's protest is revealing as well, for he engaged the argument on purely economic terms stating simply that "[Tondee] could be *employed* for the Benefit of the other Orphans."[57] What made this matter particularly galling for Parker was the timing, which happened to fall during planting season, when he needed all the hands he could muster. As William Stephens observed, growing increasingly sympathetic to the complaint against Whitefield, it was a "great [economic] Loss and Disappointment to Parker; as indeed it must be in his planting, to be deprived of the Benefit of such an Youth's Labour, now grown to a good Stature."[58] By the end of the month, Oglethorpe himself was weighing in on the controversy, saying "he thought [Whitefield] had gone beyond what the Trust intended, in taking some Orphans into his Keeping, who were well grown, and might have been of good Service this planting Time, to the Masters they lived with."[59] Revealingly, Oglethorpe also saw the matter as one with financial consequences.

The next summer, in June 1740, it appears Whitefield was at it again. This time the boy in question was a child of one of the original forty Georgia settlers, whom Oglethorpe had shown "particular Marks of his Favour to, for their Father's Sake." The lad is described as being

57. William Stephens, *A Journal of the Proceedings in Georgia* (Ann Arbor: University Microfilms, 1966), 272–73; emphasis added. For another account of this incident, see Lambert, *James Habersham*, 47.

58. Stephens, *Journal of the Proceedings*, 2:277.

59. Stephens, *Journal of the Proceedings*, 2:294–96.

"an active, diligent, and well-grown Youth . . . [who] was become service-able, in many Cases, to his good Patron, and employed by him variously, as Occasion required." In other words, the youth had become a valuable source of labor when "Mr. Whitefield came, with the Power which the trust had granted him," and took the young Mellidge away, "leaving the Elder at home." The boy's sister and brother lodged vehement protest, not only at the loss of a family member but also at the timing of this loss "when he could be of so much Use."[60] This overreach by Whitefield was more than Oglethorpe could stomach, and he immediately issued an order to have the child returned to his family, thus restoring not only their brother but a reliable source of income.

The question as to why Whitefield felt compelled to round up youths who already had decent homes is an important one. Studies of Whitefield have refrained from making any judgments about his collection of "orphans" that go beyond the overzealous ardor of his compassion.[61] Before absolving Whitefield of any illicit motivation, however, the matter is worth further exploration. Why did Whitefield go out of his way, even inviting controversy and criticism, during a time when he had many other matters vying for his attention? The common denominator in these two cases spread out over more than a year is the "usefulness" of both Tondee and Mellidge toward work that Whitefield needed to be done on the grounds of Bethesda. On more than one occasion, he appears to have forcibly taken children out of their homes because of the economic service they could render. It is possible there were philanthropic or religious motivations as well, but those were not the reasons he cited—and quite forcefully at that—when he faced criticism for his actions. It is not necessary to go as far as to insinuate that he was seeking to build a profitable business under the guise of orphan relief. Instead it is sufficient to posit that Whitefield mixed moral and religious goals with imperial and mercantile aims. More likely than a sinister explanation, in fact, is that he was fumbling his way toward a firmer understanding about what he needed in order to secure a stable footing for the orphanage. It is manifestly clear that this effort was leading him toward the sanctioning of slave labor. Despite the huge

60. Stephens, *Journal of the Proceedings*, 2:409.

61. For example, Stuart Henry is likely correct, but only partially so, to defend Whitefield, "It must not be imagined, however, that Whitefield was perpetrating pious fraud upon the colonists in his ardor to watch over the homeless." Stuart Clark Henry, *George Whitefield: Wayfaring Witness* (Nashville: Abingdon Press, 1957), 58.

sums of money he raised for his charity work in Georgia, the challenge of creating a sustainable institution dogged Whitefield throughout his life. Consciousness of his need to act as a preacher for the empire, in turn, lay behind this search for a stable institutional base.

The Merchant of Savannah

As early as August of 1740, onlookers reported signs of trouble in Bethesda's future. "Ever since Mr. Whitefield left Georgia the latter End of August in [1740] . . . it has decayed a-pace," wrote Patrick Tailfer, the Scottish Malcontent leader. Although the orphanage housed as many as a hundred at one point, it had difficulty maintaining those numbers. Tailfer went on to describe an unfinished main building, sixty feet long and forty feet wide, with a shingled roof and not much more. The houses and huts that accompanied this unfinished building added to its dilapidated appearance. There were more worrisome signs than the incomplete and ramshackle buildings, according to Tailfer, as he wondered out loud: even "if it were finished, where is the Fund for its support?"[62] Problems lay beyond Bethesda, moreover, since a thriving orphanage would have little to offer a destitute colony: "What Service can an Orphan-House be in a Desert and a forsaken Colony[?]" These words of Whitefield corroborated Tailfer when he lamented the low state of the colony's welfare. As revivals came and went, his investment in the imperial outpost of Georgia remained. It was incumbent upon him to find a means of supporting the enterprise when the support of fellow enthusiasts waned.

Therefore, although he had successfully established a sprawling revival network, Whitefield could hardly rest. If he wanted a stable institutional base for that network, he would have to work for it. He looked for creative solutions to the ebb and flow of financial support that mirrored the unstable temperature of revival fervor. It should come as no surprise that the same individual who lugged British consumer goods across the Atlantic Ocean during his first missionary trip to America sought ways to use a further supply of such goods as a funding source for his ongoing efforts at institution building. Whitefield used some of

---

62. Patrick Tailfer, Hugh Anderson, and Da. Douglas, *A True and Historical Narrative of the Colony of Georgia* (Charles-Town, SC: Printed for P. Timothy, 1741), 72.

the items he imported to provide aid to those in need, but he also functioned as a merchant, using the proceeds from the sale of British goods to finance his travels throughout the colonies. For example, during his second American trip (August 1739 to March 1741), he enlisted Benjamin Franklin's help as he frequently advertised items for sale in *The Pennsylvania Gazette*. The following notice, which appeared on November 8, 1739, was a regular feature in the paper:

> TO BE SOLD,
> At the House of the Rev. Mr. Whitefield,
> In Second-Street (the same in which Capt. Blair,
> lately dwelt) the following GOODS;
> Being the Benefactions of CHARITABLE PEOPLE
> In England, towards Building an Orphan-House
> In Georgia.[63]

The list of goods included sundry items, from brass candlesticks to pistol powder to buttons and sewing silk. This advertisement shows the complex transactions contrived in support of Whitefield's ministry. By buying English goods in London with the contributions he received there and selling them in the colonies, he was actually able to turn a profit. One can almost sense Whitefield's glee as he describes the process that yielded an extra income "as much by them at Philadelphia as nearly defrayed the Family's Expence of coming over."[64] With sixty to seventy orphans, moreover, he managed a large staff: "Sometimes (Labourers and all) I have had a Hundred and Twenty to provide for daily."[65] Responsible for the livelihood of so many people, Whitefield had to function both as a businessman and as a clergyman. Such extracurricular activities for a minister would have been unthinkable in the Puritan world of the previous century. In the second quarter of the eighteenth century, however, Whitefield had few qualms about entering the marketplace.

In fact, when all was said and done, his ministerial credentials proved an asset for his business ventures. To be sure, there were critics who found the preacher's use of commercial tactics unseemly and even

---

63. *The Pennsylvania Gazette*, November 8, 1739.
64. Whitefield, *Brief Account of the Rise, Progress, and Present Situation*, 56.
65. Whitefield, *Brief Account of the Rise, Progress, and Present Situation*, 57.

demeaning. But many more thronged to hear what he had to say, to purchase his writings, and to contribute to his many charitable causes. Because of his investments throughout the British Empire, his affairs in the world of trade proved an integral part of his growing ministry, a necessary means toward a greater end. His entrance into the world of trade gave him further opportunity to announce the work of the gospel in which he was engaged. As a peripatetic revivalist who cultivated close ties with clergymen as well as merchants, he used the colonial markets to strengthen his American labors based in Savannah.

As he labored to establish a foothold in the imperial outpost of Georgia, changing conceptions of the market whirled all around White-field. The warning of Puritan divines against the temptations and vices rampant in commercial activities were giving way to a post-Puritan endorsement of the market economy.[66] British settlers in America were becoming increasingly attuned to trends in material fashion as well as fashionable ideas. In a telling remark concerning a collection of Gilbert Tennent's sermons, Simon Frost, a devotee of Whitefield, told the Boston merchant and judge Samuel Savage that although he "shou'd have been fond to have had 'em bound up in ye best manner" since he planned to lend the copy out to friends, a "Common Cover will do."[67] Frost went on also to request the latest Whitefield items that might be available. As revivals exploded across the colonies, the demand for revival goods stirred a flurry of commercial activity. One historian has observed the significance of a merchant's obsession over details like paint color: "Timothy Orne, an eighteenth-century Salem merchant who figured among the town's 'codfish aristocracy,' contracted with a local artisan, detailing the exact paint colors for walls and trim in each room in his new house."[68] If attention to such details is a sign of membership in the new economic class of "men of moveable property," then Whitefield's instructions for the design of Bethesda—and, in particular, his living quarters—qualified him. The preacher proved a scrupulous consumer in providing instructions for the buildings at Bethesda. Revival fervor in the context of imperial expansion not only

66. See Valeri, *Heavenly Merchandize*.

67. Simon Frost to Savage, April 15, 1741, in Samuel Savage Papers, MS N-855.1, Massachusetts Historical Society.

68. Phyllis Hunter, *Purchasing Identity in the Atlantic World: Massachusetts Merchants, 1670–1780* (Ithaca: Cornell University Press, 2001), 11.

enlarged the field of religious missionary work, it heightened prospects for wealth and status.

Yet, the revivals were episodic and so was the fundraising dependent on them. Whitefield needed productive, income-generating work at Bethesda because it was impossible to raise enough subscriptions of support from converts and admirers to keep the enterprise going. Benjamin Colman, his friend and advocate as well as the moderate pastor of Brattle Street Church in Boston, harbored early uncertainties about the financial viability of the orphanage. In a letter of 1742 to a friend in Glasgow, Colman expressed those doubts: "But how it can subsist, and flourish, and answer the Founder's End, is the Enquiry here, and will be a Marvel in the Providence of God, if it do so."[69] Unlike Professor Francke's school in Prussia, Bethesda was too isolated, "the one being in the midst of Europe the other in the Confines of America."[70] Not a little miffed at Colman's words, Whitefield tried to surmount criticism by sounding a pious note, "How it can subsist and flourish for the future, I am not sollicitous about: God can help us in Georgia, as well as he helped Professor Francke in Germany."[71] Yet four years after this letter, six after Bethesda's inception, Whitefield was still struggling to find a workable scheme for the long-term viability of the orphanage. Writing in 1746, he rejoiced that "friends have raised an annual Subscription sufficient for discharging [the arrears] till the Family may be able to provide for itself." His plan for achieving self-sufficiency was "to use the Plow" and "to have many Acres of good Oats and Barley."[72] He would need a substantial labor force for it all to work.

From what we have observed, Whitefield functioned as a salesman of British goods as well as an evangelist of the gospel. His activities in the service of faith and world of trade served complementary purposes and thrust the itinerant into the marketplace of empire. As one historian noted: "Religious sanction for market exchange had become a commonplace in Boston by the 1740s."[73] In this milieu, Whitefield was merely one among a cadre of ministers who sought to leverage the market for their spiritual work. Such observations make it less surpris-

---

69. *The State of Religion in New England, Since the Reverend Mr. George Whitefield's Arrival There* (Glasgow, 1742), 44.

70. *The State of Religion in New England*, 44.

71. Whitefield, *Continuation of the Account*, 17.

72. Whitefield, *Brief Account of the Rise, Progress, and Present Situation*, 59.

73. Valeri, *Heavenly Merchandize*, 235.

ing that from the beginning of his American career, Whitefield lobbied for legal sanction of enslaved labor in Georgia. Why would an itinerant preacher merely passing through the colony take the time and go to the trouble of lobbying for slavery in the backcountry of a fledgling colony? The most plausible explanation is that he had larger designs in mind than the work of a parish priest. That plan included not just converting souls but building a movement with component pieces such as schools, storefronts, and plantations. Unsurprisingly, he came to see that all these efforts required a labor force to support the work. That he was concerned about Georgia's position on slavery bolsters evidence of a long-range strategic vision and supports the notion that more than re- vival itinerancy drove his numerous trips to the colonies.

A Plantation Owner in South Carolina

As it turns out, his plan for a self-subsisting operation in Georgia did not get very far. By the spring of 1747, Whitefield had to make the tactical switch to a plantation in South Carolina where he could employ slaves to provide for the ongoing needs at Bethesda. He justified his purchase of "a plantation of six hundred and forty acres of excellent land" by saying that "it is impossible for the inhabitants [of Georgia] to subsist themselves without the use of slaves."[74] In the same letter he mentioned the gift of "one negro" and his plans to purchase more. With his hands tied in Georgia, he found a convenient solution nearby. His excitement was palpable as he wrote numerous friends and associates about his newly acquired Carolina plantation that he intended to use for the up- keep of his work at Bethesda in Georgia.[75] This development he took to be a sign of God delivering him out of his embarrassments. Whatever moral qualms he may have had, he assuaged his conscience by telling his friends that many of the enslaved were "brought under conviction."[76] Since the intervening years had not been kind to the Bethesda project, Whitefield was under a barrage of accusations regarding his financial dealings.

74. Letter to a generous Benefactor unknown, Charles-Town, March 15, 1747, in *Works*, 2:93–95.

75. Letter on June 1, 1747, in *Works*, 2:108. Another letter on June 29, 1747, in *Works*, 2:113–15.

76. Whitefield, *Works*, 2:123–31.

Specifically, opponents charged him with traveling across the Atlantic world tugging at the heart strings of Britons to raise untold sums of money for an orphanage that continually suffered neglect in a dilapidated state. For his part, Whitefield endeavored to construct the best defense he could by going on the offense to build a prosperous institution. Yet he faced the embarrassment of arrears on his Bethesda property, even the threat of imprisonment for his debts in the early months of 1741. According to his biographer Tyerman, "Whitefield was in debt, and was constantly speaking as though he was about to be sent to prison."[77] After he purchased a plantation and slaves in South Carolina, he intended "to devote [them] to the use of Bethesda" and insisted they would help create "a visible fund for the Orphan house."[78] To close friends, he gave the impression that these financial matters were carnal annoyances beneath his dignity: "surely the Lord will deliver me from money matters by and by," he confided to Howel Harris in September of 1747.[79] To John Wesley, mentor and friend as well as rival, he sounded a more pious note: "I hope ere long to be delivered from my outward embarrassments. I long to owe no man anything but love."[80] In a February 28, 1748, letter to Harris, however, Whitefield still had not found a solution for his debts, which he described as "a load which has lain on me for years."[81] What cannot be doubted from these many references is the extent to which his financial woes troubled and humiliated Whitefield. Given his ambivalent stance on slavery at the outset, it is not surprising that the potential of profiting from slave labor grew ever more tempting in his eyes. It is true that Whitefield recoiled at the cruel realities of slavery in the New World. It is also an undeniable fact that, as he constantly skirted close to the brink of financial ruin for his initiatives in Georgia, he ultimately found it hard to resist the solution of enslaved labor. So impatient was Whitefield for change that, according to historian Thomas Kidd, he began using slave labor in Georgia in 1749, two years before it became legal.[82]

---

77. Tyerman, *Life*, 1:460.

78. Whitefield to Mr. H—, June 1, 1747; Whitefield to —, June 29, 1747, in *Works*, 2:105, 110.

79. Whitefield to Howel Harris, September 11, 1747, in *Works*, 2:125.

80. Whitefield to John Wesley, September 11, 1747, in *Works*, 2:127.

81. Tyerman, *Life*, 2:179.

82. Kidd, *George Whitefield*, 209.

Part of the problem for Whitefield was that as the revivals waned, he faced intense competition from a prospering consumer economy. By the late 1740s, his main competition was not theological, in the form of Arminianism or Antinomianism, but rather material, in the context of a culture increasingly enamored with British imperial affluence. And so Nathaniel Sargent, a Massachusetts lawyer who would later become the second chief justice of the United States, writing to Samuel Savage in the late summer days of 1747 could pivot seamlessly from singing the praises of Whitefield's sermon—"I can heartily join with you in your Sentiments, & really think him an Extraordinary person & one that is sent out from God, &c."—to asking about the price of paper, cheese, and coffee.[83] Rather than back down from fear of obsolescence and fierce competition, Whitefield fought hard to maintain a foothold in the marketplace of public opinion. Some years later, in 1759, a Philadelphia merchant, William Shippen, would in effect illustrate Whitefield's success in bringing the worlds of religion and commerce together. On Sunday, September 9, 1759, Shippen's economy of words combined Whitefield's sermon and the evening's supper into one brief and fragmentary entry: "spent at Mr DeBerdh. & hearing Mr. Whitefield with Mr. Clarkson supp'd upon Philadelphia cranberry Rye very fine."[84] On the following Sabbath, the merchant recorded his impressions of Whitefield in the same terms he might have used to describe the quality of coffee and dessert: "afternoon Mr. Candor a scholar a bad preacher Evening Mr Whitefield always ag'reable."[85]

Remorse as well as recalibration characterized Whitefield's response to the meandering course of the revivals. In an apologetic letter to the Trustees of Georgia on December 6, 1748, Whitefield attempted to mend relations. He also advanced his most forceful case to date for the necessity of slavery in Georgia and attempted to justify his investment in a slave plantation in South Carolina. Acknowledging "too great an opinion of my own sufficiency" and "misguided zeal," he nevertheless pleaded for recognition of his "disinterested" motives.[86] For the

83. Nathaniel Sargent to Savage, August 24, 1747, Ms N-885.1, Samuel Savage Papers, Massachusetts Historical Society.

84. Sunday, August 9, 1759, Mss.b.sh61, William Shippen Journal, American Philosophical Society.

85. Sunday, August 16, 1759, Mss.b.sh61, William Shippen Journal.

86. Whitefield to the Honorable Trustees of Georgia, December 6, 1748, in *Works*, 2:208–9.

troubled state of Georgia and his orphanage there, he fixed squarely on the inability to use slaves. "Upwards of five thousand pounds have been expended in that undertaking [at Bethesda], and yet very little proficiency made in the cultivation of my tract of land, and that *entirely* owing to the necessity I lay under of making use of white hands." He could not resist adding wistfully: "Had a negro been allowed, I should now have had a sufficiency to support a great many orphans, without expending above half the sum which hath been laid out."[87] Though the Trustees' resolve against slavery had weakened somewhat by this time, it is still possible to overstate the case. In other words, there was nothing inevitable about Whitefield's insistence on slavery. His position still faced considerable counterarguments. One example is a sermon Thomas Francklin preached before the Trustees as late as March 16, 1750, in which he argued "how inconsistent Negroes are with it, as likewise with the Welfare of GEORGIA; and, if GEORGIA should receive them, how prejudicial they would be to SOUTH-CAROLINA: How needless also they are for the Products which are designed to be raised there."[88] That Francklin's arguments were less moral and more pragmatic is one indication of the diminishing strength of the anti-slavery sentiment in Georgia.

Yet, determined not to be stymied any longer, Whitefield found alternative means of getting around the Trustees. He wanted the Trustees to know that he had weighed his options and found those in Georgia wanting. It was because his hands were tied, he claimed, that he was "prevailed on" to "purchase a plantation in South-Carolina, where negroes are allowed."[89] One can sense Whitefield straining to provide a justification for his actions. Likely aware of others in Georgia who were already disregarding the Trustees' prohibitions, Whitefield added: "But notwithstanding my private judgement, I am determined that not one of mine shall ever be allowed to work at the Orphan-house, till I can do it in a legal manner, and by the approbation of the honourable Trustees."[90] A generous reading would suggest that Whitefield intended to abide by the rules in 1748, though he would change his mind by the following year.

87. Whitefield to Trustees, in *Works*, 2:209; emphasis added.
88. Thomas Francklin, *A Sermon Preached Before the Honourable Trustees for Establishing the Colony of Georgia in America, and the Associates of the Late Rev. Dr. Bray; March 16, 1749–50. In the Parish Church of St. Margaret, Westminster* (London, 1750).
89. Whitefield to Trustees, in *Works*, 2:209.
90. Whitefield to Trustees, in *Works*, 2:209.

Itinerating in Bermuda

In the spring of 1748, Whitefield spent two months on a preaching tour through Bermuda during which time he reached upwards of half the population.[91] Judging from his journal entries in Bermuda, Whitefield appears to have experienced a veritable paradise: "The simplicity and plainness of the people, together with the pleasant situation of the island, much delighted me."[92] His time in the Caribbean was filled with positive encounters with all levels of society there, from government officials to slaves. Bermuda was a prospering colony with an extraordinary *sensus communis*, where people "came together across socioeconomic, racial, and gender lines."[93] It was, moreover, a society that prized refinement with regular formal balls, Masonic lodges, literary clubs, and private libraries. Governor Alured Popple's eleven-hundred-volume library was the envy of Bermudian society, and people regularly borrowed, lent, and read books together.

In addition to the fair climate, thriving economy, and social harmony, Whitefield witnessed a society where racially mixed audiences gathered for religious services and literate slaves engaged him in astute theological conversations. He was impressed enough to record in his journal: "From all which I infer, that these Bermudas negroes are more knowing than I supposed; that their consciences are awake, and consequently prepared, in a good measure, for hearing the Gospel preached unto them."[94] If Whitefield enjoyed his conversation with the enslaved Bermudians, he also learned to refine his preaching in a way that conformed to slave society: "I believe the Lord enabled me so to discourse as to touch the negroes, and yet not to give them the least umbrage to flight or behave imperiously to their masters. If ever a minister in preaching, need the wisdom of the serpent to be joined with the harmlessness of the dove, it must be when discoursing to negroes."[95]

91. Michael J. Jarvis, *In the Eye of All Trade: Bermuda, Bermudians, and the Maritime Atlantic World, 1680–1783* (Chapel Hill: UNC Press, 2010), 304. Though Whitefield stopped publishing his journals in 1741, portions of his journal entries from Bermuda are preserved in John Gillies, *Memoirs of the Life of the Reverend George Whitefield* (Meadow View: Quinta Press, 2000), 121–33.

92. March 1748 (precise date unknown), in Gillies, *Memoirs*, 121.

93. Jarvis, *In the Eye of All Trade*, 303.

94. May 7, 1748, entry in Gillies, *Memoirs*, 130.

95. May 1, 1748, entry in Gillies, *Memoirs*, 128.

Even as he made the free offer of the gospel to all, Whitefield discerned clear racial and social boundaries that he would need to tread with caution. So seriously did he take this balancing act that he called upon "the wisdom of the serpent." His travels around the empire were teaching Whitefield the possibilities for reimagining British society in the colonial margins even while maintaining and reinscribing traditional boundaries.

Slave Owner in Georgia

The long and winding path Whitefield traversed in search of a viable strategy in Georgia helps us understand his response to the legalization of slavery in 1751. Upon hearing the news, he burst into doxology. "Thanks be to God, that the time for favoring that Colony seems to be come," he wrote to a colleague in ministry. In addition to praise of the Almighty, his letter mingled relief with regret as it revealed the extent of his involvement in Georgia affairs. Relief because slave labor would provide a much-needed boost to Georgia's ailing economy. Regret because the decision had come after long and costly delay. He could not help looking back and lamenting the many lost opportunities: "What a flourishing country might Georgia have been, had the use of [slaves] been permitted years ago?"[96] The end result for Whitefield was a deepening resolve to see things through in the colony.

More than a story of one person's fluctuating fortunes, Whitefield's circumstances reflected broader realities on the ground in Georgia colony. The 1740s were a period of war and recession, where the early promise of a new enterprise had given way to stagnation and despair. After a moribund period of social and political unrest, Georgia was finally regaining its footing in the early 1750s. At its lowest point the population of the colony had dwindled to three thousand whites and six hundred blacks, but now was turning the corner toward a slow yet steady resurgence. Though many gave up and left Georgia, the few remaining Malcontents who had long protested the Trustees' land and labor policies began to see what they deemed encouraging signs of change. To the delight of many, the ban on slavery was lifted in 1749. The subsequent legalization of slavery in 1751 and the transfer of the colony to a royal

---

96. Whitefield to Mr. B—, March 22, 1751, in *Works*, 2:404.

charter in 1752 fueled a stream, if not a flood, of migration from South Carolina. By one account, nearly a thousand slaves were brought from the neighboring colony into Georgia. In a similar vein, "between 1745 and 1766, South Carolina accounted for 'more of Georgia's new settlers . . . than . . . Europe or any other American colony.'"[97] The tide had finally turned so that Georgia not only stopped losing settlers to its neighbor to the north but gained new residents to work the land and breathe new life into its economy.

Not by coincidence, it was during this time that Whitefield also began sharing some of his new insights regarding Africans. "I think now is the season for us to exert our utmost for the good of the poor Ethiopians," he wrote to a friend in March 1751. He had just observed, no doubt referring to the slavery issue, that "the time for favouring that Colony seems to be come." The letter also remains one of the few extant sources that reveal Whitefield's theological position on slavery. He applied not one but three biblical examples in support of slavery. Not always the most systematic thinker, he cited the apostles, the Gibeonites (Joshua 9), and Abraham (Genesis 21) as he jumped between the Old and New Testaments with no discernible sense of reasoning or purpose. To scriptural argumentation he added economic necessity: "it is plain to a demonstration, that hot countries cannot be cultivated without negroes." He also evinced a racial bias as he lamented: "How many white people have been destroyed for want of them, and how many thousands of pounds spent to no purpose at all?"[98]

As profit-seeking South Carolinians began moving into Georgia with their enslaved laborers, Whitefield hastened to sell his own Providence Plantation in South Carolina and set up Ephratah, a new plantation adjacent to his orphanage in Georgia. He sent instructions to sell Providence, at a loss if necessary: "I would only observe, that I had rather it should be sold for somewhat less than its real value, than to keep it any longer in my hands."[99] He wrote letters rejoicing that slave labor would improve future prospects at Bethesda: "I am glad to hear that Ephratah plantation is in some degree opened, and thereby a preparation made for a future progress this spring."[100]

---

97. Betty Wood, *Slavery in Colonial Georgia, 1730–1775* (Athens: University of Georgia Press, 1984), 91.

98. Whitefield to Mr. B—, March 22, 1751, in *Works*, 2:404-5.

99. Whitefield to Mr. H— B—, January 7, 1753, in *Works*, 2:476.

100. Whitefield to Mr. J— B—, February 1, 1753, in *Works*, 3:7.

As his plan unfolded, Whitefield was not only responsible for leading the charge to legalize slavery in Georgia; he was also very much active in reaping the benefits of slave labor. Although details of Whitefield's economic acitivity in Georgia are scant, we do know that by summer of 1753 the plantation near his orphanage had planted "about 50 acres of corn and rice."[101] Entering into the rice industry required more labor and equipment than a crop like cotton, as well as greater managerial efficiency.[102] In other words, it was not a work to be lightly engaged; rather, it took firm resolve, a large capital investment, and a long-term plan. Jonathan Bryan, a wealthy South Carolina plantation owner himself who also began investing in Georgia, was a revival convert and follower of Whitefield. In his letter to Whitefield, there is a sense of both nervousness and embarrassment that he has failed to secure the laborers needed to support Whitefield's crops: "I am sorry, those negroes expected from Doctor Brisbane are not yet bought." We do not know how Whitefield responded to this setback, but it is clear Bryan felt the need to pad his report with as much positive news as possible, as he took pains to point out: "your people are now making shingles for sale."[103] This comment also gives a helpful glimpse into the complex economic operation in process around Bethesda. We can be sure that much of the push for economic efficiency came from Whitefield, whose religious convictions led him to spurn idleness as detrimental to the soul. Though a landed member of the gentry, with holdings in both South Carolina and Georgia, Bryan sounds at times like a groveling employee before Whitefield. Judging by his earlier letter and Whitefield's own incessant writing about his financial travails, as well as his financial hopes, it is hard to exaggerate the interest with which both men followed the economic development of Whitefield's property in Georgia. Two years later, Whitefield was still struggling to maintain the orphanage and frustrated in his attempts to buy slaves: "I am determined to take in no more than the plantation will maintain, till I can buy more negroes."[104] Despite the hurdles, his resolve was as strong as ever.

---

101. Jonathan Bryan to George Whitefield, July 1, 1753, Letter 34 in George Whitefield Papers, Library of Congress.

102. Smith, *Slavery and Rice Culture.*

103. Jonathan Bryan to George Whitefield, July 1, 1753, Letter 34 in George Whitefield Papers, Library of Congress.

104. Whitefield to Mrs. C—, August 30, 1755, in *Works*, 3:217.

Slavery, Whitefield, and the Life Cycle of Revivals

Whitefield's active participation in efforts to legalize slavery in Georgia sheds fresh light on how the political and economic realities of imperial expansion influenced the work of revivalists after the revivals peaked. Despite the impossibility of establishing a direct causal relationship, there can be little doubt that his decision to use the labor of enslaved persons for supporting the work of Bethesda was tied to the fleeting fruits of revival. Whatever worries he may have had about the morality of slavery faded as the revivals themselves dwindled and other concerns took priority. He had orphans to feed and clothe. There were more preaching appointments to meet and new places to reach across the Atlantic world. He had building projects of chapels in Philadelphia, Bristol, and London. He also began to harbor dreams of building a college and seminary.

And so we come again to Whitefield's pensive words from the winter of 1750: "It tries me to hear that religion is at so low an ebb amongst You. Strange That we should grow older & yet grow worse, Receive more from Xt & yet do less for Him."[105] He appears to have been trying to make sense of what it meant that the high season of revivals had passed. At the intersection of the awakenings' downward trend and his growing interest in other ventures, including slavery, it is noteworthy that George Whitefield not only was a religious leader but had also become a formidable economic and political force. His activism led him into arenas of imperial life where the Bible had little direct bearing, at least as he interpreted it. His facile attempts at scriptural justification aside, Whitefield saw economic activity as a necessary extension of his spiritual ambitions. For this reason, he detected no contradiction between owning slave plantations and preaching to tens of thousands of people in outdoor fields. To him, both were vital demonstrations of faith in action. He moved seamlessly from one mode of operation to another, and, as we retrace those steps carefully, we might also discern a pattern to the cycle of revivals emerging in evangelical religion. To put it another way, we can see the revivals as more than a religious campaign. The evangelical renewal was also a social, economic, and political movement that progressed along a series of phases. The phenomenon

---

105. George Whitefield to William Bradford, February 24, 1750, in Miscellaneous Manuscripts Collection, American Philosophical Society.

historians call the Great Awakening began with isolated and localized awakenings, spread to a more general network of revivals, then finally entered a later phase of revivalism, where the longing for heightened religious zeal lingered more than the actual experience.

One benefit to this kind of analysis is the focus it brings to a neglected but important feature of what might be called revival twilight— the long, calmer, and cooler aftermath of the white-hot bursts that had spread with the speed and intensity of a forest fire during the awakenings. While the image of Whitefield ingrained in historical memory is a young, brash revival preacher, our view of his involvement in slavery opens a wider angle that takes his later years into account. To illuminate the latter, more opaque phase of Whitefield's public life exposes the ways in which mercantile ambitions—and not merely moral or religious motivations—energized his involvement in the emerging plantation economy of the American South at the very same time his revival project faced diminishing returns. This claim will sound like a self-evident statement of fact to some and cruel, even blasphemous, slander to others. Suspending judgment and paving a middle way through both of these evaluative responses allows us to see how post-revival dynamics set up ideal conditions for the conflation of religious, political, and economic forces. Without intending to do so, Whitefield pushed religious concerns into the realm of imperial economy and politics. His advocacy for slavery was the most obvious, and tragic, consequence of this fact.

To put this matter in broader context, even as a prospering economy expanded the number of material choices available to ordinary people, the revivals emphasized the importance of making good religious choices in all spheres of life. As one historian put it, "The revival moment . . . deepened evangelicals' sense—an often tacit assumption—that free trade and piety, market behaviors and social solidarity, were compatible."[106] After the early spectacular revivals, the challenge of maintaining and consolidating revival gains dovetailed with growing evangelical participation in the world of market exchange. At a time when the clergy were relaxing earlier strictures, ceding more economic freedom to merchants, and articulating a vocabulary of faithful engagement with imperial policies, Whitefield rushed headlong into the market system himself. As the early eighteenth-century colonial world witnessed a transformation of religious attitudes toward economic ac-

106. Valeri, *Heavenly Merchandize*, 244.

tivity, Whitefield placed himself at the forefront of that sea change. Not merely a preacher providing guidance, he became an active participant in the world of commerce.

For this reason, a fresh look at Whitefield's changing attitudes toward slavery, which the preceding pages have tried to offer, is an integral part of any attempt to understand revival religion, and for that matter any social or religious movement with a tempestuous crescendo followed by a protracted settlement period. That examination has revealed Whitefield's drive for economic stability despite his loud and repetitive denials, often with accompanying denunciations, of what he called "temporal" motives. It is not necessary to judge or deny the sincerity of Whitefield's interest in the spiritual well-being of all persons in Georgia—including British colonists *and* enslaved Africans—to recognize that he was also subject to the political and economic realities of imperial life. By placing the issue of slavery into the larger narrative arc of Whitefield's revival ministry, we can discern a relationship between slavery and the revivals that points to a pattern in which opportunities concerning the former counteracted the waning influence of the latter.

Conclusion

Whitefield's evolving stance on slavery reminds us that the expanding imperial landscape resulted in a bewildering array of socioeconomic opportunities, cultural encounters, and ethical choices, which elicited problematic responses. In addition to posing pragmatic questions about sustainable economies, the moral quagmire involved in enslaving another human being engendered a spiritual and theological crisis.[107] In this instance, the imperial experiment influenced scriptural

---

107. Whitefield lived in a time when belief in common human origins, or monogenesis, was an accepted fact of life. However, intellectual rationalizations for chattel slavery and the increasing pluralistic understandings of humankind began to undermine status quo assumptions. For a study of crumbling Mosaic foundations due to an undermining of common human origins, see Colin Kidd, *British Identities before Nationalism* (Cambridge: Cambridge University Press, 1999). To understand the complexity of the questions arising in this period, we might look ahead to the proffered solution of polygenesis in the nineteenth century that proved profoundly troubling from the perspective of European theological orthodoxy.

interpretation and theological conviction. The capitulation to slavery, moreover, attenuated the moral clarity of evangelicalism and exposed the vulnerabilities of the awakenings as a sustainable movement. In the process, the honey-tongued evangelist also tied the cause of revivalism to the engine of a growing commercial empire, consequently captivated by the allure of an expanding British state on a seemingly unstoppable arc of growth.

Whitefield's relationship to slavery allows us to discern distinct steps along this journey. Once so preoccupied with preaching to the masses that he hardly had time to write letters to close friends, he entered into another period of life during the decade of the 1740s in which he began organizing a lobby to introduce land and labor reforms in the small outpost colony of Georgia. For this reason, his life can serve as a proxy for discerning the transition in evangelical heart religion from winning souls to maintaining a movement. The awakenings in their early years had been impulsive, local events. They subsequently spread to create a more general phenomenon of revivals, which were transatlantic in scope, even international to some extent. The revivals then gave way to a process of routinization, with the spirit of evangelical religion becoming less spontaneous and more institutionalized. The focus turned from sparking revivals to sustaining revivalism and somewhere along the way the experience of revivals was supplanted by the longing for revivals. For John Wesley this sequence led to his organization of connectional Methodist societies; for Whitefield it led to his reorganization of Britain's imperial economy.

It is striking to see this sequence of stages in Whitefield's life. As he penned a public letter to the inhabitants of the southern colonies in 1740, he sounded tentative about slavery because the letter was composed at the height of revival fervor at a time when he was constantly on the move, rushing from one memorable revival triumph to another. As such, the letter sought to establish some semblance of authority over a fast-growing movement spread across a wide geographical region. Whitefield's purpose in writing the letter was not so much to formulate rules but to encourage an attitude of piety and perhaps just as much to test the boundaries of his influence. A decade later, Whitefield was in a dramatically different frame of mind. He was focused on more mundane matters—like legislative reform, rice cultivation, and real estate transactions. To account for this change in Whitefield's life is one way of getting at the adaptations of early evangelicalism to the realities of time and space.

Examining the relationship between Whitefield and slavery has revealed the ways in which the religious event of the Great Awakening conformed to the values and priorities of imperial state formation. When war erupted across the empire once more in the middle of the 1750s, the boundary between religion and society would be blurred again.

CHAPTER 5

Whitefield and War

A product of the eighteenth-century British Atlantic world, evangelicalism came of age in an era of conversion, commerce, and conquest.[1] If this is true, then it follows that any accounting of Whitefield's contributions to the birth of evangelical Protestantism would benefit by incorporating all three of these features. And yet, while we are familiar with the revival origins of evangelicalism as a religion of heart conversion, and there is broad appreciation for the commercial savvy with which evangelicals have always approached their labors, far fewer works have examined evangelicalism as a religion of conquest.[2] Examining the relationship between Whitefield and war presents an opportunity to address this lacuna in the historical record and demonstrate the influence of British imperial attitudes of theological, cultural, and racial superiority on the development of evangelical religion.[3]

1. For this triptych as a way of charactering the eighteenth century, I am indebted to David Hempton, *The Church in the Long Eighteenth Century* (London: I. B. Tauris, 2011), 55.

2. For a study of evangelicalism as heart religion, see Dallimore, *George Whitefield*. For studies that highlight Whitefield's propensity for leveraging commercial opportunities, see Lambert, "Subscribing for Profits and Piety"; Lambert, *"Pedlar in Divinity."*

3. For seventeenth-century precedents in establishing British cultural superiority, see Joyce E. Chaplin, *Subject Matter: Technology, the Body, and Science on the Anglo-American Frontier, 1500–1676* (Cambridge: Harvard University Press, 2001). In addition, what Calloway has said about European invaders of America can apply to Whitefield as well: "European colonists intended not only to take over the land; they also were determined to change it, to remake it into something more closely resembling the world they had left." Calloway, *New Worlds for All*, 13. Richter identified "the hard racial underside of the American mosaic" as an eighteenth-century phenomenon. In illuminating fash-

169

Table 2. A Chronology of Whitefield and War

July 9, 1755	Battle of the Monongahela, General Braddock's defeat
1756–1763	Seven Years' War (also called the French and Indian War in America, 1756–1763)
February–April 1756	Persecution of Whitefield at Long Acre Chapel
1756	Publication of *A Short Address to Persons of All Denominations*
February 10, 1763	Treaty of Paris

The Seven Years' War was nothing less than an international conflagration that nearly bankrupted the British Empire and set its course toward dissolution in North America. During a period in his life when he published remarkably little, Whitefield put pen to paper in order to write an important imperial tract entitled *A Short Address to Persons of All Denominations*.[4] He used the pamphlet to warn against the dangers of French victory and champion the British cause. His involvement as an Anglican cleric in the politics of imperial conflict helps explain why the colonies were so significant for British interests in this period. It also shows how the entanglement of war and religion created deeper cavities in what one historian has called a "hollow victory" that paved the way for further disappointments.[5] In addition to the precarious bal-

---

ion, he also provides a rich description of the early eighteenth-century British colonies as occupying the "foreign historical terrain" of a distinctly imperial era. Daniel K. Richter, *Facing East from Indian Country: A Native History of Early America* (Cambridge: Harvard University Press, 2001), 152–53. For a theological account of race that begins with the age of discovery and conquest and traces the development of racialized thought, see Willie James Jennings, *The Christian Imagination: Theology and the Origins of Race* (New Haven: Yale University Press, 2010). Jennings has pointed out an important theological quandary by asking how a Christian religion of love could have given rise to racial segregation. One way to solve this theological as well as historical puzzle is to show, as my work does, that between the European age of exploration and the American era of segregation there was a host of deleterious developments like the evangelical articulation of theological and cultural superiority based on British Protestant hegemony.

4. George Whitefield, *A Short Address to Persons of All Denominations, Occasioned By the Alarm of an Intended Invasion* (London, 1756).

5. For the image of a hollow empire that emerged after the Seven Years' War, see Fred Anderson, *Crucible of War: The Seven Years' War and the Fate of Empire in British North America, 1754–1766* (New York: Alfred A. Knopf, 2000), xix–xxi.

ance of geopolitical power and the high stakes involved in transoceanic commercial networks, the contentious battles for religious renewal and freedom that raged during and after the war provides another angle for understanding the perilous course of British expansion in the mid-eighteenth century.[6]

Whitefield the Imperial Propagandist

Even as Whitefield was sorting out the implications of slave labor for his Georgia project, Britain once again entered into war with France. Whitefield placed himself at the center of the religious commentary on this epic imperial struggle as he sounded the alarm for the British-American front. The speed with which the itinerant trumpeted his country's role in the Seven Years' War and the ease with which he identified British victory as a matter of international Protestant interest reveal the power of imperial culture in the theological imagination of this evangelical minister.[7] British nationalism and biblical spirituality became hardly distinguishable in Whitefield's message, which freely mixed the affairs of empire and faith. In the aftermath of the Great Awakening as war raged all around him, he retooled his message and reconciled the religious and political goals of the kingdom of God and the Hanoverian empire. Paying attention to Whitefield's developing war rhetoric brings into sharper focus the relationship between revival religion and imperial politics. Indeed, the process of British state formation and the building of a Protestant empire aligned closely against the threat of French Catholic invasion. That Britain's hard-won victory proved fleeting and hollow in the end is also an essential part of the story as we trace Whitefield's steps in plotting yet another course for revival consolidation.

To appreciate Whitefield's alignment of religion and war on the imperial landscape, it will be helpful to see the development of his anti-

6. For an analysis of Britain's economic transition from an agricultural to a manufacturing nation, see Paul Mapp, "British Culture and the Changing Character of the Mid-Eighteenth-Century British Empire," in *Cultures in Conflict: The Seven Years' War in North America*, ed. Warren R. Hofstra (Lanham: Rowman & Littlefield, 2007).

7. Thomas Kidd noted the development of Whitefield's patriotism in this way: "[Whitefield] certainly left traces of his patriot sympathies after his turn toward politics, which began with the Louisbourg campaign and peaked during the Seven Years' War." Kidd, *George Whitefield*, 255.

Catholic sentiments during the decade of the 1750s. An examination of Whitefield's visit to Lisbon, Portugal, and the reaction of his Protestant sensibilities to the Catholic festivities there will help set the stage for his more forceful rhetoric against the French Catholic threat to British power in the Atlantic world. The *Four Letters* of Whitefield written from Portugal to a friend in England provide insight into Whitefield's view of Catholicism in 1754.[8] In those letters, he criticized Catholics for their theological errors but also revealed admiration for their devotional rigor, going as far as to lament Protestant laxity in comparison. Two years later, when he published *A Short Address to Persons of All Denominations*, Whitefield had undergone a noticeable shift in his tactical response to Catholicism as he sought to mobilize a broad Protestant audience against the gathering Catholic threat. Ranging from liturgical and ecclesiastical critique to social and political commentary, these two documents show development in the ways Whitefield used suspicion of papist conspiracies to support his Protestant cause. The changes we detect in Whitefield's deployment of anti-Catholic rhetoric help us to see this revival preacher adjusting to his post-revival world.

Whitefield in Catholic Portugal

In March 1754, on the way to America for his fifth visit, Whitefield welcomed the opportunity to make a stop in Lisbon. He wrote his friend that he believed "it might be serviceable to me, as a Preacher and Protestant, to see something of the superstitions of the Church of Rome." Being the season of Lent as well as drought, Whitefield witnessed intense displays of Catholic piety, including public processions and petitions for rain accompanied by elaborate rituals and relics. All was not abhorrent to Whitefield, however, and on several different occasions, he expressed admiration for the "great earnestness" and "extempore prayer" of the people. In the final analysis, Whitefield lamented the perversion of the gospel he detected in "such a mixture of human artifice and blind superstition." There is also, however, an undeniable tension in the tone of Whitefield's letters. He could not help admiring their sincerity and

---

8. George Whitefield, *A Brief Account of Some Lent and Other Extraordinary Processions and Ecclesiastical Entertainments Seen Last Year at Lisbon: In Four Letters to An English Friend* (London: W. Strahan, 1755). Referenced as *Four Letters* for brevity.

fervency. God even appeared to answer the people's prayer for rain, with impeccable timing no less, for as Whitefield reports, "The third Day in the Forenoon it rained."[9]

We might sense Whitefield's discomfort as he was "received and entertained with great Gentility, Hospitality, and Friendliness" while being bombarded to the point of sensory overload by the sight of such direct affronts to his Protestant sensibilities.[10] To put it another way, his doctrinal and theoretical biases ran up against the reality of flesh-and-bone people. After some disorientation, Whitefield managed to cling to dogmatic certitudes in the face of these novel encounters. Before rushing with Whitefield to those standard conclusions, however, we can learn a great deal more about the state of evangelical and imperial flux in the mid-eighteenth century if we linger over his initial shock and tension in the face of Catholic devotion in Lisbon.

In a second letter to the same friend in the same month, Whitefield expressed "disgust" and "horror" at the sight of numerous processions and physical, superstitious displays of penitence. He concluded his letter with a litany of praise for the Reformation and by noting his tears of grief at the sights he had witnessed. But embedded within this text of intense disapproval is a notable interjection that beckons deeper consideration. Expressing joy that Portugal was not his nation, nor Catholicism his religion, Whitefield declared, "But, blessed be God, the snare is broken, and we are deliver'd—Oh for Protestant Practices to be added to Protestant Principles!—Oh for an obediential Acknowledgment to the ever blessed God for our repeated Deliverances!"[11] The middle statement is the curious one, for he enjoined practices to be added to principles, and urged the acting out of faith in addition to the cognitive assent to faith. If one did not know better, one might suspect Whitefield of envying the Catholics for their impassioned devotional living. It is as if Whitefield were saying: Catholics may have it wrong, but to their credit they are passionately wrong. Protestants, on the other hand, were guilty of lacking sufficient visible fruits and outward demonstrations of their faith.

At this juncture it is helpful to remember that the Great Awakening was a distant memory by the 1750s, even if occasional bursts of revival per-

9. Whitefield, *Four Letters*, 6.
10. Whitefield, *Four Letters*, 3.
11. Whitefield, *Four Letters*, 15.

sisted. In fact, as converts backslid and the fire of renewal fizzled, White-field recalibrated expectations. He confided to a friend in March 1753, a year before he sailed into the port of Lisbon, "There are so many stony-ground hearers that receive the word with joy, that I have determined to suspend my judgment, till I know the tree by its fruits." Numerical growth did not translate into spiritual vitality and Whitefield expressed sorrow that "Scotland is so dead" despite congregations being "larger than ever."[12] Moreover, the transatlantic community of saints and the international network of revival—which appeared unstoppable in the 1740s—was in the process of fragmenting in the 1750s. As an example, when Samuel Da-vies and Gilbert Tennent traveled to Britain to raise funds for the College of New Jersey, they made delicate evasions of meeting publicly with White-field, who had become a lightning rod of division. Faced with the reality of revival on the wane, Whitefield recognized the need to consolidate revival gains. Less than the actual experience of awakenings, we may surmise, it was the efforts at revival making that characterized evangelical faith in the eighteenth century. And if it is true that revivals by their very definition could only enliven that which was dead to begin with, then more closely examining the valleys of spiritual lethargy and plains of ordinary time that preceded and followed the mountaintop experiences is vitally important to understanding the history of revivals.

Acknowledging this climate of post-revival decline as an essential category of historical analysis, we may see that Whitefield's Lisbon let-ters reveal ritual envy and a longing for similar vitality in Protestant spirituality. Though far from advocating the "horrific" papal prostra-tions he had just witnessed, Whitefield made little effort to moderate his plaintive cry—"Oh for Protestant Practices to be added to Protestant Principles!" This slip into lament is especially telling when we remem-ber not only his immediate Catholic context in Lisbon but also a lon-ger view that accounts for Whitefield's disappointment at the fleeting effects of revival.

In his third letter from Lisbon, Whitefield recorded observations of Maundy Thursday events in that great profligate city. Whitefield was taken by the extravagance of church adornments where "all was so magnificently, so superstitiously grand, that I am persuaded several thousands of pounds would not defray the expenses of this one day."[13]

12. *Works*, 3:8, 27.
13. Whitefield, *Four Letters*, 11, 18.

The day must indeed have been strange for Whitefield, who scorned such lavish embellishments but also marveled at the king and queen of Portugal traveling about the city separately, washing the feet of the poor and worshiping alongside their subjects. Whitefield himself was one of the gawkers at one point, straining his neck to get a better look at the queen. Later in the day, Whitefield bumped into the king walking along the streets "with his Brother and two Uncles, attended only with a few Noblemen in black velvet, and a few guards without halberts."[14] Though we cannot say for sure, Whitefield possessed too imaginative a theatrical mind to miss the echoes of the incarnation in his own descriptions of royal figures who condescended to walk amid their people.

The fourth and final letter contains Whitefield's description of Lisbon's Good Friday observations as "Tragi-comical, superstitious, idolatrous droll."[15] In the middle of his puritanical condemnations, however, there is a moment when the old theater enthusiast in Whitefield cannot remain silent and offers some stage directions of his own to enhance the dramatic scene unfolding before him—mentioning that the soldier should have pierced the side of Christ and the preacher could have improved "the passions of his auditory" by wiping the head of Christ with a bloodied cloth. Whitefield's interjections show deep-seated ambivalence about the Catholic ritualization of faith. Theologically deviant in his view, these liturgical devices still reflected life and a passionate living, which in his mind was the primary deficiency of Protestant spirituality. So he opined, "Surely our English preachers would do well to be a little more fervent in their address. They have truth on their side. Why should superstition and falsehood run away with all that is pathetic and affecting?"[16] The intensity of Whitefield's contempt for Catholic idolatry is not what is so noteworthy about Whitefield's words. Such expressions, especially for someone like him, would have flowed freely without much thought or effort. Whitefield's admiration for the spiritual affections of the Catholic priests, on the other hand, stands out in stark relief. To be sure, Whitefield did not relent one inch to Catholic doctrine. But his admiration of Catholic devotion contrasted sharply with his criticisms of Protestant backsliding.

---

14. Whitefield, *Four Letters*, 20.
15. Whitefield, *Four Letters*, 27.
16. Whitefield, *Life*, 2:332.

Whitefield's letters from Portugal provide a window into his developing anti-Catholicism from abstract and inchoate theory to a hardening conviction based on his personal experience of the broader Atlantic world. It was very much a contested landscape filled with religious differences that could easily morph into geo-political dangers. One biographer, Luke Tyerman, put it this way: "He was learning lessons which could not be learned in England or America, and which, he hoped, would make him a better man and a better preacher, to the end of life. He became a stauncher Protestant, and felt more than ever how invaluable were the privileges enjoyed by the inhabitants of Great Britain."[17] His anti-Catholic sentiments were not merely reified or inherited beliefs he held onto in unchanging form, but rather dynamic forces that grew in intensity as he traveled the Atlantic world. Observing the distinct shift of an incipient notion articulated in 1754 amid the Lenten festivities of Lisbon toward a more strident point of view in 1756 against the specter of war helps us to see the influence of the imperial world on Whitefield's worldview.

Whitefield and the French Catholic Threat

Historians have long puzzled over how the heightened patriotism inspired by the Seven Years' War gave way so soon after military triumph to the dismantling of Britain's imperial holdings in North America. While an in-depth exploration of that question lies outside the scope of this study, Whitefield's contributions are a significant part of the broader narrative of the process of Anglicization that influenced British state formation in the mid-eighteenth century. His activism, both religious and political, during this period shows the ways in which the ideals of British liberty were held alongside of, even if distinct from, imperial patriotism. The former was a matter of indissoluble principle whereas the latter was inspired by an ephemeral polity that could be traded in for another. In other words, peeling away the outward paradox reveals an inner consistency at work. This apparent tension is present in Whitefield's activities during a period of life when he authored his most political and patriotic writings even as he engaged in his fiercest battles over civil and religious freedom. Whitefield's fight for ecclesial

17. Tyerman, *Life*, 2:331.

and political freedom put enormous pressure on him to show loyalty to the British imperial cause in order to allay widespread charges of methodist disloyalty to the crown—an easy association considering Whitefield's own activism against the establishment clergy and churches. This contorted alliance between the progress of religious liberty and a war of imperial conquest, as we will see, had the incongruous effect of ratcheting up the tension between ideals of British liberty and loyalty to Britain itself so much that a rupture was all but inevitable.

Despite Whitefield's narrative of providential necessity throughout the Seven Years' War, the acquisitive spirit of British imperial activity in North America was fraught with problems for the Christian conscience of evangelical Protestants. A reflexive tendency demanded that the war be portrayed as a just cause. The reality was more complex and many of the underlying motivations for war—far from noble or holy—flowed from economic protectionism, political corruption, and cultural imperialism. British politics in general after the Glorious Revolution had come to more and more justify, in the words of one historian, "an absolutist parliamentary regime."[18] Say what they might, many religious leaders beheld the specter of political coercion and worried about the intrusive power of the state. For instance, Samuel Davies, fourth president of the college in Princeton, took the opportunity while eulogizing George II to emphasize political restraint as one of the virtues of the late monarch: "George the Great but Un-ambitious, consulted The Rights of the People, as well as of the Crown; and claimed no Powers but such as were granted to Him by the Constitution and celebrated political freedom."[19]

Seemingly impervious to such concerns, however, Whitefield threw himself into the political fray and tried to rally as much popular support as possible. In the same way that the goal of economic solvency swayed Whitefield's attitudes toward slavery, his quest for influence

18. Jack P. Greene, *Creating the British Atlantic: Essays on Transplantation, Adaptation, and Continuity* (Charlottesville: University of Virginia Press, 2013), 50; Helmut Georg Koenigsberger, "Composite States, Representative Institutions and the American Revolution," *Historical Research* 62, no. 148 (1989): 135–53.

19. Although Davies articulated suspicions of encroaching arbitrary power against liberty for Britons, he also celebrated the defeat of French and Native American forces. This kind of double standard was common among evangelical leaders. Samuel Davies, *A Sermon Delivered At Nassau-Hall, January 14, 1761. On the Death of His Late Majesty King* (Boston, 1761), 7–9.

forced him to overlook the dispossession of Native Americans during the Seven Years' War. Practically speaking, Whitefield lent his name to the task of recasting an aggressive war of expansion into a defensive war of necessity. Critics of imperial propaganda demurred, showing Whitefield's position was not the only option.[20] For example, Samuel Johnson expressed his discomfort with the war's effects on native peoples by writing in the voice of an Indian chief, condemning both English and French claims:

> The sons of rapacity have now drawn their swords upon each other, and referred their claims to the decision of war; let us look unconcerned upon the slaughter, and remember that the death of every European delivers the country from a tyrant and a robber; for what is the claim of either nation, but the claim of the vulture to the leveret, of the tiger to the fawn? Let them then continue to dispute their title to regions which they cannot people, to purchase by danger and blood the empty dignity of dominion over mountains which they will never climb, and rivers which they will never pass.[21]

Such a scathing view of the Seven Years' War provides helpful context for understanding Whitefield's own words endorsing war and expressing support for the crown in its expansionist schemes as a matter of Christian duty. Johnson's words were not those of a lonely prophet in

20. For many of the examples in the next two paragraphs of literature and art, I am indebted to John Richardson, "Imagining Military Conflict during the Seven Years' War," *Studies in English Literature 1500–1900* 48, no. 3 (2008): 585–611. Though alienating in its caustic tone, a work that thoroughly critiqued Francis Parkman's (and, inadvertently, George Whitefield's) interpretation of the Seven Years' War as the triumph of good over evil is Francis Jennings, *Empire of Fortune: Crowns, Colonies, and Tribes in the Seven Years War in America* (New York: W. W. Norton, 1990). To offer a sample, characteristic quote: "The war was brought on and directed by some very ugly, powerful men motivated by greed, self-aggrandizement, and the desire for yet more power. It was conducted in the usual bloody, dirty way of war by officers who relied on the strategy of massacre and terror over troops and civilians alike, by methods that had become integral to European culture." Jennings, *Empire of Fortune*, 172. While Jennings has been accused of superimposing presentist values on a past event, Richardson's article shows a cast of eighteenth-century writers and artists who had similar qualms about the cruelty of war.

21. Samuel Johnson, *The Yale Edition of the Works of Samuel Johnson: The Idler and the Adventurer*, vol. 2 (New Haven: Yale University Press, 1963), 254.

the wilderness; in fact, there was a chorus of viewpoints that balked at the corrosive effects of a war of conquest.[22] Even the hawkish *Daphnis and Menalcas*, a work appearing after the British victory in Canada that extolled the virtues of the late General Wolfe, could not help referring repeatedly to Britain's triumph as a "conquest" (up to ten times) and proclaimed relief at the war's conclusion, since: "Now murder, fraud, and impious warfare cease."[23] For many Britons, the celebration of conquest also included frank acknowledgment of the inherent "impious" horrors of war.

Other artists used a variety of means to illuminate the moral dilemma of a so-called war for liberty that led to rape, indiscriminate massacre, and other appalling atrocities. When William Whitehead, future poet laureate, warned against the "Pride of War" in 1764, he had already seen enough to worry that military victory did not guarantee an easy or enduring civil peace. He rightly fretted about the consequences of a hard-fought victory that too easily sacrificed the moral high ground. It is telling that Whitefield's writings about the war, in contrast, displayed none of the careful ethical parsing that marked the commentary of many of his contemporaries. Rather, his words more closely resembled a painting by Edward Penny, *The Marquis of Granby Giving Alms to a Sick Soldier and His Family*, which depicted a scene of charity from the hand of a military leader. By eliminating any hint of death and destruction from battle, the painting offered a sterilized picture of war excised of any unpleasant details. Instead, it presented economic squalor as one of the threats that war would ameliorate. It was an example of how some patriotic Britons attempted to portray the war in a way that comported to their ideals of heroism and providential destiny. (Even in this painting, however, there is a lone image of dissent—a toddler with her back toward the gallant Granby, shoulder raised in defensive posture and eyes askance with suspicion, instinctually sensing danger.) By offering a perspective on the war that celebrated the religious virtues of the British Empire, Whitefield allied himself with a particular view of the conflict that competed with other perspectives. In this light, his enthusiastic embrace of a narrative of British and Protestant triumphalism requires explanation.

22. For more examples, see Richardson, "Imagining Military Conflict."
23. *Daphnis and Menalcas: A Pastoral. Sacred to the Memory of the Late General Wolfe* (London, 1759), 10.

Nearly twenty years after the outbreak of evangelical revivals, White-field had made some gains in respectability, but he and other evangel-icals remained an embarrassment to many Anglican colleagues and a laughingstock to most elites. There were breakthroughs and victories but also setbacks and disappointments—not only in a military sense but also culturally and religiously. As a person who embodied this tension, Whitefield's body of work during this period illuminates the fragile, and increasingly conflicted, process of empire building. In fact, Whitefield had been down this road of managing heightened fervor and fighting apostasy before, in the aftermath of the Great Awakening.

Tracing links between the post-revival years and the onset of im-perial war, the remainder of this chapter will examine two contrasting types of Whitefieldian rhetoric: his celebration of British Protestant liberty and his condemnation of French Catholic tyranny. Whitefield spoke ardently for the British cause, yet he unabashedly criticized the abuses of power that threatened the already embattled revival religion of evangelicals, both at home and abroad. With respect to the latter, he rallied Christians of all denominations to support the British im-perial project by trumpeting its virtues. But with respect to the former, he faced conflict at home: riots in England, controversy in Scotland, and stoning in Ireland. In each of these cases, opposition came from those Whitefield and his coreligionists viewed as insufficiently re-formed Protestants or their longstanding rivals, the Catholics. Such a story of evangelical chastening represents the dark side of British imperial triumphs and can further illuminate the paradoxical gains of imperial victory as well as evangelical revivalism. For revivalists and imperialists alike contended with dramatic victory that then had to be preserved.

Stewarding victory was not as easy as the exuberant British thought. Some English leaders viewed the colonists as inferior, while others ap-prehended the need to tread more gently. Whether in Braddock's and Loudoun's arrogance toward provincials that translated into policies of coercion, or in Pitt's more tactful approach of cooperation, we can see the troubled waters of intercultural interaction that not only po-litical and military leaders but also religious figures had to navigate.[24] This alliance between the cause of religion and that of empire in the

24. For more on military leaders, coercion, and cooperation, see chapter 46, "The Fruits of Victory and the Seeds of Disintegration," in Anderson, *Crucible of War*.

mid-eighteenth-century British Atlantic world was tenuous at best, as Whitefield painfully came to learn.

Whitefield's Appeal to All Protestants

Before we turn to a close reading of Whitefield's *A Short Address to Persons of All Denominations*, published in the early part of 1756, a survey of the imperial landscape will help set the context. The year 1755 witnessed military disasters for Britain as well as natural catastrophes in numerous parts of the world. In July, General Braddock was fumbling one task after another in an ill-fated march on Fort Duquesne in the Ohio territory of North America, which was aimed at dislodging the French from their southernmost fortress.[25] Later in the same month, likely before news of Braddock's defeat reached him, Whitefield weighed in on Britain's imperial battles. "God only knows what a trying season lies before us. It is to be feared, that we are upon the eve of a bloody war," he wrote to a friend. Nevertheless he welcomed the fight, framing it as a war against the evils of Catholicism: "O that the war between Michael and the Dragon may go on! The prospect is promising. Several ministers preach Christ boldly; and as for my own poor feeble labours, the blessed Jesus vouchsafes to crown them with success."[26] In his stark and binary view of the world, Britain was the angel entrusted with the heroic task of slaying France. With the battleground so clearly laid out, he could move seamlessly from hoping for victory in war with France to declaring success in gospel preaching because he saw continuity between these purposes. Even when setbacks on the battleground piled on, Whitefield continued to express hope in Britain's providential destiny, oddly mixing military and soteriological metaphors by praying for "the late defeat" to "be sanctified."[27] When projecting confidence in eventual military victory, he used the biblical language of triumph in salvation, proclaiming, "I doubt not but we shall be more than conquerors through the love of Christ."[28] To defeat France was to overcome the forces of darkness and evil, and everything else—including lesser evils—paled in comparison.

---

25. Anderson, *Crucible of War*, 109.
26. Whitefield to the Rev. Mr. H—, July 25, 1755, in *Works*, 3:130.
27. Whitefield to Mr. V—, Aug. 30, 1755, in *Works*, 3:136.
28. Whitefield to Mr. V—, in *Works*, 3:138.

Not surprisingly, as he found himself blocked from travel to the colonies, Whitefield was hungry for any word he could get of the war's progress, telling a friend on August 30 that he "was looking out for more news from dear America" and to a colonel in September, "O for good news from dear New England!"[29] For Whitefield there was little daylight between the cause of Christ and the fight for empire.

In fact, his numerous references to the American theater of war show that Whitefield acted not only as a servant of Christ but also as a foot soldier for the empire. In this role, he consoled the wife of a soldier, going as far as to tell her that Jesus was her husband's captain: "He is gone upon a good cause, and under the conduct of the best general, even the Captain of our salvation."[30] He likewise prayed for a colonel, "May your head, and the heads of all engaged, be covered in every day of battle; and may our troops be made in the end more than conquerors through the love of God!"[31] That his words were not mere patriotic bluster can be seen in his wish for friends to participate in the war effort as much as they could. "I am glad to hear, that the Ladies are employed in making the soldiers cloaths; I trust my female friends are some of the most active," he wrote to an official in Boston.[32] Busy as he was in so many affairs, he also stressed the importance of broad social engagement in supporting Britain's cause.

Most significant for our purposes, Whitefield frequently noted a direct correlation between the progress of war and growth in piety: "O that this time of outward danger, may be sanctified to the exciting of greater zeal against our inward spiritual enemies!"[33] Whitefield held out hope that the spiritual lethargy that had followed revival fervor might be reversed by the imperial battles engulfing the British world. War with Catholic France, he thought, could lead to the return of evangelical zeal, indeed sanctification, in spiritual matters. It is no wonder that he preached about the importance of war with France even as he encouraged his hearers to fight against sin and evil. He boasted to a friend in November of that same year, "I seldom preach, without men-

29. Whitefield to Mr. V—; Whitefield to Colonel P—, September 1, 1755, in *Works*, 3:138, 141.

30. Whitefield to Lady P—, September 1, 1755, in *Works*, 3:137.

31. Whitefield to Colonel P—, September 1, 1755, in *Works*, 3:140.

32. Whitefield to Honourable J— R—, November 7, 1755, in *Works*, 3:148.

33. Whitefield to A— O—, November 8, 1755, in *Works*, 3:149.

tioning dear New England."[34] In his view, British imperial victory was tantamount to the triumph of Protestant Christianity.

Far from deflating Whitefield, news of military defeats served to heighten spiritual expectations. When the situation did not change for the better after the disaster of Braddock's failed attack on Fort Duquesne in July 1755, Whitefield remained indefatigable as he doubled down on his own efforts to rally a pan-Atlantic community of Protestant saints. August was filled with the mishaps of William Shirley, royal governor of Massachusetts who assumed the role of commander in chief after Braddock's death. This former hero of King George's War saw little of his old successes in the new war. Instead, he bent his energies toward expelling the Acadians, natives who were loyal to France, from Acadia in what is now Nova Scotia and New Brunswick. Anderson describes this religious persecution of the Catholic Acadians as "perhaps the first time in modern history a civilian population was forcibly removed as a security risk" and "so chillingly reminiscent of modern 'ethnic cleansing' operations."[35] It was in such a climate of heightened anti-Catholic sentiment and sheer human tragedy that Whitefield issued his address to Protestants of all denominations.

A Short Address showcases a vehement, militant polemic that sought to mobilize an army of like-minded Protestants who happened to share a national bond. Noted for its widespread appeal, the pamphlet sailed through seven popular editions and became the number two bestseller of the period.[36] Showing the geographical breadth of Whitefield's influence, only the first edition was published in London, with subsequent editions printed in places as far afield as Edinburgh, New York, Philadelphia, and Boston. All seven editions appeared in 1756. From England (as he would be unable to return to America for the duration of the war), he sounded an alarm to "persons of all denominations," repositioning himself as a leader who transcended denominational identity for the sake not only of gospel ministry but also of national and imperial security. With concern for "British borders," the piece resounded with Old Testament allusions to the holiness of Israel in contrast to their gentile neighbors, drawing on a cast of well-known Hebrew characters such

34. Whitefield to A— O—, in *Works*, 3:149.

35. Anderson, *Crucible of War*, 113, 114.

36. Whitefield, *A Short Address*. Jerome Mahaffey writes of five editions, but there were actually seven. Mahaffey, *Preaching Politics*, 170.

as Esther, Mordecai, and Jonah. Casting the French as pagan enemies menacing the chosen people of Yahweh made it possible for Whitefield to assume the role of a new Moses whose vision of postmillennial peace represented movement toward a new promised land.

Whitefield did not merely fill his polemic with biblical references; he engaged in military and political exposition as well. His references to the six nations of Indians allied against the colonies, his discussion of the breach of the Treaty of Aix la Chapelle that had concluded King George's War in America, and his eloquent appeal to just war rationale all worked in concert to demonstrate that more than religious motivations animated his call for vigilance and action. Reminding readers of devastating natural disasters in Africa, Spain, and Portugal, he fixed France in the crosshairs of divine judgment. The catastrophic effects of an earthquake in Lisbon in November 1755, a year and a half after his own visit there, must have made a profound impression on Whitefield. He described that devastation experienced by Portugal, another Catholic state, as being "beyond conception, beyond the power of the most masterly pen to describe. It is to be questioned, whether the like hath ever been heard of since the deluge."[37] These were, in other words, events of biblical proportions that demanded the attention of faithful Protestants everywhere.

The stakes could not be higher, as Whitefield saw it. For the great disaster that befell Portugal would pale "in Comparison of our hearing that a French Army, accompanied with a Popish Pretender, and Thousands of Romish Priests, was suffered to invade, subdue, and destroy" the Protestant land of freedom and righteousness, which Britain represented.[38] The tyranny of evil France must be avoided at all costs, and it was his responsibility to sound the alarm at the prospect of such a ruthless invasion of "this happy isle." In this way, Whitefield stoked xenophobic alarm against the French even as he fanned the flames of British religious exceptionalism.

Just over four thousand words in length, the letter's pace is brisk, moving from a brief sketch of the historical circumstances for the war to biblical justifications for war to finally a rallying cry for all Protestants to unite in common cause under the banner of British freedom. In the latter half of *A Short Address*, Whitefield focused especially on an ap-

37. Whitefield, *A Short Address*, 12.
38. Whitefield, *A Short Address*, 12.

peal to reason and common sense: "But how any serious and judicious, much less religious and devout person, can be so stupid to all principles of self-interest, and so dead even to all maxims of common sense, as to prefer a French to an English government . . . must be imputed to nothing else but an awful infatuation."[39] Ever the orator, Whitefield was not one to mince words. Against such folly, he called for a sensible rejection of French aggression and Roman Catholicism. As one example of French brutality in contrast to British liberty, Whitefield quoted a French decree dating back to July 1686, which called for the death of any non-Catholic ministers daring to preach in French territory: "we do command that all preachers, who shall call assemblies, preach in them, or discharge any other function, be put to death."[40] Rising to the challenge, Whitefield sang the praises of martyrdom for so worthy a cause as the British and Protestant interest. He concluded the letter by declaring his confidence in the God of universal monarchy under whose reign Britain held a central place.

Not only the fresh experience of his American trip, which would have highlighted the need for a reassessment of his American strategy, but also increasing French hostility, indeed the very real prospect of war on the homeland, influenced Whitefield's thinking about the need for an expanded role for himself in the context of a British Empire under strain. In reconfiguring the war as one of defense rather than conquest, Whitefield matched the audacity of addressing persons of all denominations with an anti-Catholic rhetoric that soared with as much militant triumphalism as religious passion and conviction.

Viewed against the larger backdrop of his life, Whitefield's war rhetoric in the mid-1750s displays a marked shift in his philosophy and strategy. Gone is the reticence of young Whitefield who had balked at helping his friend Colonel Pepperell raise troops for the Cape Breton expedition in 1746. Only after his good friend's persistent persuasion had he relented on that earlier occasion. Ten years later in 1756, however, it appears Whitefield needed no coaxing or encouragement. In fact, it speaks volumes about the changes wrought in Whitefield that this British-born Anglican priest described his years away from America during the Seven Years' War as a period of exile and mounting anxiety

39. Whitefield, *A Short Address*, 15.
40. Whitefield, *A Short Address*, 15.

for his cause in America. Far from sitting idly by, he used this time away to reevaluate his transatlantic ministry.

This reassessment came in the context of Whitefield's growing engagement with imperial military campaigns. Britons during this time, including Whitefield, spoke of a "critical juncture" to describe the times in which they lived. The term may apply also to Whitefield's vocational life, for it was a personal juncture that increasingly combined the interests of revival religion and British Empire into one common cause. When we ignore these developments in his thinking during the 1750s, we also miss out on significant shifts taking place in evangelical Protestant engagement with British imperial culture. By the end of this period, Whitefield would make up his mind to turn his Georgia orphanage into a college in the American South to rival schools like Harvard and Yale to the north. Something else happened as well. Whitefield turned from an amateur critic who dabbled in touristic observations of Catholicism into a full-fledged anti-Catholic spokesperson. Indeed, imperial battles raged on many fronts. But that was not all. Coming to grips with post-revival disappointments, and the work of sorting through Awakening remains after the dust had settled, also lay heavy on Whitefield's heart.

With the blazing fires of revival now banked and incendiary war all around, evangelical Protestants faced the daunting challenge of keeping their religious movement alive in the face of an increasingly hostile world. Anti-Catholicism provided one way of addressing both the religious setbacks and political perils rampant in this period. By identifying a clearly discernible enemy in French Catholics, evangelicals like Whitefield attempted not only to rally a fractious coalition but also carve out a more credible and respectable space for themselves in the national imagination. It was a path filled with danger, moreover, not only from non-Protestant forces outside the nation but from what these evangelicals viewed as quasi-Catholic forces within.

Contending for British Liberties

After arriving back in England in the middle of 1755, Whitefield did not return to America again until the summer of 1763. In the intervening eight years, he traveled around Britain and Ireland, attempting to spark ongoing fires of revival. He also spent much of his time during these years in London, working to bring together scattered Calvinistic methodists who had long endured schisms and lacked (unlike Wesley's methodists) strong, stable leadership. As an institutional base, he already had his Tabernacle at Moorfields, built in 1741 and rebuilt in 1753. By the end of 1756, he would build another Tabernacle, this time on Tottenham Court Road in London. It was a building project he likely did not have in mind when he began the year with commitments to preach several times a week at Long Acre Chapel in London.

When Whitefield accepted the invitation to Long Acre he had little idea what a litigious affair his ministry there would prove to be. With the London theaters on one side of the chapel and Wesley's West Street chapel on the other, the revivalist threw himself into this busy commercial area of London.[41] It was not long before this controversial preacher, who had weathered many attacks, was taken aback by the force of violent opposition he faced there. The great irony is that the Long Acre episode occurred at just the time Whitefield was preparing his *Short Address* for publication. In other words, at the very moment when he was extolling the freedoms enjoyed by British subjects he was undergoing one of the severest tests of his own liberties.

His time of trial began with a letter from the new Dean of Westminster, Zachary Pearce, freshly arrived in London after serving eight years as Bishop of Bangor in the northern edge of Wales. He wrote to forbid Whitefield from preaching at Long Acre. Perhaps out of deference, but more likely in an effort to highlight the bishop's recent arrival in London, Whitefield addressed his letter "To the Bishop of Bangor" (and not to the "Dean of Westminster," which would have been more accurate). The Grand Itinerant who had traveled the breadth of the empire and made London his British base of operations might have wondered what a bishop from Bangor knew of ecclesiastical business in the capital city. Whitefield was, moreover, by this time well practiced at fielding such prohibitions and delved into particulars by appealing immediately to his civil liberties:

> For I looked upon the place as a particular person's *property*, and being, as I was informed, not only unconsecrated, but also licensed *according to law*, I thought I might innocently preach the love of a crucified Redeemer, and for his great name's sake, loyalty to the best of princes *our dear sovereign King George*, without giving any just of-

41. Tyerman, *Life*, 2:355.

fence to Jew or Gentile, much less to any bishop or overseer of the church of God.[42]

In his carefully crafted rejoinder, Whitefield made two tangential issues central. First he pointed out that the chapel belonged to an individual and as private property lay outside the jurisdiction of the bishop. Not content to rest his case on legal technicalities, Whitefield went on to spell out in some detail the matter in which the bishop was meddling. The second part of Whitefield's defense then was his preaching "loyalty to the best of princes our dear sovereign King George." How could any British subject, let alone the Bishop of Bangor, be opposed to such an important task, particularly in a time of war? In this way, Whitefield hoped that his bellicose imperial message would provide cover for his religious work. Lest there be any doubt about the matter, Whitefield went on to state: "I trust the irregularity I am charged with, will appear justifiable to every true lover of *English* liberty." He was not merely determined but confident that the law was on his side and that his English rights would prevail in the end. It is not clear if Whitefield himself noticed the irony, but at the very same time he found himself in conflict with the bishop, the congregation at Long Acre raised £80 for "the poor persecuted French protestants."[43] Though beset by ecclesiastical bullying, the worshipers at Long Acre saw a difference between their lot and the suffering of the French. Apparently, there was reason to hope that the bishop's opposition was merely a passing storm.

Two weeks later, on February 16, 1756, it became clear that the struggle was to be a protracted one. While we do not have the text of the bishop's letter, the fact that Whitefield sat down the same evening he received the letter to write a nearly 2,500-word response gives some indication that neither side was anywhere near backing down. The preacher again tied his struggle to the larger British fight for liberty by declaring the slightest acquiescence to the bishop unthinkable, especially "at this juncture, when all our civil and religious liberties are as it were at stake." Such surrender, he opined, "would to me be worse than death itself."[44]

42. Whitefield to the Bishop of Bangor, February 2, 1756, in *Works*, 3:157; emphases added.
43. Whitefield to the Bishop of Bangor, in *Works*, 3:158; emphasis in original.
44. Whitefield to the Bishop of Bangor, February 16, 1756, in *Works*, 3:164.

Connecting his cause at Long Acre with the British war against the French, Whitefield sent a copy of his pamphlet, *A Short Address to Persons of All Denominations*, to the bishop a week later. "I can only entreat the continuance of your Lordship's blessing, and begging your Lordship's acceptance of a short address I am now publishing," Whitefield wrote even as he supplied further evidence for the legality of his preaching ministry at the meeting house. Far from endorsing his letter, the bishop in the middle of March 1756 again sent disturbers to the chapel who threw large stones through the windows, badly injuring several worshipers. Once again appealing to his rights as "a subject of King George, and a minister of Jesus Christ," Whitefield threatened to "lay a plain and fair narration of the whole affair, together with what hath passed between your Lordship and myself, before the world."[45] In turn, the bishop invoked his authority to prevent the publication of such letters and threatened grave legal consequences. Though Whitefield complained that the persecution he faced was "not to be met with in English history," the intensity of the attacks only grew. Using instruments such as a copper furnace, bells, drums, clappers, marrow bones, and cleavers, various kinds of "the baser sort" who had been "hired by subscription" assaulted the chapel, timing the most intense part of their attack to coincide with the sermon. These attacks continued throughout the month.[46]

The appearance of a threatening letter from another hand further escalated an already tense situation. This anonymous note warning of "a certain, sudden, and unavoidable stroke" was left for Whitefield on a chair near the pulpit. It perturbed Whitefield enough that he forwarded a copy of the letter to a magistrate friend, describing the situation at Long Acre as "an affair that hath reference to the welfare of civil government."[47] In other words, it was a matter not merely of personal but national safety. He also sent a copy of the letter to his friend and patroness, the Countess of Huntingdon, telling her "indeed the noise hath been infernal."[48] Eight days later he wrote her again, perhaps concerned that he had sounded too craven in his last letter. Framing his situation in the context of broader geo-political struggles, he declared his willingness to

---

45. Whitefield to the Bishop of Bangor, in *Works*, 3:167.
46. Whitefield to the Bishop of Bangor, in *Works*, 3:168.
47. Whitefield to Honourable Hume C—, April 9, 1756, in *Works*, 3:171.
48. Whitefield to the Lady Huntingdon, April 10, 1756, in *Works*, 3:172.

serve as a martyr: "Glad should I be to die by the hands of an assassin, if popery is to get footing here."[49]

What may have begun as merely an intramural ecclesiastical conflict, Whitefield managed to turn into an urgent contest for civil liberty with the hallmark feature of the British Empire at risk. "Such an infernal continued noise, on such an occasion, at such a juncture, under such a government, I believe was never heard of before."[50] It was a particular source of consternation for Whitefield that such civil injustices should be occurring at what he and many others called this "critical juncture" in British history. After receiving a third ominous letter portending bodily harm, Whitefield's rhetoric reached a fevered pitch. Beyond a matter of national security, the battle at Long Acre became for him a matter of divine justice: "Our cause, in my opinion, is *the cause of God*, and the cause of civil and religious liberty."[51] More than an alignment of interests, this was a conflation of two distinct matters into one. So much did Whitefield immerse himself into the mindset of imperial war that he began to describe his own preaching tours as "expeditions," as if they were acts of reconnaissance and incursion into enemy territory. And so as he planned a trip to Scotland, he described it as his "northern expedition."[52] Extending the metaphor, he explained his inability to travel to America in this way: "The attraction towards America is as strong as ever, but at present I am *stationed* here."[53] Each and every Briton had a role to play in the struggle against France and Whitefield had found his own. Under this kind of religio-political rhetoric, the fight for British imperial expansion, a geopolitical campaign, became also a divine and spiritual struggle. It was a conflict, above all, where fractures threatened to undermine British and Protestant liberty.

On May 2, 1756, Whitefield preached his final sermon at Long Acre before setting out for Wales on a preaching tour. In a letter to the Countess of Huntingdon on that day, he made a special announcement: "and this brings you the further news of my having taken a piece of ground, very commodious to build on."[54] Not to be deterred by the likes of Bishop Pearce, he thus commenced plans to build the Tabernacle at

49. Whitefield to the Lady Huntingdon, April 18, 1756, in *Works*, 3:173.
50. Whitefield to Mr. C—, April 25, 1756, in *Works*, 3:176.
51. Whitefield to Mr. C—, in *Works*, 3:177; emphasis added.
52. Whitefield to the Lady Huntingdon, July 17, 1756, in *Works*, 3:187.
53. Whitefield to Mr. S—, November 17, 1757, in *Works*, 3:220; emphasis added.
54. Tyerman, *Life*, 2:372.

Tottenham Court Road, his second chapel after the Moorfields Tabernacle. Located near the theater district in London's West End, the chapel provided an ideal location for extending Whitefield's influence in England, a strategy that had long been on his mind.[55] After spending the summer months in the west of England and completing an expedition through Scotland, he was back in London to build and open his new chapel. Whitefield would be detained from America a good deal longer.

Conclusion

One summer day in 1757, a mob of Irish Catholics stoned George Whitefield nearly to death. Earlier in the day he had exhorted his audience "not only to fear God, but to honour the best of kings."[56] On his way home after preaching this political homily, Whitefield ran into Christian ruffians of the worst kind—they were disgruntled by his sermon and determined to do something about it. "Vollies of hard stones came from all quarters, and every step I took, a fresh stone struck, and made me reel backwards and forwards, till I was almost breathless, and all over a gore of blood," he later recounted.[57] Whitefield barely survived. In a March 1758 letter to Professor Francke in Germany, he disclosed further information about the events that led to his near stoning: "Last year, while I was preaching in the fields in Ireland, a popish mob was so incensed at my proclaiming the Lord our Righteousness, and at my praying for our good old King, and the King of Prussia, that they surrounded, stoned, and almost killed me. But we are immortal till our work is done."[58] From this letter, it is evident that Whitefield practiced what he preached in his *Short Address*. He measured Christian faithfulness by devotion to the British Protestant cause against the French Catholic threat and mingled gospel sermons with political prayers. Unlike the aggressors at Long Acre, however, the popish mob did almost murder him. Whatever anxieties he may have harbored about assaults on English liberties, the belligerence of that Irish mob gave him further education about eighteenth-century realities. A corrupt British Protes-

---

55. Jones, Schlenther, and White, *The Elect Methodists*, 148.

56. Tyerman, *Life*, 2:395.

57. Whitefield to Mr. —, July 9, 1757, in *Works*, 3:207. Also a slightly different version is in Tyerman, *Life*, 2:396.

58. Tyerman, *Life*, 2:405.

tant government that threatened with the letter of the law was preferable to a mob of papists that actually hurled stones.

There were subtler lessons as well. For coercion was as much a temptation in the religious struggle for renewal as it was in the great war for empire. Inasmuch as Whitefield stood for liberty, he also wielded power and privilege in a way that reinforced the imperial attitudes of his time. In a time when Britons embraced with little nuance or hesitation their responsibility to "reduce" Native Americans to civility and enslave African Americans for productivity, evangelical leaders echoed similar attitudes of cultural chauvinism in the exercise of their religious duties.[59] In the case of Whitefield, he applied force with his belief that the evangelical message of new birth was the greatest hope for an ascendant British culture. If it was a straightforward thesis, the path to turning this dream into reality was a more convoluted undertaking. In the face of opposition to such a lofty enterprise, he may have been more inclined to use excessive force. Alongside the spiritual goal of repentance, therefore, Whitefield had to consider economic necessities as well as military and political realities. The resulting admixture tells the story of religion as a culturally embedded force that is as much acted upon as it is an agent unto itself. In an era of conversion, commerce, and conquest, evangelical leaders like Whitefield embraced an ideology of empire. More than a religion of dramatic conversion, and not merely a commodity peddled for common consumption, evangelicalism came to ascendancy as a means of establishing British cultural superiority and rationalizing imperial expansion. It must not be forgotten that from the beginning an army of evangelicals who tried to convert the world also sought to conquer the world. In an environment where British Protestants held deep convictions about their theological, spiritual,

---

59. David Hempton has insightfully used phrases like "European Christian chauvinism" and "cultural chauvinism" to describe British attitudes in the eighteenth century. Hempton, *The Church in the Long Eighteenth Century*, 28–30. My argument moves beyond Hempton, however, who said "missionaries were not so much advocates of imperialism as they were genuine religious enthusiasts who could not avoid interacting with agencies of imperial control," to highlight ways in which Whitefield acted as an imperial agent. Building on the works of Henry Fielding and Sir John Fortescue, Jack Greene has written about the imperial identity of Britons in the eighteenth century that often led to espousal of British "superiority" in relation to other nations and cultures. See especially the chapter "Empire and Identity from the Elizabethan Era to the American Revolution," in Greene, *Creating the British Atlantic*, 253–77.

and cultural superiority, revivalistic evangelicals were quick to jump on the bandwagon of such imperial hubris.

A study of Whitefield's evolving views on slavery and war touches on two of the preeminent issues facing the British Empire in the eighteenth century. Both were the result of imperial expansion and both complicate our understanding of the long trajectory of the Great Awakening and its relationship to the complex process of British state formation. What one historian has called the "prodigal victory" of the Seven Years' War also applies to our view of the ongoing struggle of evangelical revivalism to reinvent and reassert itself in the face of persistent challenges.[60] In trying to articulate a way forward through these cultural floodwaters, Whitefield found himself awash in a sea of imperial developments.

60. Anderson, *Crucible of War*, xxi.

CHAPTER 6

Whitefield and His Colleges

Losing sight of Whitefield's later years not only distorts a compelling biographical story but also obscures the shifting tides of British imperial history in the mid-eighteenth century. For it was in these final years that the preacher's long brewing interest in the empire became most pronounced. At a time when the British Empire was growing at a rapid pace, Whitefield's ongoing revision of revival strategies contributed much to the remaking of his world. Therefore, following this indomitable preacher into his latter years shows that his most creative work happened after the height of revival, as he struggled to work out alternatives to the revival successes that faded away. During the Great Awakening he lambasted institutions like Harvard and Yale for dead, reified religion, only to spend his years in the aftermath of revival fervor supporting—in many cases fundraising and helping to establish—institutions of higher learning such as Dartmouth, Princeton, and the University of Pennsylvania. Far from evincing outright inconsistency, such changes signify a hierarchy of values and evolution in strategy. In fact, Whitefield went beyond supporting others' college ventures; he set out to establish a college of his own. Examining the political, theological, and cultural dimensions of the campaign to turn his Bethesda Orphanage into a college provides additional evidence for the significance of Whitefield's later years in understanding British imperial developments in the mid-eighteenth century. In so doing, this chapter argues that extending attention into the last decade of his life holds the key to understanding religion's ongoing, albeit tempered, influence in British imperial culture and politics.

Throughout the 1760s, Whitefield poured his remaining energy into a campaign to establish Bethesda College in Georgia, revealing ambitions that reached across the British Empire. In a 1763 remark describing the purpose of his college to the Archbishop of Canterbury, Thomas Secker, he said it was to prepare "persons of superiour rank" to "serve their king, their country, and their God, either in church or state."[1] In this telling comment, Whitefield made it clear that he was not content to limit his influence to the church. His aim rather was an institution that would serve the state as well. Beyond the region surrounding Savannah, moreover, he also announced designs on a broader southern area of the empire, so that his college might rival older institutions in New England. Bethesda and Georgia were no longer side occupations to which Whitefield would turn when he had time to spare. Rather, they became the essential elements of a comprehensive program for empire-wide influence. In these ways, Whitefield showed little interest in continuing to export British culture into the American colonies. To the contrary, he saw the outlying provinces as themselves contributing to the cause of building a worldwide British Empire.[2]

During these years, Whitefield proved that he was more than the central architect of an international Protestant revival movement; he became an outspoken advocate of the American colonies. Although he had established himself as a chaplain to the London gentry as well as a leader of the Calvinistic methodists scattered across Britain, Whitefield was far from content in the metropole. While demand for his presence remained at a high pitch in the cosmopolitan centers of the British Empire, Whitefield consistently made a beeline for the periphery. A Briton deeply committed to both the heart and outer edges of the empire, the famous itinerant helps us to appreciate the centrifugal force of British imperialism. That a person of such international prominence and widespread transatlantic connections should set his sights so persistently

1. "To His Excellency James Wright, Esq; Captain General and Governor in Chief of his Majesty's province of Georgia, and to the members of his Majesty's council in the said province. The Memorial of George Whitefield," in *Works*, 3:470.

2. As one historian has written, "Now the 'new' world became not only a challenge to the comfortable intellectual assumptions of the old; it became a possible replacement for it." Anthony Pagden, "The Challenge of the New," in Canny and Morgan, *The Oxford Handbook of the Atlantic World: 1450–1850*, 461. Pagden also quotes William Robertson, a Scottish historian in the eighteenth century, who gave expression to the new possibilities teeming during this period: "[It was the age] when Providence decreed that men were to pass the limits within which they had been so long confined, and open themselves to a more ample field wherein to display their talents, their enterprise and courage" (450).

on a rural project in the American South speaks volumes about the allure of emerging provincial centers in the colonial landscape. Notwithstanding Whitefield's vaunted ambitions for Bethesda's regional impact in the southern colonies, Savannah was located at the geographical margins of colonial life. With Congregationalism dominant in New England, Protestant pluralism thriving in Pennsylvania, and Anglicanism entrenched in Virginia, however, Georgia was a fitting site for the experiments of a lifelong outsider like Whitefield. That he attempted to make the hinterlands of colonial society the center of his imperial enterprise was one of Whitefield's most significant innovations, the culmination of his lifelong devotion to a theology of the margins. His Bethesda efforts were only the most visible activities of a wide-ranging involvement in developing institutions across the American colonies. In his view, the center of influence in the empire had shifted from Britain to America, and from London to—of all places—Savannah and other colonial towns.

Far from a schismatic or a revolutionary, however, Whitefield saw himself as a loyal subject of the king and servant of the church. As such he toiled to make contributions toward a transatlantic and pan-Protestant British society. In this labor, Bethesda allowed Whitefield the satisfaction of local entrenchment without the loss of an international platform.[3] From the brief sketch in the following pages, a much more complex image of Whitefield will emerge than that simply of revival preacher. From the beginning of his career he declined the role of a parish priest, and he disregarded parish boundaries throughout his life. His preferred title was "presbyter at large," and he saw culture-making as a critical component of his vocation. In this combination of self-invention, imperial fixation, and long-term projects that reflected both, he eventually articulated a distinct role for America in the empire.

Along the way, we will also see the Achilles's heel in the process of British state formation in the eighteenth century. It was not because Anglicization failed that a final rupture between the colonies and their motherland occurred. Instead, it was because the process of transplanting British culture, along with its values and ideals, succeeded so spec-

---

3. Whitefield knew how to negotiate the empire's characteristic tension, which Jack P. Greene has described as existing "between centripetal impulses toward centralization and centrifugal tendencies toward localism." Greene, *Creating the British Atlantic*, 36.

tacularly that activities like the building of colleges and the making of culture shifted easily into a movement for liberty and independence (albeit after Whitefield's death).[4] There is no evidence to suggest that Whitefield had premonitions of a coming revolution. Yet there are ample reasons to argue that the preacher's lifelong and intensifying emphasis on British liberties contributed to the formation of a distinctly American style of religion and culture.[5] In other words, Whitefield's life is an object lesson in the corrosive effects, in the long term, of Anglicization on imperial cohesion. As the empire grew and subjects like Whitefield sought to carry British liberties to the colonial fringes, solidarity with fellow Britons buckled under the burden of distance. Although not evident at the time, Whitefield's attempts to build a college in the Georgia forests represented a subversion of the imperial cause as well as an outworking of the imperial logic.

With Whitefield's campaign for Bethesda College as an entry point, this chapter argues for the enduring if emended role of religion in mediating the torrent of political and cultural change in the period between the Great Awakening and the American Revolution. My approach centers on unifying a heretofore patchwork understanding of Whitefield's struggles to establish Bethesda College against the backdrop of broader colonial agitation for a place in the wider imperial landscape.

The chapter begins with a survey of various efforts to establish colonial colleges in which Whitefield had some degree of involvement. We will then trace the development of Whitefield's dreams for his own Bethesda College, which had origins in the complex crucible of post-revival ennui, the growing web of transatlantic evangelicalism, the strategic frontier position of Georgia with the other southern colonies, and Britain's growing imperialism during and after the Seven Years' War.

---

4. The comparison of British state formation in the seventeenth and eighteenth centuries made by Patrick Griffin provides a helpful backdrop to this discussion. To summarize: "ideas that underwrote stability could support rebellion. Ideas that animated the state could also be used to undo it." Griffin, *America's Revolution*, 114.

5. My analysis stands in contrast to Michael Zuckerman's contention that the American Revolution was merely a political dissolution and "that the colonists of British America always strove to be Britons and that they attained political independence at the end of the eighteenth century without ever declaring their common character or distinctive identity." Michael Zuckerman, "Identity in British America: Unease in Eden," in Nicholas P. Canny and Anthony Pagden, *Colonial Identity in the Atlantic World, 1500–1800* (Princeton: Princeton University Press, 1987), 115.

In examining this period, recognition of the post-war reconstruction character of colonial life is vital; in this vein, the Seven Years' War of the immediate past looms larger as an interpretive factor than the specter of the Revolutionary War in the not-so-distant future. After tracing the history of Whitefield's quest for a college charter in this way, we will proceed to explore the meaning of his Bethesda vision, from his tactical accommodation of imperial politics to his theological affection for the margins to finally his vision of social and cultural renewal. Understood in its larger context, the Bethesda project was an attempt to further the vision of an ascendant Protestant society, through both triumph and turmoil, on the fluid canvas of colonial life.

Whitefield and Colonial Colleges

Whitefield came into contact with numerous colonial colleges at one point or another in the course of his American career. These interactions shaped his interest in a college project of his own. Though his first encounters with Harvard and Yale during the height of the Great Awakening were bitterly antagonistic, he sought to mend relations with these institutions in his later years. He also directed his energies toward helping not only fellow revivalists but also friends like Benjamin Franklin in their respective college-building efforts. Since these activities influenced his vision for Bethesda College, the first part of this chapter will explore Whitefield's various connections to colleges in the New World.

An allegorical pamphlet by William Smith published in 1753 can help us understand the general appeal of colonial colleges in the mid-eighteenth century. Smith was a graduate of the University of Aberdeen who assisted in the campaign for a college in New York. Upon the publication of his pamphlet, he received an invitation to Philadelphia from Benjamin Franklin, who was duly impressed with Smith's vision. The guest lecture led to a permanent position, and so valuable were Smith's contributions to Franklin's efforts that he became the first provost of the new college. An excerpt from the conclusion of his pamphlet is instructive for our purposes, especially as he explains the benefits of a provincial college:

> A single Province has a vast Advantage, in the Execution of a Scheme of this Nature, above an extensive Monarchy. In large and populous

Countries, Education cannot be immediately the Care of the Legislature; they can only enact good Laws for Education, and devolve the
Execution of them upon fit Persons, in every particular Seminary: But
in a single Province, where all the Youth may be collected into one
general Seminary, the Legislature, or those commission'd by them,
may, and should, be the immediate Superintendents of Education;
than which nothing can be more worthy their Care.[6]

As Smith saw it, a provincial college helped establish a direct line of
influence within the local region and without relying on ties to the imperial center by way of "immediate superintendents." Education par-
ticularized to a province, in other words, contributed to a cohesive local
or regional culture.

This dynamic of greater provincial independence is likely what
Thomas Penn, son of Pennsylvania colony's founder, had in mind when
he wrote to Governor Hamilton on February 12, 1750, expressing doubts
about the advisability of a college in Philadelphia. "I find people here
think we go too fast with regard to the matter," wrote Penn, "and it gives
an opportunity to those fools who are always telling their fears that the
Colonies will set up for themselves."[7] A colonial college not only served
to bring greater stability to a province distant from the metropole; it
also reinforced the separation that existed between the two. By setting
out to establish colonial colleges, provincial leaders like Franklin in
Pennsylvania, Gilbert Tennent and Samuel Davies in New Jersey, and
Eleazar Wheelock in Connecticut (and later New Hampshire) contributed to the building of a colonial infrastructure that set the colonies
on a centrifugal course away from the centralizing tendencies of imperial culture. With this larger colonial backdrop in mind, we can better
assess Whitefield's labors in provincial Georgia as well as the potent
resistance he met in his efforts to establish Bethesda College.

This college project was far from a novel idea that dawned on him
during the twilight of his life; there are hints of it in Whitefield's writings from early in his American career. At the beginning of his second
American trip in a letter dated November 10, 1739, he said as much:

6. William Smith, *A General Idea of the College of Mirania* (New York: J. Parker and
W. Weyman, 1753), 75.
7. Cited in Joshua L. Chamberlain, *The University of Pennsylvania: Its History, Influence, Equipment and Characteristics* (Boston: R. Herndon Company, 1901), 55.

"I have had great intimations from above concerning Georgia. Who knows but we may have a college of pious youths at Savannah?"[8] Perhaps for this reason, he paid careful attention to the colleges he visited during his early travels around the colonies, writing down largely negative judgments about their state. In those early years, Whitefield's primary concern was revival preaching and his eyes were fixed upon these institutions' moral and spiritual deficiencies. Yet it is also possible that his early criticism of colonial educational institutions was motivated by an ambition to build his own college that fit his particular vision of spiritual renewal.

Alongside criticism, Whitefield also recorded quite specific details about their organization. In a visit to Williamsburg, Virginia on December 15, 1739, he noted there were "eight scholars, a president, two masters, and professors in the several sciences."[9] The fact that "Christ or Christianity is scarcely so much as named amongst them" led Whitefield to dream about a remedy: "we may hope for some primitive schools to be erected and encouraged amongst us."[10] In September of the following year, he was at Harvard, where again he was meticulous to note: "one president, four tutors, and about a hundred students." Here too, he was not impressed, writing, "The college is scarce as big as one of our least colleges at Oxford." Even more disconcerting, "Discipline is at a low ebb. Bad books are become fashionable among the tutors and students. Tillotson and Clark are read, instead of Shepard, Stoddard, and such-like evangelical writers."[11] Yale College in New Haven was even less inspiring, being "about one-third part as big as that of Cambridge." Whitefield continued to jot down very specific details, as if sizing up his would-be competitors: "It has one Rector, three Tutors, and about a hundred students." As we will see in the following narrative, Whitefield's relationship with colonial colleges evolved over the course of his career. First was criticism and then came cooperation; both led to the idea of his own chartered college.

8. Whitefield to Mr. ——, November 10, 1739, in *Works*, 1:84.
9. December 15, 1739, entry in Whitefield, *Journals*, 407.
10. Whitefield, *Journals*, 408.
11. Whitefield, *Journals*, 505–6.

A College in New Jersey

Whitefield was not merely an obstructionist critic when it came to colonial colleges. In fact, there were a number of schools he supported with the full weight of his considerable influence. He early expressed enthusiasm for William Tennent's Log College, a forerunner of the College of New Jersey at Princeton.[12] In a November 21, 1748, letter that shows his broad reach, he wrote from London of his efforts in Scotland to raise funds for schools in America: "I have been endeavoring in Scotland to do all the service I could to [Wheelock's] Indian school and the New-Jersey college whilst I was there."[13] Two years later, he expressed enthusiasm for the strategic geographical location of the college in New Jersey, since "the spreading of the gospel in Maryland and Virginia in a great measure depends upon it."[14]

He was no doubt familiar with the efforts of Gilbert Tennent and Samuel Davies in promoting the college in New Jersey. The rationale held out by these revival preachers featured a strong imperial theme. For instance, Tennent and Davies, revivalists like Whitefield, transferred their immense energies to the college in New Jersey even as the fruits of revival withered. In 1754, they spelled out what they had in mind just as tensions between the British and French empires were breaking out into open warfare. Their explanation took a distinct step beyond religious to political rationales: "Nor would such a Seminary answer a *religious* End only; it would also serve a *political* View: For sure, if from us Learning and good Manners could be propagated thro' these Savages, it would be a Means of engaging them more firmly in the British Interest."[15] In their view, as the colonies grew, there were emerging

---

12. David Calhoun writes, "George Whitefield's early contact with the Log College and his unstinting praise for the school and its founder elevated the whole enterprise in the minds of American Christians, especially as Whitefield moved from his earlier controversial reputation (which divided Christians, including Presbyterians, over his emphases and tactics) to a revered status, among Protestants, as a kind of American church father." Archibald Alexander, *The Log College: Biographical Sketches of William Tennent and His Students* (London: Banner of Truth Trust, 1968), iv. According to Archibald Alexander, "the Log College was the germ of the College of New Jersey."

13. Whitefield to Rev. Mr. P—, November 21, 1748, in *Works*, 2:206.

14. Whitefield to Rev. Mr. M—, May 14, 1750, in *Works*, 2:349.

15. Samuel Davies and Gilbert Tennent, *A General Account of the Rise and State of the College, Lately Established in the Province of New-Jersey, in America* (Edinburgh, 1754), 3; emphasis added.

needs that "the Two Colleges in New-England . . . [were] unable to sup-ply."[16] If there was the possibility of inter-colonial competition, they were also quick to point out the imperial dimensions:

> A Design! which is not calculated to promote the low Purposes of a Party, but in its Views and Consequences affects the Protestant Inter-est in general, and Great-Britain in particular, both in Religious and Civil Respects; since by this, the filial Duty of her Descendants will be inculcated, their Manners reformed, and her Trade increased, which is the Basis of her Empire, Glory and Felicity.[17]

Not only would an "English College," as they called it, help preserve British culture in the colonies. Such an institution would also be vital in the process of assimilating non-English settlers. Tennent and Davies went out of their way to stress the importance of teaching English to the Germans among them "so national Prejudices may be removed, and they more easily incorporated with the rest of His Majesty's Subjects."[18]

A College in Pennsylvania

Around the same time that Tennent and Davies made their appeal, in nearby Pennsylvania Whitefield showcased his ability to juggle a variety of tasks as he communicated with Franklin over the latter's efforts to establish a school in Philadelphia. Back in 1740 during the height of the revivals, Whitefield's preaching in that city had led to the construction of an edifice to accommodate his religious services. The "New Build-ing" as it came to be known was principally used by Whitefield for his revivalistic purposes in its early days. In fact, he was the first to preach there in November 1740, before its roof had even been placed. From the beginning, however, those who initiated the building project had a larger purpose in mind. The New Building was sponsored by lead-ing merchants and religious leaders who wanted to provide space for a charity school as well as revival services. In a July 1740 advertisement, the proponents of the building described their purpose as "to erect a

16. Davies and Tennent, *A General Account*, 4.
17. Davies and Tennent, *A General Account*, 7–8.
18. Davies and Tennent, *A General Account*, 1–2.

large building for a charity school for the instruction of poor children gratis in useful literature and the knowledge of the Christian religion and also for a house of publick worship, the houses in this place being insufficient to contain the great numbers who convene on such occasions and it being impracticable to meet in the open air at all times of the year because of the inclemency of the weather."[19] Whitefield was not only the most popular preacher at the New Building; he was also selected one of its Trustees. In a letter he wrote to a friend on December 4, 1740, he sounded an enthusiastic tone: "As I am chosen one of the Trustees and have promised to procure a master and mistress for the first scholars, I think it my duty to make what interest I can towards carrying on so good a work."[20]

As with so many other colonial projects of Whitefield, however, this one too languished while the preacher devoted himself to his first love, proclaiming the new birth across the Atlantic world.[21] In the meantime, it fell to Benjamin Franklin to revive the work for a college; in 1749 he opened the campaign with a letter in *The Pennsylvania Gazette* saying that "those times are come, and numbers of our inhabitants are both able and willing to give their sons a good education, if it might be had at home, free from the extraordinary expense and hazard in sending them abroad for that purpose."[22] In a lengthier piece entitled "Proposals Relating to the Education of Youth in Pensilvania" that was also published in 1749, Franklin urged the necessity of a school that "might supply the succeeding Age with Men qualified to serve the Publick with Honour to themselves, and to their country."[23] He may even have been trying to provoke a competitive spirit among his peers in Philadelphia by going as far as to say: "The present Race are not thought to be generally of equal Ability. For though the American Youth are allow'd not to want Capacity; yet the best Capacities require Cultivation, it being truly with them, as with the best Ground,

19. Chamberlain, *The University of Pennsylvania*, 48.

20. Cited in Chamberlain, *The University of Pennsylvania*, 48. This letter is not found in any of Whitefield's published writings.

21. A detailed history of the transfer of the "New Building" to a new Trusteeship intending to build an academy and eventually a college can be found in Chamberlain, *The University of Pennsylvania*, 47–55.

22. Cited in Chamberlain, *The University of Pennsylvania*, 51.

23. Benjamin Franklin, *Proposals Relating to the Education of Youth in Pensilvania* (Pennsylvania, 1749), 5.

which unless well tilled and sowed with profitable Seed, produces only ranker Weeds."[24]

Franklin shared his plans for the college with Whitefield, who replied promptly with an honest critique. For starters, he was not happy that Franklin included Archbishop Tillotson in his list of recommended readings, whom Whitefield had reviled as knowing no more about Christianity than Mohammed.[25] Yet he also expressed support for his old friend and tactfully, if firmly, offered some choice suggestions for improving the plan, which he described as deserving of "general approbation," while hastening to add, "I think there wants *aliquid Christi* [something of Christ] in it, to make it so useful as I would desire it might be."[26] Whitefield went on to stress the need "to convince [students] of their natural depravity," as well as the services of "a well-approved Christian Orator" whose lessons would be as frequent as one to two hours a day. Furthermore, he reminded Franklin, who took pride in his own narrative of self-made success, about the importance of a "free education of the poorer sort." He almost certainly had his own life story in mind when he said, "It hath been often found, that some of our brightest men in church and state, have arisen from such an obscure condition."[27]

Franklin went on to build his college, and today a statue of Whitefield stands on the campus of the University of Pennsylvania, identifying him as a founder of the university. The plaque in front of the statue bears a quotation from Benjamin Franklin: "I knew him intimately upwards of thirty years. His integrity, disinterestedness and indefatigable zeal in prosecuting every good work I have never seen equalled and shall never see excelled."[28] In spite of profound disagreements over the course of their long friendship, it is clear Franklin saw Whitefield as a likeminded partner in the colonial enterprise.

---

24. Franklin, *Proposals Relating to the Education of Youth*, 6.

25. Franklin, *Proposals Relating to the Education of Youth*, 13. In a letter to a friend, he defended his statement, noted the controversy that erupted around his comment, and attributed the idea to John Wesley, who "if I mistake not, first spoke it in a private Society." Whitefield, *Three Letters From the Reverend Mr. G. Whitefield*, 2.

26. Whitefield to Benjamin Franklin, February 26, 1750, in *Works*, 2:336.

27. Whitefield to Benjamin Franklin, in *Works*, 2:337.

28. The statue was commissioned by a group of alumni who wanted to mark the bicentennial of Whitefield's birth for his key role in the founding of the institution.

A College in Connecticut and New Hampshire

We saw in the previous chapter how war in North America kept White-field in Britain from 1755 to 1763. Once war ended, however, the restless itinerant once again threw himself into a variety of projects in America. The general interest he harbored toward colonial colleges took on more specific form as he provided aid to Eleazar Wheelock's efforts to establish an Indian school. A Congregational minister, Wheelock was a recent Yale graduate and a young itinerant preacher during the awakenings of the 1740s when he first became acquainted with White-field's stunning ministry. When he turned to the task of establishing a school later in life, he naturally turned to Whitefield. "I have preferr'd a Memorial to the Assembly now sitting here, for such an Incorporation as may perpetuate my School, & secure the Design of the Benefactors," he wrote Whitefield on May 18, 1764. He valued the wisdom Whitefield might have to impart to his cause, saying "I wish I had thot of desiring you by Mr Smith to send one, or some minuits of ye Form of such a Society."[29] In August of that year, Wheelock again wrote Whitefield, informing him, "My prospects are daily increasing. It looks as tho' God had been laying out for this design for many Years past."[30]

This partnership between kindred spirits, however, was not without difficulty. The strains in their friendship reveal the extent to which Whitefield involved himself in colonial matters. Over the course of their tenuous relationship, a number of episodes heightened the tension between them. For instance, when Wheelock sent one of his most trusted and talented converts, Samson Occom, as a missionary to the Oneida in New York in the summer of 1764, it became the occasion for an open disagreement. Believing Occom to lack what Whitefield deemed sufficient funds and other means of support, he chastised Wheelock for his "imprudent scheme" regarding "Mr. Occum and His Companion in their intended mission."[31] Refusing to concede the point, Wheelock made Whitefield's lack of good judgment toward the Indians the issue, complaining to a friend: "He labors under the discouraging apprehen-

29. Eleazar Wheelock to George Whitefield, May 18, 1764, MS764318.1, The Papers of Eleazar Wheelock, Dartmouth College.
30. Eleazar Wheelock to George Whitefield, August 7, 1764, MS764457, The Papers of Eleazar Wheelock, Dartmouth College.
31. George Whitefield to Eleazar Wheelock, September 5, 1764, MS764505, The Papers of Eleazar Wheelock, Dartmouth College.

sion that the Pagans of America are Canaanites, to be cut off before God's people, and never to be gathered into his Family. However I hope in God he will yet have the Pleasure of seeing himself mistaken."[32] Apart from the theological disagreement, what is so illuminating about this incident is the wide range of Whitefield's involvement in the affairs of a burgeoning Indian school in the hinterlands of Connecticut (later Wheelock would move the school to New Hampshire and establish it as Dartmouth College). Whitefield felt confident enough in his role as elder statesman to take the liberty of sending Samson Occom back to New England from New York. Eleazar Wheelock could hardly contain his anger when he heard the news. Writing a fellow minister, John Brainerd, he complained about the severe consequences of Whitefield's intervention: "The blow which Mr. Whitefield gave this school in sending Mr Occom back from New York was beyond any it has received from the first."[33] Whitefield continued to meddle, however, and Wheelock could ill afford to lose Whitefield's assistance in England.

When the Grand Itinerant formulated a plan to send Occom on a preaching and fundraising tour through England, Wheelock set aside any lingering resentment and readily gave his consent. From February 1766 to July 1767, Occom proved a sensation throughout England, winning support for Wheelock's school from the king himself and the Earl of Dartmouth among numerous others and totaling contributions of £12,000. Whitefield relished his role in guiding Samson Occom through his sojourn in England; although the specific cause was Wheelock's school, the wide publicity for colonial schools could only have bolstered the cause in Georgia as well.

Beyond his support, Whitefield also evinced a paternalistic and controlling temperament, expressing irritation where he saw Occom overstepping the bounds of propriety he had set up in his own mind. To take one example, he took enough interest and had sufficient influence to provide advice on where Occom should vacation, as well as the places a proper Indian should avoid: "Mr. Occum should not go to Bath, Coltan is a proper retirement for body & soul. Honest Indians love a straight

32. Eleazar Wheelock to J. Erskine, September 29, 1764, MS764529, The Papers of Eleazar Wheelock, Dartmouth College.

33. Eleazar Wheelock to John Brainerd, January 14, 1765, MS765114.3, The Papers of Eleazar Wheelock, Dartmouth College. The incident is also described in Kidd, *The Great Awakening*, 209–10.

path."[34] The following year in a letter to Wheelock, he showed similar concerns for Occom maintaining a sense of his place in English society and not forgetting his eventual return to the American context: "Occum still attracts the approbation of all. He really behaves well. Only I wish His continuance in England may not spoil Him for the wilderness."[35] Even on his best behavior, Occom was incapable of completely allaying Whitefield's fears.

Wheelock himself was not beyond the reach of Whitefield's critical judgments. In fact, Whitefield felt free to nitpick Wheelock over his expenditures and his lack of transparent bookkeeping: "But how came you to draw for so many hundreds this last year? And why no account of the disbursements? This must be annually and punctually remitted."[36] Whitefield may have forgotten the accusations of financial corruption made against his orphanage in Georgia, or it is possible he wanted to spare Wheelock the pain of such an ordeal. What is most remarkable is that Whitefield had the boldness to demand Wheelock disclose to him the details of the Indian school affair.

Colleges and the Long Path of Protestant Renewal

Whitefield's long and varied involvement in colonial colleges reveals a pattern of engagement that goes beyond ephemeral revival services. Criticisms of Whitefield's "ready, fire, aim" approach are valid, and there is no denying his inability to linger in any one place for too long.[37] At the same time, extending our study into his latter years shows that his rapid movements across the Atlantic world did not preclude a bigger, more comprehensive vision of Protestant renewal. Few accounts of his life trace the ways his longstanding involvement in a variety of educational efforts throughout the colonies culminated in his own college building project in the final decade of his life. By paying attention to the full scope of his life, including "the final discharge of his public duty," which this chapter seeks to flesh out, we will be in a better position to understand

34. George Whitefield to N. Whitaker, August 11, 1766, MS766461.4, The Papers of Eleazar Wheelock, Dartmouth College.

35. George Whitefield to Eleazar Wheelock, February 9, 1767, MS767159.4, The Papers of Eleazar Wheelock, Dartmouth College.

36. George Whitefield to Eleazar Wheelock, February 9, 1767.

37. Noll, *The Rise of Evangelicalism*, 108; Kidd, *The Great Awakening*, 44.

how the grassroots dimension of popular revival services gave rise to a program of cultural institutions that moved beyond the revival emphasis on individual piety. The awakenings represented more than bursts of religious energy released by socioeconomic crises or the catalytic charisma of traveling preachers. Beyond isolated socio-cultural episodes or a transatlantic religious movement, the history of evangelical revivals in the eighteenth century is also an essential part of the story of British imperial growth and the ongoing need for cultural adaptation in the face of relentless change. As a response to tectonic shifts in the broader social and political landscape, developments in evangelicalism during the eighteenth century illuminate revival religion and British and American cultures in the long term. Not content with the passing fruits of revival as an adequate answer to the challenges of imperial expansion and cultural enlightenment, Whitefield sought an alternative means of further reformation. By his evolving strategy, Whitefield displayed the conviction that more than an outward revival of religion would be needed to make an enduring evangelical impact on British culture.

While Bethesda represented a regional work in the colony of Georgia, Whitefield traversed far-flung networks that connected America to the British Empire.[38] Whitefield's understanding of educational institutions in England had an inevitable impact on his understanding of his own endeavors. Schools were deemed so essential to building British national character that King George III once justified his interest in Eton College and his "regard for the education of youth" by declaring it as the site where "most essentially depend my hopes of an advantageous change in the manners of the nation."[39] As Oxford and Cambridge grew increasingly aristocratic and thus lay further beyond the reach of the common people in England, however, a simultaneous proliferation of academies and colleges sought to fill the spaces those older, venerable institutions vacated in broader society. Reaching for intellectual and cultural influence in America, Whitefield's Bethesda project in the South stands as a sensible enterprise in the face of these emerging trends.[40] Whitefield's Bethesda College would seek to sustain

38. Of Whitefield's international connections, Boyd Schlenther has commented: "Whitefield's career is a parable of [the] transatlantic context." Schlenther, "Religious Faith and Commercial Empire," in Marshall, *The Oxford History of the British Empire*, 2:144.

39. Langford, *A Polite and Commercial People*, 83.

40. According to Paul Langford: "Numbers at both universities [Oxford and Cam-

the work of cultural renewal that elite colleges in the British Empire seemed to be forsaking.

Bethesda College in Georgia

In the light of his involvement in a wide range of college experiments in the colonies, Whitefield's interest in building a college of his own in Georgia takes on greater significance. For the remainder of this chapter, we will study the sequence of events in his Bethesda College campaign and offer an analysis of his activities and their significance for the changing imperial landscape of the mid-eighteenth century.

To understand what Whitefield might have had in mind for these last years of his life, a contemporary observer can provide perspective. Just as the imperial war came to a close in 1764, Eleazar Wheelock wrote a letter to John Erskine in Scotland revealing his view on the state of Whitefield's present health and future plans. "Mr. Whitefield's low State of Health has forbid his preaching very frequently in America," he wrote, referring to Whitefield's diminished preaching ministry. Furthermore, Wheelock appeared to resent Whitefield's preoccupation with his Georgia affairs, which came at the expense of projects like his Indian school in New England: "And his own Necessities (apprehending he shall soon be incapable of public service) and the necessities of his orphan House (which have far exceeded his expectation) have engross'd the most he has had opportunity to collect in America."[41] This remark by Wheelock is helpful because it points out the ways in which Whitefield was growing old and was also accommodating his ministry strategy based upon this irrefutable fact of life.

The dream of a college in Georgia underwent a long period of gestation, in part due to Whitefield's busy preaching schedule, but also because his attention was scattered in so many different directions across the British Empire.[42] On December 9, 1749, Whitefield wrote explicitly

---

bridge] fell markedly in the mid-eighteenth century. Together they admitted about five hundred annually in the 1720s. By the 1760s the figure was not much above three hundred. It rose somewhat to four hundred by the 1780s but hardly in line with the population growth of the period." Langford, *A Polite and Commercial People*, 89.

41. Eleazar Wheelock to J. Erskine, September 29, 1764, MS764529, The Papers of Eleazar Wheelock, Dartmouth College.

42. Robert L. McCaul, "Whitefield's Bethesda College Project and Other Attempts

of his plan for a college: "We propose having an academy or college at the Orphan-house in Georgia."[43] Almost a decade later, he mentioned "the proposals about the Georgia college" to a possible benefactor in April 1757.[44] His absence from America during the Seven Years' War, however, delayed action, and it was not until February 1760 that he was able to write, "thoughts of a College are revived."[45]

In the aftermath of war, finally able to return to America, Whitefield perceived a changed playing field in which the revivals were but a distant memory and new challenges abounded. His letters to friends and supporters mark this shift in Whitefield's thinking and his apprehensions about the start of a new phase in his Georgia labors. "[T]o America," he wrote a friend on January 15, 1763, "I think there is a manifest call at this time, both as to the bracing up my poor, feeble, crazy body, and *adjusting all things* relating to Bethesda."[46] Six months later he was crossing the ocean to begin his American work anew. In a sharp break with former patterns, his sense of call to America at this juncture made no mention of preaching, identifying instead the reordering of Bethesda as the matter of highest priority. Signaling his intentions to mark a new beginning for Bethesda, Whitefield sent instructions on December 7, 1763, to "have the family lessened as much as may be, and all things contracted into as small a compass as possible."[47] He spent the first part of his trip traveling through the Middle Colonies and New England raising support for the college. By December of the following year he was on his way to Georgia with a resolute plan in mind. It was a season of new beginnings, and Whitefield wanted to clear the ground for an ambitious restart. Though he would not announce his plans until the following year, Whitefield was finding his stride to launch a college of his own at Bethesda.

At long last on December 18, 1764, Whitefield submitted his official proposal for Bethesda College, "The Memorial of George Whitefield," to magistrates in Georgia.[48] To preempt the criticism he expected, White-

to Found Colonial Colleges: Part I," *The Georgia Historical Quarterly* 44, no. 3 (1960): 263–77.

43. Whitefield to Mr W— L—, December 9, 1749, in *Works*, 2:297.
44. Whitefield to Lord H—, April 20, 1757, in *Works*, 3:203.
45. Whitefield to Mr. D—, February 5, 1760, in *Works*, 3:259.
46. Tyerman, *Life*, 2:457; emphasis added.
47. Tyerman, *Life*, 2:470.
48. "To His Excellency James Wright, Esq.; Captain General and Governor in Chief

field described the college as a logical extension of his charity work, which had already helped so many people and thereby kept them "from leaving the colony in its infant state." He emphasized the fact that he had spent over twenty-five years and expended upwards of twelve thousand pounds sterling to help establish the colony. As he described the full extent of his benefactions for the colony in his memorial, he emphasized the numerous strategic benefits that Bethesda College would bring to Georgia. Whitefield had good reasons to feel confident about the prospects of a college charter. The president of the state senate was his longtime friend and one-time disciple, James Habersham. The royal governor of Georgia, James Wright, fully backed the plan, pointing out its "utmost utility to this and the neighbouring provinces" and calling it "beautiful, rational, and practicable." As further encouragement, he was finally debt-free at Bethesda, declaring on February 18, 1765: "All arrears are paid off . . . so that one great load is taken off."[49] This milestone brought welcome conclusion to a constant struggle of two-and-a-half decades. The resulting financial freedom enabled Whitefield to focus on higher pursuits.

More specifically, the benefits Whitefield cited for the college were cultural, economic, and empire-wide. First, he argued that a college in Georgia would help build the region's cultural base. The fact "that several gentlemen have been obliged to send their sons to the northern provinces" was not merely a matter of strain on familial ties. He feared "their affections being alienated from their native country." In this way, Whitefield identified a distinct region in the southern provinces that he called its own "native country." He also noted that the existence of an institution like Bethesda College would "keep considerable sums of money from being carried out of this into other provinces." His was a sensible and straightforward case, Whitefield believed, for a self-sufficient economy that could enter into competitive trade relations with other parts of the empire. For this reason, he was not at all trying to seal the colony off from the flow of imperial traffic, especially since he envisioned Georgia becoming a center of learning and culture for a strategically targeted segment of

---

of his Majesty's province of Georgia, and to the members of his Majesty's council in the said province. The Memorial of George Whitefield," in *Works*, 3:469–70; emphasis added. For brevity, this document will hereafter be referred to as "The Memorial of George Whitefield to Governor Wright."

49. Whitefield to Mr. R— K—n, February 13, 1765, in *Works*, 3:323.

the empire. He reckoned the proposed college "would probably occasion many youths to be sent from the British West India islands and other parts." Whitefield's interest in slavery had no doubt served to deepen his familiarity with imperial topography. He knew the lay of the land not only because he itinerated through it but also due to the business interests and relationships he had built along the way. With good reason, he expected such an imperial appeal would be easily apprehended by his hearers. It merely sufficed for him to observe: "The many advantages accruing thereby to this province, must be considerable."[50]

It took only two days for Whitefield's memorial to garner an enthusiastic response from both Houses of Assembly in Georgia as well as the governor. A statement dated December 20, 1764, addressed to the governor and signed by James Habersham, president of the upper House, and Alexander Wylly, speaker of the Commons House, sounded a ringing endorsement:

> The many and singular obligations Georgia has continually laid under that Reverend gentleman, from its very infant state, would in gratitude induce us, by every means in our power, to promote any measure he might recommend; but in the present instance, where the interest of the province, the advancement of religion, and the pleasing prospect of obtaining proper education for our youth, so clearly coincide with his views, we cannot in justice but request your Excellency to use your utmost endeavours to promote so desirable an event, and to transmit home our sincere and very fervent wishes, for the accomplishment of so useful, so beneficent, and so laudable an undertaking.[51]

Whitefield could not have asked for a stronger statement of support, with the House mounting a religious, social, cultural, and political argument for the valuable contributions of the proposed college. Governor Wright provided an immediate response on the same day, telling the legislature and Whitefield that they "may rest assured, that I shall transmit your address home, with my best endeavours for the success

---

50. "The Memorial of George Whitefield to Governor Wright," in *Works*, 3:470.
51. "The Address of Both Houses of Assembly in Georgia," in *Works*, 3:471.

of the great point in view."[52] The chasm, however, between the colony and metropole was wider than any of the players anticipated.

After securing the support of the Georgia magistrates, Whitefield spent the first half of 1765 traveling north in the colonies and preaching and raising funds for Bethesda. In those ventures he commonly referred to it as a future college rather than an orphanage. When he returned to England in July, propitious developments in English politics at first augured well for his college dream. Lord Dartmouth, a friend of the Countess of Huntingdon, was head of the Board of Trade, and Whitefield counted on his support as his proposal went before the Privy Council. In the following year, however, prospects soured. The government of the First Rockingham ministry, headed by the Marquess of Rockingham, fell and Lord Dartmouth resigned. These developments deprived Whitefield of a powerful ally in Dartmouth. Making matters worse, Thomas Secker, Archbishop of Canterbury and a long-time critic of Whitefield, showed no amenable signs of cooperation.[53] As a supporter of the Society for the Propagation of the Gospel (SPG) and, for a season, its president, Secker had taken strong exception to Whitefield's criticism of SPG missionaries during the awakenings of the early 1740s. Though Whitefield did not need Secker's approval to move forward with his college plans, he misjudged his odds, overestimated the weight of his own popularity, and became embroiled in a protracted game of bureaucratic brinkmanship.

It soon became evident that the archbishop would be a markedly different kind of audience for Whitefield than his allies in America. Sensing the nature of the challenge before him, he made a few telling revisions to the memorial he had earlier written to the governor and magistrates of Georgia when he sent it to the archbishop a few years later in 1767.[54] Rather than naming "the British West India islands and

52. James Wright to the Houses of Assembly in Georgia, December 20, 1764, in *Works*, 3:472; emphasis added.

53. In 1746, Whitefield had written Secker to point out how in a recent sermon the latter was "misinform'd as to some particulars." Whitefield also thought he had a better perspective on a range of matters due to his travels: "As I have lately been in most parts of America, I am better able to judge of some things than those who live in England." George Whitefield to Secker, June 9, 1746, MS1123/1, Lambeth Palace Library. An account of this early "icy exchange" can be found in William Gibson, "Whitefield and the Church of England," in *George Whitefield: Life, Context, and Legacy*, ed. Geordan Hammond and David Ceri Jones (Oxford: Oxford University Press, 2016). Also in Ingram, *Religion, Reform and Modernity in the Eighteenth Century*, 223–24.

54. "To the King's most Excellent Majesty. The Memorial of George Whitefield,"

other parts" as he had to the Georgia magistrates, Whitefield mentioned "the neighbouring southern provinces" as the geographical region that would benefit from the founding of a college in Georgia. The itinerant preacher may have seen the greater appeal of a more general region to an archbishop of the established church who was farther removed and less informed about the geographical nuances of the New World. His request for two thousand acres of land to support the college in his earlier memorial to the Georgia officials having already been granted, Whitefield happily noted this development. He importuned the archbishop "that numbers both in Georgia and South-Carolina are waiting with impatience to have their sons initiated in academical exercises." He pointed to the plan of New Jersey College as an inspiring precedent and template for Bethesda. As if all that were not enough, and in what might have been a sign of desperation, he pledged to give the entirety of his considerable possessions in Georgia—"all lands, negroes, goods, and chattels, which he now stands possessed of in the province of Georgia"—toward the founding of the college.[55] In other words, Whitefield was fully committed to the enterprise. The college was to be the final, culminating achievement of his long career.

Secker, however, was not impressed. More than that, he was decidedly opposed to setting up schools for Dissenters in America. He had already turned down an entreaty of support for Wheelock's school in Connecticut. To be sure, it was not for lack of interest in the colonies or imagination for strategic thinking. "My first Notion was, that our Society might send children to be educated there, who might afterwds be sent out by us as Missionaries," Secker wrote in 1767, displaying an agile missionary interest in America. Being apprised of the school's distinctly Presbyterian emphasis, however, he wrote "in the civillest Terms I could, that we thought it would be best, that the Church of England & the Dissenters from it should each maintain their own Schools."[56] Despite similarities, dealing with Whitefield's petition was not as straightforward a matter as Wheelock's. Whitefield was an ordained minister of the Church of England and notwithstanding his past acrimony with church officials, the priest expressed a submissive spirit and willingness to cooperate.

---

in *Works* 3:473–75. This document will hereafter be referred to as "The Memorial of George Whitefield to Archbishop Secker."

55. Whitefield to Thomas Secker, June 17, 1767, in *Works*, 3:479.

56. Folio 74, 1764, in Thomas Secker, *The Autobiography of Thomas Secker, Archbishop of Canterbury* (Lawrence: University of Kansas Libraries, 1988), 58.

Secker decided to test the extent of Whitefield's loyalty to the church. Taking a ruthless pen to the plan of the charter, he "proposed several Alterations in it." Though extant details are sparse, the archbishop appears to have mandated rules regarding its governance and liturgy that would have secured the college as an institution of the church.[57] In response, Whitefield trod carefully and acknowledged his high esteem for the church but also appealed to the fact of a broad fundraising base, with many Dissenters from outside the church having already contributed toward the college. In the end, the primate and his priest were unable to find common ground on essential matters. Secker noted Whitefield's efforts to comply, but it is also clear that in key matters there was no disposition toward compromise from either side, as Whitefield wrote:

> He agreed to almost all of them; but refused his Consent to two: which were, that, as in the charter of New York College, the Head shd be always a Member of the Church of England, & the publick Prayers in the College shd be not extempore, but either the Liturgy of the Church of England, or part of it, or some Form approved by the Governors.[58]

During this period, Secker rejected another petition for a colonial academy, a Rhode Island college that in his view "tended to Perpetuate the Notions of the Anabaptists there."[59]

The archbishop's rejection of three colonial colleges in the course of 1767 reveals a pattern of both engagement and detachment. Not only did colonial leaders see some kind of connection to the Church of England as helpful to their enterprise; Secker also recognized the strategic value of colleges as sites for missionary training and ecclesiastical control. He disliked, nevertheless, the idea of nonconformist colleges spreading their influence in the colonies. Also noteworthy is the fact that, in these colonial matters, Secker had a network of informants who kept him updated on fresh developments in America. The archbishop mentioned receiving more accurate insights from a Mr. Apthorp, an SPG missionary in New England, regarding Wheelock's

57. Whitefield to Thomas Secker, June 17, 1767, in *Works*, 3:475-77.
58. Folio 88, 1767, in Secker, *Autobiography*, 65.
59. Folio 90, 1767-1768, in Secker, *Autobiography*, 66.

Indian school.[60] As he considered Whitefield's plans for a college, he heard from at least two informants who provided unfavorable news.[61] William Smith, the provost of the college in Philadelphia we encountered earlier, shared his misgivings with the secretary of the SPG, who likely passed the word on to the archbishop.[62] Evangelicals were not the only group with a sophisticated network of communication.

For Secker, the Bethesda affair was one administrative detail in a sea of urgent ecclesiastical matters vying for his attention, but for Whitefield it was the dearest cause of his final years. In noting the blow of this failure, it must also be asked why he sought a charter from the archbishop in the first place. According to one historian, "Not one of the six colleges founded between 1745 and 1775 had been chartered by the Crown. All had been incorporated directly, without referring to Whitehall."[63] In 1749, Bishop George Berkeley advised against such a move: "I would not advise the applying to England for Charters or Statutes (which might cause great trouble, expense and delay), but to do the business quietly within themselves."[64] Why then did Whitefield pursue a royal charter? While historians generally point to the practical reasons, such as Whitefield's confidence in the successful bid for a charter or his desire for as many advantages as possible for the college, our study of the imperial dimension of Whitefield's revival ministry provides yet another angle for answering this question.[65] We can only surmise that Whitefield pursued royal endorsement for his work in Georgia because of his desire to see Bethesda serve as an imperial institution for the furtherance of the British Protestant cause in a turbulent world. Watching Samson Occom's gallant success throughout England (including a personal contribution of £200 from the king himself) at the very same time he had locked horns with Thomas Secker could only

---

60. Folio 74, 1767, in Secker, *Autobiography*, 58.

61. Folio 87, 1767, in Secker, *Autobiography*, 64.

62. McCaul, "Whitefield's Bethesda College Project," 276.

63. McCaul, "Whitefield's Bethesda College Project," 272.

64. Cited in McCaul, "Whitefield's Bethesda College Project," 273.

65. McCaul points out Whitefield must "have felt confident that his application for a charter would move smoothly and expeditiously through the English governmental channels." He also points out Whitefield's desire to secure as many "positive advantages" for his institution as possible—including freedom from criticisms, especially since the charter for the College of New Jersey granted by Governor Belcher was challenged. McCaul, "Whitefield's Bethesda College Project," 274.

have served to deepen his resolve. Wheelock would not need to worry himself with a charter application for his Indian school, but Whitefield persisted because he had more lofty ambitions for his college.

It is significant that when plans for the college charter finally ran aground, it was not because of challenges in Georgia but due to opposition in England. Whitefield faced a formidable opponent in the implacable Archbishop Secker. In the face of Whitefield's pleas, by turns unctuous and truculent, Secker harbored many misgivings about what the college might mean for provincial life and imperial culture. In an indirect way, the prelate's opposition highlights the potential of what Whitefield's dream college could have meant. A man of considerable piety and genuine concern for the welfare of the church, Secker's resistance signified more than petty politicking with a longtime critic and thorn in his side. The clash between Whitefield and Secker represented competing views of the role of religion in the empire's future. Although an ordained Anglican cleric, Whitefield's view of religious life in the Atlantic world was expansive and ecumenical. In contrast, Secker wanted to tighten the reins of control.

With his centrifugal vision of empire, Whitefield piously expressed concerns for the colony: "I humbly hope, the province of Georgia, in the end, will be no loser by this negotiation." As for his next steps, he intended to pursue a "public academy," which would circumvent the need for a royal charter. Even so, Whitefield persisted in his hopes for a college: "In the mean time, a proper trust may be formed to act after my decease, or even before, with this proviso, that no opportunity shall be omitted of making fresh application for a college charter."[66] In this way, death itself should prove no barrier to the dream of a college in Georgia.

The Meaning of Bethesda

Based on the foregoing survey of Whitefield's petition for a college charter, we are now ready to examine the meaning of the Bethesda project. The vision of a college in Georgia provides a clue to understanding both Whitefield and the British Empire in the mid-eighteenth century. For Bethesda became the contentious focal point of Whitefield's final drive for Protestant renewal and Archbishop Secker's efforts to maintain ec-

---

66. Whitefield to Thomas Secker, February 12, 1768, in *Works*, 3:484.

clesiastical uniformity. As such, Bethesda was nothing less than a test site for the limits of imperial expansion and coercion. Significantly for evangelical religion, Bethesda also represented an effort to harness the revival spirit in an ongoing institutional form.

There are few better examples of Whitefield's evolving sense of purpose than his efforts to build an academic college out of his philanthropic project in Georgia. In a colony where disillusioned abandonment outpaced fresh arrivals for the first twenty years, Whitefield's orphanage helped sustain the colony and even raised a number of colonial leaders. When the economic prospering of the colonies throughout the 1750s created new opportunities, Whitefield proved himself a skilled entrepreneur despite being an absentee landlord. By the beginning of the 1760s, Georgia had a population of approximately ten thousand, a few libraries dotted the landscape as symbols of growing refinement, and the establishment of *The Georgia Gazette* in 1763 signaled its progress toward becoming a mature colony.

As circumstances in the colony changed, so did the religious emphases of Whitefield's ministry. The revival soil that the gifted preacher tilled with great enthusiasm in his early years did not bear the kind of widespread and long-lasting fruit for which its participants hoped. Rather than persisting with the same tried-and-failed revival tactics of the 1740s, Whitefield came to the realization that the awakenings had made only an ephemeral impact. Precisely because of this realism, he reemerged in America for his sixth visit—which also marked the commencement of his Bethesda College campaign—responding to new trends and formulating revised strategies, all the while reaching for lasting fruits the revivals had failed to deliver. The time of his return to America in 1763 also coincided with the end of the Seven Years' War, and Whitefield apprehended a time of ripening opportunity in America. Georgia had benefited from the war—with an expanded territory secured in the Proclamation of 1763, a new phase of friendly relations with Native Americans, and a popular governor who worked well with the legislature. Encouraged by these developments, Whitefield expressed eagerness to reengage the work at Bethesda.

The shift in his approach was unmistakable. No longer did preaching to the masses represent Whitefield's primary occupation, nor did maintaining the orphanage at Bethesda. Instead, the vision of establishing a southern college absorbed most of his energy. How do we account for this dramatic turn in the life of a person who had devoted his life to preaching the evangelical new birth? To understand White-field's unwavering commitment to Bethesda College in his latter years requires an exploration of its imperial significance. Only by examining the place of Whitefield's proposed colonial college in the larger con-text of the British Empire and the expanded opportunities for influ-ence that it represented to the evangelical statesman can we explain his absorption with it. Toward that end, we will observe the ways in which Bethesda served as the meeting place of a number of different interests that had animated Whitefield throughout his public career, much of which had been a balancing act between imperial and religious ambitions. By containing, if not melding, these divergent and at times vigorously conflicting forces, Bethesda became a rehearsal site for the ideological contests of cultural formation in America. A tour of the vari-ous possibilities inherent in Bethesda, to which we now turn, will reveal how much the meaning of Bethesda intersected with developments in the outlying frontiers of British imperialism.

An Imperial Institution

Whitefield went to a great deal of trouble in his efforts to attain a royal charter for Bethesda College. To understand why, it may help to re-member that the successful establishment of Bethesda College would have dramatically increased Whitefield's profile in the mid-eighteenth-century British Empire. Georgia lay not only at the southernmost tip of the mainland colonies but also represented a fast-growing edge of the empire. Whitefield himself emphasized the recent changes to imperial boundaries that resulted from victory over the French, when he wrote on December 18, 1764, "the late addition of the two Floridas renders Georgia more *centrical* for the southern district." In other words, he was familiar enough with the map of empire to highlight the shift of Georgia's posi-tion from the periphery to the emerging center of the American South. As Whitefield took pains to observe, "The many advantages accruing thereby to this province," as well as to his own interests we might add, "must be very considerable."[67] To explore the extent of Whitefield's involvement

---

67. "The Memorial of George Whitefield to Governor Wright," in *Works*, 3:470; emphasis added. In his petition to Secker, Whitefield changed "this province" to "Geor-gia." "The Memorial of George Whitefield to Archbishop Secker," in *Works*, 3:474.

in the imperial dimensions of his work in America, we will examine a letter from Franklin to Whitefield in 1756 and a farewell sermon by the itinerant in 1763, marking his cognizance of imperial politics at the beginning and end of the Seven Years' War. Both documents reveal the ways in which the preacher's empire-wide aspirations influenced his enduring concern for the usefulness of the southern outpost that was Georgia. In addition, a diary of an unidentified Bostonian visiting England will help us understand how Whitefield's message was heard and interpreted in a time of heightened political tension in the British Empire. This source presents a helpful reminder that the preacher's college in Georgia was part of a wider transatlantic program of Protestant renewal.

Whitefield's contact with imperial politics could only have grown through his unlikely friendship with Benjamin Franklin. This influential colonial leader once invited Whitefield to dream with him about starting a new colony together, in a letter dated July 2, 1756:

> I sometimes wish, that you and I were jointly employ'd by the Crown to settle a Colony on the Ohio. I imagine we could do it effectually. . . . What a glorious Thing it would be, to settle in that fine Country a large Strong Body of Religious and Industrious People! What a Security to the other Colonies; and Advantage to Britain, by Increasing her People, Territory, Strength and Commerce.[68]

Whitefield's response to Franklin is unknown, yet it cannot have been far from enthusiastic affirmation of the dream, perhaps a line or two offered toward embellishing—even improving (as he did with Franklin's plan for an academy)—the vision. At the very least he would have agreed that such work, if unrealistic in remote regions, merited pursuit in more immediate and present circumstances. Indeed, he might have replied to Franklin that the very thing his friend proposed to do, he himself was already attempting in the outskirts of Savannah.

The timing of Franklin's musings as well as his choice of Whitefield as confidant offer a portrait of the famous preacher that may not be gleaned from his own writings. Franklin wrote his letter in the early phase of the Seven Years' War, a time when tensions and fears ran high.[69] The

68. Benjamin Franklin to George Whitefield, July 2, 1756, in *The Papers of Benjamin Franklin*, 6:468–69.
69. Silver, *Our Savage Neighbors*.

horrors of war would ravage the very territory where Franklin dreamed of settling a new colony. In fact, it was most likely French and Indian aggression that led him to contemplate, "What a Security to the other Colonies" such an enterprise would become. In other words, Franklin was not recruiting Whitefield to the pipe dream of a social and spiritual commune; he was inviting him, albeit hypothetically, to partner with him in an expansionist political, even military, venture. By invoking the "Advantage to Britain" such an enterprise would have secured, Franklin wooed Whitefield the imperial citizen. Far from mere idle words of an armchair dreamer, this 1756 letter to Whitefield reveals Franklin's apprehension of the rebel priest as a patriotic imperial subject and shrewd political strategist. We may not know all of what Whitefield said to give Franklin such ideas; we do know, because Franklin himself mentions it in the same letter, that the preacher had often expressed a desire to become an army chaplain. At any rate, Franklin had heard or seen enough to believe his dream of an Ohio settlement—wishful banter though it may have been—would not fall on deaf ears with Whitefield.

Likely boosting Franklin's confidence in this regard was the active interest Whitefield had earlier taken in his school building efforts in Philadelphia. The alliance between Franklin and Whitefield continued to deepen so that when Franklin in 1766 testified before the House of Commons during the Stamp Act crisis, Whitefield was there by his side. Joseph Galloway, a leading figure in colonial politics from Pennsylvania, wrote a letter to William Franklin, recounting his father's admirable performance before Parliament. In that letter, he also mentions Whitefield, showing how much the preacher's reputation had grown since 1743 when he was seen as too much of an embarrassment and liability to testify before the House (see chapter 2). "Who Dare deny Mr. Whitefield's authority?" wrote Galloway. "Will the Church? Will the Presbyterians?"[70] In this way, Franklin's longstanding relationship with his preacher friend underscores the point that Whitefield's interests went far beyond evangelistic preaching to matters of empire.

Understanding the ways Whitefield's vision both embraced and transcended regional and colonial spheres of influence helps identify the extent of his ambition. In "Jacob's Ladder," his farewell sermon preached in England in June 1763 (four months after the war ended), he

---

70. Joseph Galloway to William Franklin, April 29, 1766, B:F85 XLVIII, 123, American Philosophical Society.

expressed his love for both the colonies and England. Before embarking on yet another Atlantic crossing, he went so far as to pronounce a benediction on the imperial bond:

> And the gentlemen of America, from one end to the other, are of such an hospitable temper, as I have not only been told, but have found among them upwards of thirty years, that they would not let public houses be licensed, that they may have an opportunity of entertaining English friends. May God, of His infinite mercy, grant this union may never be dissolved![71]

In this way, Whitefield praised America and hastened to add a word about the indissoluble bond shared with Britain. Lest there be any doubt of his love for the mother country, he voiced his sincere desire to return to England: "For, let people say what they will, I have not so much as a single thought of settling abroad, on this side eternity."[72] Whitefield was evidently apprised of naysayers who questioned his devotion to England—not without reason, given his ceaseless travels. Yet, ever the sojourner, he avoided the prospect of becoming a settler. While he always knew where his eternal home would be, he also appears to have had no qualms about being an Englishman throughout his life, despite his many years of traveling abroad and the many conflicts he endured with the Anglican establishment. He viewed himself as a connective link between Britain and America, and, more than that, a mediating figure who sought to bring together the best of both worlds. In this way, the older Whitefield was a man urgently seeking reform yet also keen for conciliatory union as he devised plans for a college with which to engage a hollow political landscape.

Whitefield returned from his sixth visit to America in the late summer of 1765. Even as he engaged in the struggle of his life in trying to attain a charter for the college in Georgia, his ministry of preaching Christian and British liberties continued, though on a reduced basis. The remarks of an unidentified tourist from Boston traveling in England from 1768 to 1769 can shed light on the kind of political climate

71. George Whitefield, "Jacob's Ladder," in *The Works of George Whitefield, Additional Sermons* (Meadow View: Quinta Press, 2000), 226.
72. Whitefield, *The Works of George Whitefield, Additional Sermons*, 237.

that prevailed during this time and the place of Whitefield's influence in this volatile period. The Bostonian's impressions of Whitefield's sermons in the context of other speakers and events during his visit provide an additional vantage point that lies outside the usual perspectives on the Grand Itinerant, which tend toward either fierce criticism or fawning admiration.

We know little about this American visitor except that he came from Boston, stayed for a little over a year in London, and exhibited a wide-ranging interest in the life of the imperial capital. His interests fell primarily into political and religious categories. He was a close follower of parliamentary activities (especially obsessed with controversies surrounding the radical English politician John Wilkes) and enjoyed listening to preachers of all stripes, from Whitefield and Wesley to the Sandemanians (a sect originating from Scotland that denied the need for a national and institutional church since the body of Christ is essentially spiritual). As a colonial visitor, the Bostonian displayed sensitivity throughout his diary to the abuses of the British government with their "Arbitrary Insults" against liberty.[73]

It becomes apparent from the entries of this unknown diarist that Whitefield still possessed his homiletical genius in the last years of his life. After attending one of his services at the Tabernacle in London, the Bostonian wrote for two pages reflecting on how Whitefield's sermon taught him "what [it] is to be really Dead to Sin in the World & alive to God in Christ Jesus by a Strict Adherence to the Denial of our Selves & by our Mortifying every Carnal Lust." But Whitefield also brought the spiritual message to bear on political circumstances, so that his sermon on Isaiah was "a very Serious & Instructive Discourse and a Solemn Warning to the Wicked with his Earnest Petition to God that he would Avert these Threating [*sic*] Judgments from our Land & Town."[74] For the visitor from Boston, applying Whitefield's sermon to his life meant siding with the freeholders who continued voting Wilkes into office despite his imprisonment for libel against political opponents, because they were "determined not to have such Arbitrary Insults and Encroachments on their Liberties as Englishmen."[75] For hearers like this Bostonian, whose diary alternated between sermon notes and political reflections, the re-

---

73. *Diary of an Unidentified Bostonian*, HM175, Huntington Library, 31.
74. *Diary of an Unidentified Bostonian*, 14.
75. *Diary of an Unidentified Bostonian*, 31.

ligious message of salvation in Christ turned seamlessly into a rallying cry for the protection of British liberties.

Whitefield's continuing popularity might be explained by the fact that whether in Britain or America, whether petitioning for a college charter or preaching the virtues of British Protestantism, he proclaimed a message that conflated evangelical and imperial concerns. Because of his high ambitions, and despite Bethesda's physical location in the margins, his vision for the college from the beginning had an unabashedly elitist focus, marking a decisive shift from the mission of Bethesda Orphanage. In fact, Whitefield's primary goal for the college, as noted earlier, was to make "further provision for the education of persons of superiour rank, who thereby may be qualified to serve their king, their country, and their God, either in church or state."[76] Just as Whitefield was not content to leave Bethesda an orphanage, neither was he satisfied with the mere goal of training ministers. His was a lofty vision reaching for significant contributions to church and state, reverberating in not only spiritual but also social, cultural, and political influence, which can be inferred from his expansive reference to "church or state," an intentionally ambiguous statement that reflected a blurring of the boundaries, which Whitefield intended for strategic purposes.

In addition to transcending church and state, or religious and political, boundaries, Whitefield also included in his Bethesda plan a broad geographical reach. He intended Bethesda College to serve not only Georgia but the entire southern region. His ambitions aligned him with the cause of the empire; in addition, Whitefield had no qualms about using the tide of worldly affairs to his advantage. He would not hesitate to translate the political fortunes of war, however pyrrhic, into religious opportunities. The indefatigable itinerant harbored not merely religious motivations but extensive social and political aspirations. As the only college south of Virginia's College of William and Mary, Bethesda would have enabled Whitefield to play a major role in the intellectual, social, and political life not only of Georgia but the larger southern region.[77] Having not quite fit in at Oxford during his student days and with Harvard and Yale snubs of the revival years lingering, even if faintly

76. "The Memorial of George Whitefield to Governor Wright," in *Works*, 3:470. This statement also appears in "The Memorial of George Whitefield to Archbishop Secker," in *Works*, 3:474.

77. Harold E. Davis, *The Fledgling Province: Social and Cultural Life in Colonial Georgia, 1733–1776* (Williamsburg: Institute of Early American History and Culture, 1976), 247.

by now, Whitefield set out to build an ivory tower of his own. In that venture, he would draw prospective students away from elite northern colleges and help a thriving southern culture to hold its own.

A Subversive Kingdom

Bethesda's geographical position on the imperial frontier not only afforded a chance for Whitefield's appropriation of Britain's imperial expansionism; it also placed his labors squarely in the margins of colonial life. Yet here too was an opportunity, for the margins were where Whitefield felt most comfortable. Overcoming great odds was what this preacher with a booming voice that could rise above the cacophony of detractors did best. To put it another way, the political openings Whitefield apprehended required, for a man steeped in his religious beliefs, a theological interpretation. In a context of imperial languor and institutional frailty, geographical outposts provided the ideal playing field for Whitefield's activism late in life. Despite his Oxford education and extraordinary ministry successes, Whitefield continued to be acutely aware of his outsider status. Perhaps he never forgot the intimidation he felt upon first meeting the Wesleys during college. Certainly he sensed a calling greater than traditional ecclesiastical categories could hold. At any rate, it is nearly impossible to imagine Whitefield settling into a parish post in New England or even London. Georgia, on the other hand, was a place fit for his outsized personality.

An incident that happened after Archbishop Secker's rejection of a college charter for Bethesda further shows Whitefield's ongoing struggles with seemingly arbitrary authority. Whitefield was back in London, catching his breath before his seventh trip to America. He was still smarting from the defeat of his campaign for a college charter before an archbishop who insisted that it follow Anglican forms. When he heard in the spring of 1768 about the expulsion of six students from Oxford for their practice of extempore prayer, Whitefield forgot the moderate persona he had been attempting to cultivate in his later years and threw himself once again eagerly into the fray. In an openly indignant twelve-thousand-word epistolary parry, the old combative Whitefield was back. He appeared to relish the dual role of one who was simultaneously an insider as well as outsider. Embracing the tension, Whitefield fancied himself close enough in social status to the Vice Chancellor of Oxford,

David Durell, to confront him. He did so, all the while fixing his own position outside the corrupt institutional culture that Durell represented. Whitefield came to the defense of the British students who, he protested, were being treated unjustly not only for their religious practices but also for their socioeconomic standing. He wrote, "It is true indeed, one article of impeachment was, 'that some of them were of Trades before they entered into the University.' But what evil or crime worthy of expulsion can there be in that?"[78] He declared with righteous anger that originating from the "meanest mechanic employ" was no just grounds for prejudice or persecution.

Whitefield pulled out all the stops in his letter, going as far as to declare even papists more lenient than Durell. His tirade is worth quoting at length:

> Popish countries, Popish seminaries, think it no shame, no disgrace to be heard singing the high praises of their God in their Convents, their Houses, or even in their Streets; and why Protestants in general, and Protestant Students in particular, should be any more ashamed of, or restrained from the free exercise of such acts of devotion, either in secret or in private societies, no good reason can be given; unless it be proved to be good reasoning to assert, that Protestants ought to be less devout than Papists.[79]

Whitefield thus maneuvered through dangerous accusations by deft and delicate argumentation, conjuring up the Catholic threat that remained a live issue in England and just as much (if not more so) in the southern colonial region where settlers still harbored lingering memories of French and Spanish incursions. Lest he be judged to have gone too far, Whitefield also added later in the letter: "But what a mercy is it, Reverend Sir, that we live under a free government . . . and under a King who in his first most gracious and never-to-be-forgotten Speech from the throne, gave his people the strongest assurances [of religious freedom]."[80] The goal of Whitefield's reveling in the margins, after all, was to attain for himself a foothold in the empire's center of influence.

---

78. George Whitefield, *A Letter to the Reverend Dr. Durell, Vice-Chancellor of the University of Oxford; Occasioned By a Late Expulsion of Six Students From Edmund-Hall* (Boston, 1768), 7.

79. Whitefield, *A Letter to the Reverend Dr. Durell*, 12.

80. Whitefield, *A Letter to the Reverend Dr. Durell*, 19.

As Whitefield self-consciously straddled the line between Anglican and dissenting churches, detractors often highlighted his Methodist associations as a sign of his outsider status. Flexing his nonconformist muscles, Whitefield did not shy away from the title of methodist in his letter, clarifying by declaring: "If you should desire, Reverend Sir, a definition of Methodism itself, as well as of a Methodist, you may easily be gratified—It is no more nor less than Faith working by love—A holy method of living and dying, to the glory of God—It is an universal morality, founded upon the love of God shed abroad in the heart by the Holy Ghost."[81] In other words, as far as Whitefield was concerned, to be a Methodist was to be what any good Anglican should have been in the first place. In the face of efforts to exclude him from influence, Whitefield turned the table on his opponents by redefining what it meant to be an outsider. To find oneself excluded from the fellowship table of patent hypocrites was an occasion for boasting.

The fiery response occasioned by the Oxford incident provides a window into the charged religious landscape in which Whitefield labored. This context also helps us understand the resolve that shaped Whitefield's aspirations for Bethesda College. In colonial Georgia, far (though not far enough as it turned out) from the meddling tentacles of ecclesial politics but still within the bounds of English and Anglican identity, Whitefield found the ideal site for community experimentation. A college in these distant regions would have provided the base of operations Whitefield needed to reimagine what was possible for faith and social formation. No wonder he found it to be the one abiding passion that could even surpass his devotion to preaching the gospel. During his last visit to Bethesda, on January 11, 1770, he wrote: "Every thing exceeds my most sanguine expectations. I am almost tempted to say, it is good for me to be here; but all must give way to gospel ranging—divine employ!"[82] Bethesda was a place he could hardly tear himself away from, even for the sake of preaching, that other prized calling of his life.

Consideration of Bethesda's hold on Whitefield reveals a strain of personal redemption, or compensation, which seems to have infused Whitefield's extensive involvement with colonial educational enterprises. His familiarity with social margins encouraged his preference

81. Whitefield, *A Letter to the Reverend Dr. Durell*, 24.
82. Gillies, *Memoirs*, 205.

for imperial outposts and allowed him to negotiate a path to influence from a position of obscurity. He was the model ideological frontiersman for a literal, colonial frontier. Hence, flowing from his past life on the margins and his future hope of an influential center, there was a two-pronged principle to Whitefield's educational philosophy: train the elite but also raise up the lowly, and, in a hinterland like Georgia, establish a base for the British Empire as well as the kingdom of God. Instead of building a church, Whitefield pursued a college, intentionally blurring religious, social, and political boundaries. His Bethesda campaign reflects and presages broader trends in American ambivalence toward established religion. That he attempted to make the margins of colonial society the center of his colonial community making was Whitefield's true innovation, reflecting a persistent theology of the margins.

In a sermon preached before Georgia officials in the last year of his life, Whitefield more fully articulated his vision for the community Bethesda College would help fashion. He announced hopes of social and cultural as well as religious renewal:

> the wished-for period is now come, after having supported the family for thirty-two years, by a change of constitution and the smiles of government, with liberal donations from the northern, and especially the adjacent provinces, the same hands that laid the foundation, are now called to finish it, by making an addition of a seat of learning, the whole products and profits of which, are to go towards the increase of the fund, as at the beginning, for destitute orphans, or such youths as may be called of God to the sacred ministry of his Gospel.[83]

In this late expression of the Bethesda vision, three key aspects of Whitefield's aspirations emerge in bold relief. First, Whitefield makes no mention of the transatlantic support he has gathered for Bethesda, instead highlighting the support of "adjacent provinces" and presenting Bethesda as an inter-colonial project. Second, the financial benefits of a college, the "whole products and profits" that are cited as an incentive for the colony, bespeak not only pragmatic motivations but also Whitefield's recognition of the vital role of local economic systems.

---

83. Sermon LVII, "A Caution Against Despising the Day of Small Things," preached before the Governor, and Council, and the House of Assembly, in Georgia, on January 28, 1770, in *Works*, 6:358–75.

His embrace of Bethesda's role in the colonial marketplace reinforces the notion of his bid for a regionally sufficient and perpetuating social ecosystem.[84] Finally, Whitefield stated his intentions to continue care for orphans and training for ministry even with the "addition of a seat of learning." With a nod to critics leery of his shift away from charity work, Whitefield reaffirmed the philanthropic component of Bethesda while simultaneously extending the purpose of Bethesda into a distinctly academic institute. Several years after the failure of his quest for a college charter, in other words, Whitefield made key concessions even while solidifying his core agenda for a college. Far from attenuating zeal, he displayed a focus as sharp and determined as in the heydays of the Great Awakening. If it is difficult to recognize the revivalist fighter in the elderly Whitefield, it is because the scope of his religious work had grown to include broader social and cultural dimensions. The ease with which Whitefield pivoted between the roles of evangelistic preacher and determined college founder not only sheds light on his religious convictions but also illuminates the ways these convictions interacted with the political and cultural climate in which he lived.

Whitefield's work on behalf of the colonies and the empire did not go unnoticed. In a note on January 29, 1770, appreciation for Whitefield overflowed into the Journals of Georgia's House of Assembly, remarking that neighboring residents "were sensibly affected, when they saw the happy success which has attended Mr. Whitefield's indefatigable zeal for promoting the welfare of the province in general, and the Orphan House in particular."[85] The appreciation was mutual. To the very end, Whitefield not only sought international support for Bethesda but also welcomed Savannah neighbors and Georgian politicians. On the very same day the Georgia legislature was gushing about Whitefield, the minister posted a public invitation to Savannah's leading residents to

---

84. According to Boyd Schlenther, the increased economic autonomy of British citizens during the eighteenth century had religious foundations: "The Great Awakening had taught men to make new choices in open market terms and had greatly increased the sense of individual destiny in America. As they revolted against an Empire based on commercial control to claim free trade and open access to new lands, the Americans at the same time laid claim to an unhindered religious life." Schlenther, "Religious Faith and Commercial Empire," in Marshall, *The Oxford History of the British Empire*, 149. For a discussion of the power of commercial goods and choice in the pre-revolutionary period, see Breen, *The Marketplace of Revolution*.

85. Tyerman, *Life*, 2:575.

come and visit Bethesda: "A more particular application being impracticable, the Rev. Mr. Whitefield takes this method of begging the favour of the company of as many gentlemen and captains of ships in and about Savannah, as it may suit to accept this invitation, to dine with him at the Orphan House next Sunday."[86] His special designation of gentlemen and ship captains revealed once again his eye for the commercial and maritime dimensions of empire.

Conclusion

With his health failing, grudging acceptance of his limitations as well as growing awareness of his mortality pressed Whitefield to look for a college with not only a "broad bottom" but a long legacy. As it turned out, the Bethesda campaign demanded a great deal from him. In the bigger picture, Whitefield's commitment to the Bethesda enterprise marked his entire American career, from beginning to end. That commitment charted not only his overall course but also its points of retrenchment and redirection. Support for the orphanage was the initial charge that brought him to America, and it was an unfinished project that occupied much of his time and space in his letters to the very last days of his life. Not only did Bethesda provide bookends for Whitefield's American career; it was the central anchor, as he confided in a letter to Benjamin Franklin in 1747: "if the Orphan-house should be given up [before] my departure to my Native Country, America, in all probability, would see me no more. Whilst that stands, I shall have a visible call to visit these parts again."[87] In the same letter, Whitefield called the orphan house "my darling," foreshadowing the many years of toil he would pour into caring for this labor of love. That he did not tire of such a costly operation, which became only more burdensome throughout his life, is a testament to the central importance Bethesda held in Whitefield's vision for his life and ministry. In fact, as we have seen, far from waning, the Grand Itinerant's intentions for Bethesda only intensified in his last decade as he worked to turn the orphanage into a college.

---

86. Originally published in *The Georgia Gazette* on January 29, 1770; quoted in Tyerman, *Life*, 2:577-78.

87. Whitefield to Benjamin Franklin, June 23, 1747, in *The Papers of Benjamin Franklin*, 3:144.

Whitefield's quest for Bethesda College in Georgia reveals that he was more than a controversial revival preacher. Without detracting from the prominent homiletical feature of his career, the Bethesda campaign provides a wider frame for understanding the famous preacher's vision for his life and ministry. In addition, the broader implications of Whitefield's campaign for Bethesda are instructive for understanding life in the American colonies during a period surrounded by two epochal events, the Great Awakening and the American Revolution. The peripatetic Whitefield labored during a time when the bonds of imperial community were undergoing rapid changes in the eighteenth century. Similarly, shifting circumstances exerted profound pressures on conceptions and practices of Christianity in America. As the fruits of revival withered and the effects of British imperial expansion became more pronounced in the American colonies, evangelical ministers like Whitefield did not sit idly by in the face of vacillating spiritual interest. Instead, they threw themselves into the public arena, jockeying for position and vying for influence. Whitefield's labors in the American South were especially important because of his regional as well as international prominence.

To understand the meaning of Whitefield's religious motivations, this study has sought to expand an understanding of the political and cultural climate of regional, colonial affairs in the larger context of the British Empire. At the height of unprecedented imperial strength after victory over France, the colonies presented British rulers with the unforeseen challenge of making peace, which proved a more fluid and complex task than waging war. Whitefield's activities during this period offer an alternative entry point into colonial life and culture during the 1760s.[88] Approaching Whitefield's quest for Bethesda College in this way affirms the meaning of ideas in their lived context, and the imbricated nature of theological and political influences on colonial life. That a transatlantic celebrity poured himself into cultivating the margins of colonial society, bypassing traditional centers of political and cultural power while locating religious creativity and activism outside the institutional church, provides the outlines of the story. At its heart stands a spirit of evangelical improvisation emerging in the context of a growing

88. Even as Colin Calloway has sought to view this period in the light of the Treaty of Paris of 1763, this chapter represents an attempt to understand the interwar years as a period of creative reassessment of what was deemed possible in the expanding empire. Colin G. Calloway, *The Scratch of a Pen: 1763 and the Transformation of North America* (New York: Oxford University Press, 2006).

empire under duress. In this process, Whitefield's appropriation of British imperial politics, his theological use of the margins, and his vision for cultural renewal, all focused through his efforts at institution building, remind us that religion remained a vital force in the British colonies in America during the 1760s. After all, Whitefield continued to attract large crowds in his preaching tours even if he expanded the repertoire of his kingdom-building techniques beyond exegeting Scripture and exhorting the swooning masses. And he never gave up pursuing individual conversion even as he sought to make lasting cultural contributions.

Absent the fervor of revivals and predating the surge of revolutionary mobilization, and in a period lacking extraordinary, epochal markers, the contours of colonial life took form through the efforts of pioneers like Whitefield. Through Bethesda he worked the borders of political and religious worlds to present new schemes for imagining community life in ordinary time. In the context of an enlarged yet hollow imperial space, Whitefield's efforts to start a college did not necessarily foreshadow the building of a new nation. Rather, the fits and starts of the Bethesda project reflected a society in flux, where in one corner some labored to establish a colony out of a forest and others an institution of higher learning out of an orphan charity. In this process, Georgia proved to be a field of community making, the patterns of which would be retraced on numerous occasions in the years ahead as liberated colonists—no longer the subjects of an empire—forged ahead to become the shapers of a new republic. In that new space of independence and free enterprise, the earlier halting steps toward community building would provide the outlines of one new nation formed out of many, disparate ideological threads. Because of efforts like Whitefield's to reconcile divergent political, theological, and social worlds, seemingly incompatible ideas would prove moveable and surmountable, if recurring, obstacles in the decades to come.

Epilogue

Three hundred years after Whitefield's birth, his legacy remains largely ambiguous. He has long stood in uneasy company with towering figures like Jonathan Edwards and John Wesley, a sort of third wheel among undisputed leaders of the evangelical awakening. A case might be made that Whitefield serves as an awkward accessory for the sake of completing a triune symmetry. Edwards was the indubitable intellectual leader of the early evangelicals and Wesley the sophisticated organizer who laid the groundwork for worldwide Methodism.[1] Whitefield's significance is harder to define. For some he was a belligerent preacher who peaked early and just as quickly faded away from the limelight, though not soon enough. For others he was a rousing performer the likes of whom the world has not seen since. For young evangelical preachers today, he is the embodiment of everything they aspire toward—converts and critics and all. While Edwards and Wesley enjoy security in the evangelical triumvirate for the foreseeable future, Whitefield's place is more tenuous. He slips easily, perhaps too easily, into mention with extremist preachers of questionable repute such as Gilbert Tennent and James Davenport.[2] In addition, there are other early evangelicals vying for attention, perhaps even edging Whitefield aside. Sarah Osborn, a revival leader in her own right who has recently been dubbed "A Protestant Saint," deserves at least a place in the con-

1. Marsden, *Jonathan Edwards*; David Hempton, *Methodism: Empire of the Spirit* (New Haven: Yale University Press, 2005).

2. See for instance a recent study that juxtaposes Whitefield, Tennent, and Davenport as "newsmakers of the Awakening": Smith, *The First Great Awakening in Colonial American Newspapers*.

versation.[3] Even if she is unlikely to take the place of Whitefield, new scholarship may raise further questions about how, and to what extent, Whitefield fits into the larger history of evangelicalism.

The concern of this book, however, has not been so much to secure Whitefield's legacy as to more fully understand the reciprocal influence between the person and his world. Its aim has been to bring clarity to a crowded interpretive field teeming with caricatures by turning once more to the context in which he lived. The iconic preacher may be a fascinating subject, but the world in which he lived proves even more so. Over the course of the eighteenth century, England's population grew at a rate of 72 percent. In North America, that pace was even more brisk at 3 percent per year. Starting at 250,000 in 1700, the European population in the colonies had increased to 2,150,000 by 1770, the year Whitefield died.[4] The traveling priest had an uncanny ability to locate himself at the center of action as the era of proto-industrialization witnessed soaring incomes with corresponding increases in trade, commerce, and communication. Growth can be measured not only in population and currency but also in physical distance. With the discovery of "the Bering Straits in 1728; Alaska and the Aleutian Islands in 1741; Tahiti, the Solomon Islands, and New Guinea in the late 1760s; Botany Bay in 1770; and Hawaii in 1778," the known world was constantly expanding.[5] It has been my contention that placing Whitefield and the grand scale of his ambitions in this context of startling cultural change is essential to understanding what happened during the Great Awakening, its aftermath, and more broadly across the British Empire.

This effort to reinsert the religious Whitefield into his secular world faces formidable challenges. More to the point, assumptions underlying hagiography (the most common genre in studies about Whitefield) pose the greatest difficulties. With false confidence in the deceptive clarity of hindsight, the temptation is ever present to impose artificial boundaries between matters of religion, economics, and politics. In fact, the vexed historiography of eighteenth-century religious revivals, with its many divergent interpretations, is the result of compartmentalizing various spheres of life that were experienced in vital, syner-

3. Brekus, *Sarah Osborn's World*, 337–44.
4. Much of the information in this paragraph is drawn from David Hancock, *Citizens of the World: London Merchants and the Integration of the British Atlantic Community, 1735–1785* (Cambridge: Cambridge University Press, 1995), 25–33.
5. Hancock, *Citizens of the World*, 31.

gistic tension by contemporaries. Historians have created a needless conundrum since, in the lived experience of eighteenth-century people, these realities were inseparable. Attempting to view the period as a whole allows for the recognition that as evangelicals preached, converted, traded goods, bought slaves, took up arms, built institutions, and prayed for revival, they were responding to a complex web of life ceaselessly emerging and intertwining in their transatlantic, imperial context.

Building on this perspective of life and society as a unified whole, my study of the Great Awakening has taken seriously the British Empire as its cultural setting. The grandiose spirit of an empire-building people not only provided a critical backdrop for the revivals but also supplied the very air in which they erupted. Imperial hubris also provided the long arc along which revival religion lost its way. Paying attention to empire leads to a wider perspective that may still locate the core impulse of the Great Awakening in spiritual concerns but recognizes that a host of nonreligious factors were also important. Consideration of the religious emphases at the center of the awakenings, therefore, should not detract from the broader contextual realities that also shaped the evangelical revivals. By approaching our study in this way, we have explored how acquisitive forces, both economic and political, embedded in imperial culture impacted the course of religious revivals. From the resulting long view, we have also come to appreciate the vital part that religious awakenings played in the larger process of British state formation. Evangelicals, as proponents of cultural as well as religious renewal, contributed to a principled rhetoric of empire. They accomplished this feat by participating in religious activities that depended upon state and commercial infrastructure stretching across the Atlantic world.

As a way to bring evangelical religion and the imperial dimension together, this study has focused on George Whitefield, the most famous preacher of the British Empire during the era of the Great Awakening. While students of history have assumed that we already know everything worth knowing about him, the foregoing chapters have been an effort to dispel that unwarranted conclusion. In point of fact, the imperial Whitefield reveals complex entanglements in the cultural streams of his lifetime. A subject of the British Empire, the celebrity preacher was as much a cultural and political emissary as he was a religious missionary. He so accommodated to the emerging transatlantic world that he also became one of its most creative entrepreneurs in the cultural marketplace, where his religious message competed with a wide array of other consumer goods. In the twilight of his life, he became more weary but also more enamored with institution building. Though he did not succeed in the effort, he concluded his life trying to establish a college that would continue to expound his evangelical message. In this movement from conventicle to college, Whitefield sought to make sense of his world by combining the forces of religion and empire in ways that were distinctly Protestant, maritime, commercial, and free. There is no assailing the familiar trope that he was an unstoppable preacher of heart religion. This view of the ubiquitous preacher is etched in our textbooks and rightly so. That he approached all of his life as a product of the empire, however, has the potential to change—or at least enrich—how we think and write about this religious figure. Along these lines, a new focus on his later years reminds us that more than the account of a great historical figure, what we have before us is the story of an ordinary human being. For we have learned that Whitefield the honey-tongued preacher was a person subject to the vagaries of economic and political fortunes, like most people then and now.

Sobriety about George Whitefield brings greater clarity to the imperial world he inhabited. It was not merely Matthew Tindal's encroaching deism and William Hogarth's prints of moral laxity that the evangelical revivals were meant to counteract.[6] Whitefield lived in a bewilderingly expansive world that was only growing larger by the day, amid a "superheated atmosphere of geographical, scientific, and technological discovery."[7] And so it may be most fitting to conclude in the way we began, by picturing the young Whitefield in early Georgia and appreciating the extent to which he was reimagining his world. For some, it was the far edge of the world. For others with eyes to see, it was the future center of a new Protestant empire. To recall the central place that Georgia occupied on maps of the eighteenth century may be the best stimulus for trying, as this book has, to also view this extraordinary preacher as an ordinary Englishman who lived much of his life as an imperial itinerant, a presbyter at large who saw the world as his parish.

6. Hempton, *The Church in the Long Eighteenth Century*, 145–46.
7. Hancock, *Citizens of the World*, 32.

Bibliography

Manuscripts

Diary of an Unidentified Bostonian in London, Huntington Library.
Eleazar Wheelock Papers, Dartmouth College.
George Whitefield Papers, Library of Congress.
Gratz Collection, Historical Society of Pennsylvania.
James Habersham Papers, Georgia Historical Society.
Samuel Savage Papers, Massachusetts Historical Society.
Various, Lambeth Palace Library.
William Becket's Letterbook, 1727–1742, Historical Society of Pennsylvania.
William Shippen's Journal, American Philosophical Society.

Newspapers

The Pennsylvania Gazette
The Georgia Gazette

Published Sources

An Account, Shewing the Progress of the Colony of Georgia in America, From Its First Establishment: Published Per Order of the Honorable the Trustees. Annapolis: Jonas Green, 1741.
Alexander, Archibald. *The Log College: Biographical Sketches of William Tennent and His Students.* London: Banner of Truth Trust, 1968.

Amory, Hugh, and David D. Hall. *A History of the Book in America*. New York: Cambridge University Press, 2000.

Anderson, Fred. *Crucible of War: The Seven Years' War and the Fate of Empire in British North America, 1754–1766*. New York: Alfred A. Knopf, 2000.

Anderson, J. R. "The Genesis of Georgia: An Historical Sketch." *The Georgia Historical Quarterly* 13, no. 3 (1929): 229–83.

Armitage, David. "Greater Britain: A Useful Category of Historical Analysis?" *American Historical Review* 104, no. 2 (1999): 427–45.

———. *The Ideological Origins of the British Empire*. Cambridge: Cambridge University Press, 2000.

Axtell, James. *The Invasion Within: The Contest of Cultures in Colonial North America*. New York: Oxford University Press, 1985.

Belcher, Joseph. *George Whitefield: A Biography, With Special Reference to His Labors in America*. New York: American Tract Society, 1857.

Bickham, Troy. "Eating the Empire: Intersections of Food, Cookery and Imperialism in Eighteenth-Century Britain." *Past and Present* 198, no. 1 (2008): 71–109.

Bolton, Herbert Eugene, and Mary Ross. *The Debatable Land*. Berkeley: University of California Press, 1925.

Bonomi, Patricia U. *Under the Cope of Heaven: Religion, Society and Politics in Colonial America*. Oxford: Oxford University Press, 2003.

Boven, H. V. *War and British Society, 1688–1815*. Cambridge: Cambridge University Press, 1998.

Breen, T. H. *The Marketplace of Revolution: How Consumer Politics Shaped American Independence*. New York: Oxford University Press, 2004.

Brekus, Catherine A. *Sarah Osborn's World: The Rise of Evangelical Christianity in Early America*. New Haven: Yale University Press, 2013.

Butler, Jon. *Awash in a Sea of Faith: Christianizing the American People*. Studies in Cultural History. Cambridge: Harvard University Press, 1990.

———. "Enthusiasm Described and Decried: The Great Awakening as Interpretative Fiction." *The Journal of American History* 69, no. 2 (1982): 305–25.

Calloway, Colin G. *New Worlds for All: Indians, Europeans, and the Remaking of Early America*. Baltimore: The Johns Hopkins University Press, 2013.

———. *The Scratch of a Pen: 1763 and the Transformation of North America*. New York: Oxford University Press, 2006.

Candler, Allen Daniel. *The Colonial Records of the State of Georgia*. Vol. 1. Atlanta: Franklin Print. and Pub. Co., 1904.

———. *The Colonial Records of the State of Georgia*. Vol. 3. Atlanta: Franklin Print. and Pub. Co., 1905.

———. *The Colonial Records of the State of Georgia*. Vol. 5. Atlanta: Franklin Print. and Pub. Co., 1906.

Canny, Nicholas. *Making Ireland British, 1580–1650*. New York: Oxford University Press, 2003.

Canny, Nicholas, and Philip Morgan, eds. *The Oxford Handbook of the Atlantic World: 1450–1850*. Oxford: Oxford University Press, 2011.

Canny, Nicholas P., and Anthony Pagden. *Colonial Identity in the Atlantic World, 1500–1800*. Princeton: Princeton University Press, 1987.

Cashin, Edward J. *Beloved Bethesda: A History of George Whitefield's Home for Boys, 1740–2000*. Macon: Mercer University Press, 2001.

———. *Setting Out to Begin a New World: Colonial Georgia; A Documentary History*. Savannah: Library of Georgia, 1995.

Chamberlain, Joshua L. *The University of Pennsylvania: Its History, Influence, Equipment and Characteristics*. Boston: R. Herndon Company, 1901.

Chaplin, Joyce E. "The British Atlantic." In *The Oxford Handbook of the Atlantic World, 1450–1850*, edited by Nicholas Canny and Philip Morgan, 219–34. Oxford: Oxford University Press, 2011.

———. *Subject Matter: Technology, the Body, and Science on the Anglo-American Frontier, 1500–1676*. Cambridge: Harvard University Press, 2001.

Chauncy, Charles. *Enthusiasm Described and Caution'd Against. A Sermon. With a Letter to the Reverend Mr. James Davenport*. Boston: S. Eliot & J. Blanchard, 1742.

Clive, John, and Bernard Bailyn. "England's Cultural Provinces: Scotland and America." *The William and Mary Quarterly* 11, no. 2 (1954): 200–213.

Coleman, Kenneth. *Colonial Georgia: A History*. New York: Scribner, 1976.

———. *A History of Georgia*. Athens: University of Georgia Press, 1977.

———. "The Southern Frontier: Georgia's Founding and the Expansion of South Carolina." *Georgia Historical Quarterly* 56 (1972): 163–74.

Colley, Linda. *Britons: Forging the Nation, 1707–1837*. New Haven: Yale University Press, 1992.

———. *Britons: Forging the Nation, 1707–1837*. Revised Edition. New Haven: Yale University Press, 2005.

Corry, John Pitts. "Racial Elements in Colonial Georgia." *The Georgia Historical Quarterly* 20, no. 1 (1936): 30–40.

Coulter, E. Merton. *Georgia: A Short History.* Chapel Hill: University of North Carolina Press, 1960.

Crane, Verner Winslow. *The Southern Frontier, 1670–1732.* Ann Arbor: University of Michigan Press, 1956.

Dallimore, Arnold A. *George Whitefield: The Life and Times of the Great Evangelist of the 18th Century Revival.* 2 vols. Carlisle: Banner of Truth, 1970.

Davies, Samuel. *A Sermon Delivered At Nassau-Hall, January 14, 1761. On the Death of His Late Majesty King.* Boston, 1761.

Davies, Samuel, and Gilbert Tennent. *A General Account of the Rise and State of the College, Lately Established in the Province of New-Jersey, in America.* Edinburgh, 1754.

Davis, Harold E. *The Fledgling Province: Social and Cultural Life in Colonial Georgia, 1733–1776.* Williamsburg: Institute of Early American History and Culture, 1976.

Ettinger, A. A. *James Edward Oglethorpe, Imperial Idealist.* Hamden: Archon Books, 1968.

Evans, Thomas, Alexander Garden, and George Whitefield. *The Querists, the Rev. Mr. Whitefield's Answer, the Rev. Mr. Garden's Letters.* New York: J. P. Zenger, 1740.

Fischer, David H. *Albion's Seed: Four British Folkways in America.* New York: Oxford University Press, 1991.

Flavell, Julie. *When London Was Capital of America.* New Haven: Yale University Press, 2010.

Foster, Stephen. *The Long Argument: English Puritanism and the Shaping of New England Culture, 1570–1700.* Chapel Hill: University of North Carolina Press, 1991.

Francklin, Thomas. *A Sermon Preached Before the Honourable Trustees for Establishing the Colony of Georgia in America, and the Associates of the Late Rev. Dr. Bray; March 16, 1749–50. In the Parish Church of St. Margaret, Westminster.* London, 1750.

Franklin, Benjamin. *Autobiography.* Boston: Houghton Mifflin & Company, 1906.

———. *Proposals Relating to the Education of Youth in Pensilvania.* Pennsylvania, 1749.

Gallay, Allan. "The Origins of Slaveholders' Paternalism: George Whitefield, the Bryan Family, and the Great Awakening in the South." *The Journal of Southern History* 53, no. 3 (1987): 369–94.

Games, Alison. *The Web of Empire: English Cosmopolitans in an Age of Expansion, 1560–1660.* New York: Oxford University Press, 2008.

Georgia Historical Society. *Collections of the Georgia Historical Society,* vol. 1. Savannah: Printed for the Society, 1840.

Gillies, John, ed. *Memoirs of the Life of the Reverend George Whitefield, Faithfully Selected From His Original Papers, Journals, and Letters.* London: Edward and Charles Dilly, 1772.

———. *Memoirs of the Life of the Reverend George Whitefield.* Meadow View: Quinta Press, 2000.

———. *The Works of the Reverend George Whitefield M.A.* 7 vols. London, 1771–72.

Goff, Philip. "Revivals and Revolution: Historiographic Turns since Alan Heimert's Religion and the American Mind." *Church History* 67, no. 4 (1998): 695–721.

Goon, Robert. "The Classical Tradition in Colonial Georgia." *The Georgia Historical Quarterly* 86, no. 1 (2002): 1–17.

Greene, Jack P. *Creating the British Atlantic: Essays on Transplantation, Adaptation, and Continuity.* Charlottesville: University of Virginia Press, 2013.

———. "Empire and Identity from the Glorious Revolution to the American Revolution." In *The Oxford History of the British Empire.* Volume 2: *The Eighteenth Century,* edited by Peter Marshall. Oxford: Oxford University Press, 1998.

Griffin, Patrick. *America's Revolution.* New York: Oxford University Press, 2013.

Hammond, Geordan, and David Ceri Jones, eds. *George Whitefield: Life, Context, and Legacy.* Oxford: Oxford University Press, 2016.

Hancock, David. *Citizens of the World: London Merchants and the Integration of the British Atlantic Community, 1735–1785.* Cambridge: Cambridge University Press, 1995.

Hatch, Nathan O. *The Sacred Cause of Liberty: Republican Thought and the Millennium in Revolutionary New England.* New Haven: Yale University Press, 1977.

Heimert, Alan. *Religion and the American Mind: From the Great Awakening to the Revolution.* Cambridge: Harvard University Press, 1966.

Heimert, Alan, and Perry Miller. *The Great Awakening: Documents Illustrating the Crisis and Its Consequences.* Indianapolis: Bobbs-Merrill, 1967.

Hempton, David. *The Church in the Long Eighteenth Century.* London: I. B. Tauris, 2011.

————. *Methodism: Empire of the Spirit*. New Haven: Yale University Press, 2005.

Henry, Stuart Clark. *George Whitefield: Wayfaring Witness*. Nashville: Abingdon Press, 1957.

Hinderaker, Eric, and Peter C. Mancall. *At the Edge of Empire: The Back-country in British North America*. Baltimore: Johns Hopkins University Press, 2003.

Hindmarsh, D. Bruce. *The Evangelical Conversion Narrative: Spiritual Autobiography in Early Modern England*. New York: Oxford University Press, 2005.

Hofstra, Warren R. *Cultures in Conflict: The Seven Years' War in North America*. Lanham: Rowman & Littlefield, 2007.

Hunter, Phyllis. *Purchasing Identity in the Atlantic World: Massachusetts Merchants, 1670–1780*. Ithaca: Cornell University Press, 2001.

Ingram, Robert G. *Religion, Reform and Modernity in the Eighteenth Century: Thomas Secker and the Church of England*. Woodbridge: Boydell Press, 2007.

Isaac, Rhys. *The Transformation of Virginia, 1740–1790*. Chapel Hill: University of North Carolina Press, 1999.

Jackson, Harvey H. "Prophecy and Community: Hugh Bryan, George Whitefield, and the Stoney Creek Independent Presbyterian Church." *American Presbyterians* 69, no. 1 (1991): 11–20.

Jackson, Harvey, and Phinzy Spalding, eds. *Forty Years of Diversity: Essays on Colonial Georgia*. Athens: University of Georgia Press, 1984.

Jarvis, Michael J. *In the Eye of All Trade: Bermuda, Bermudians, and the Maritime Atlantic World, 1680–1783*. Chapel Hill: University of North Carolina Press, 2010.

Jennings, Francis. *Empire of Fortune: Crowns, Colonies, and Tribes in the Seven Years War in America*. New York: W. W. Norton, 1990.

Jennings, Willie James. *The Christian Imagination: Theology and the Origins of Race*. New Haven: Yale University Press, 2010.

Johnson, Samuel. *The Yale Edition of the Works of Samuel Johnson: The Idler and the Adventurer*. Vol. 2. New Haven: Yale University Press, 1963.

Jones, David Ceri. *A Glorious Work in the World: Welsh Methodism and the International Evangelical Revival, 1735–1750*. Cardiff: University of Wales Press, 2004.

————. "'So Much Idolized By Some, and Railed At by Others': Towards Understanding George Whitefield." *Wesley and Methodist Studies* 5 (2013): 3–29.

Jones, David Ceri, Boyd Stanley Schlenther, and Eryn Mant White. *The Elect Methodists: Calvinistic Methodism in England and Wales, 1735–1811*. Cardiff: University of Wales Press, 2012.

Kamrath, Mark, and Sharon M. Harris. *Periodical Literature in Eighteenth-Century America*. Knoxville: University of Tennessee Press, 2005.

Kidd, Colin. *British Identities before Nationalism*. Cambridge: Cambridge University Press, 1999.

Kidd, Thomas S. *George Whitefield: America's Spiritual Founding Father*. New Haven: Yale University Press, 2014.

———. *The Great Awakening: The Roots of Evangelical Christianity in Colonial America*. New Haven: Yale University Press, 2007.

Koenigsberger, Helmut Georg. "Composite States, Representative Institutions and the American Revolution." *Historical Research* 62, no. 148 (1989): 135–53.

Lambert, Frank. *Inventing the "Great Awakening."* Princeton: Princeton University Press, 1999.

———. *James Habersham: Loyalty, Politics, and Commerce in Colonial Georgia*. Athens: University of Georgia Press, 2005.

———. *"Pedlar in Divinity": George Whitefield and the Transatlantic Revivals, 1737–1770*. Princeton: Princeton University Press, 1994.

———. "Subscribing for Profits and Piety: The Friendship of Benjamin Franklin and George Whitefield." *The William and Mary Quarterly* 50, no. 3 (1993): 529–54.

Landsman, Ned. *From Colonials to Provincials: American Thought and Culture, 1680–1760*. Ithaca: Cornell University Press, 2000.

Langford, Paul. *A Polite and Commercial People: England, 1727–1783*. New York: Oxford University Press, 1989.

Lanning, John Tate. *The Diplomatic History of Georgia: A Study of the Epoch of Jenkins' Ear*. Chapel Hill: University of North Carolina Press, 1936.

Larabee, Leonard W., et al., eds. *The Papers of Benjamin Franklin*. 42 vols. to date. New Haven: Yale University Press, 1959–.

Livesey, James. *Civil Society and Empire: Ireland and Scotland in the Eighteenth-Century Atlantic World*. New Haven: Yale University Press, 2009.

Lovelace, Richard F. *Dynamics of Spiritual Life*. Downers Grove: InterVarsity Press, 1979.

Mahaffey, Jerome Dean. *The Accidental Revolutionary: George Whitefield and the Creation of America*. Waco: Baylor University Press, 2011.

———. *Preaching Politics: The Religious Rhetoric of George Whitefield and the Founding of a New Nation*. Waco: Baylor University Press, 2007.

Marini, Stephen A. *Radical Sects of Revolutionary New England*. Cambridge: Harvard University Press, 1982.

Marsden, George. *Jonathan Edwards: A Life*. New Haven: Yale University Press, 2003.

Marshall, Peter J., ed. *The Oxford History of the British Empire*. Volume 2: *The Eighteenth Century*. Oxford: Oxford University Press, 1998.

McCaul, Robert L. "Whitefield's Bethesda College Project and Other Attempts to Found Colonial Colleges: Part I." *The Georgia Historical Quarterly* 44, no. 3 (1960): 263–77.

McConville, Brendan. *The King's Three Faces: The Rise & Fall of Royal America, 1688–1776*. Chapel Hill: University of North Carolina Press, 2006.

Morgan, Edmund S. *The Puritan Dilemma: The Story of John Winthrop*. Boston: Little, Brown and Company, 1958.

———. *Visible Saints: The History of a Puritan Idea*. New York: New York University Press, 1963.

Murrin, John M. "A Roof without Walls: The Dilemma of American National Identity." In *Beyond Confederation: Origins of the Constitution and American National Identity*, edited by Richard R. Beeman, Stephen Botein, and Edward C. Carter, 170–206. Chapel Hill: University of North Carolina Press, 1987.

Nash, Gary. *The Urban Crucible: The Northern Seaports and the Origins of the American Revolution*. Cambridge: Harvard University Press, 1986.

Noll, Mark A. *America's God: From Jonathan Edwards to Abraham Lincoln*. New York: Oxford University Press, 2002.

———. *The Rise of Evangelicalism: The Age of Edwards, Whitefield, and the Wesleys*. Downers Grove: InterVarsity Press, 2003.

Noll, Mark A., David W. Bebbington, and George A. Rawlyk. *Evangelicalism: Comparative Studies of Popular Protestantism in North America, the British Isles, and Beyond, 1700–1990*. New York: Oxford University Press, 1994.

O'Brien, Susan A. "A Transatlantic Community of Saints: The Great Awakening and the First Evangelical Network, 1735–1755." *The American Historical Review* 91, no. 4 (1986): 811–32.

Pencak, William. "Beginning of a Beautiful Friendship: Benjamin Franklin, George Whitefield, the 'Dancing School Blockheads,' and a Defense of the 'Meaner Sort.'" *Proteus: A Journal of Ideas* 19, no. 1 (2002): 45–50.

Perry, William Stevens. *Historical Collections Relating to the American Colonial Church*. Hartford: The Church Press, 1871.

Pestana, Carla. *Protestant Empire: Religion and the Making of the British Atlantic World*. Philadelphia: University of Pennsylvania Press, 2009.

Pocock, J. G. A. "British History: A Plea for a New Subject." *The Journal of Modern History* 47, no. 4 (1975): 601–21.

———. *The Machiavellian Moment: Florentine Political Thought and the Atlantic Republican Tradition*. Princeton: Princeton University Press, 1975.

Prince, Thomas. *A Sermon Delivered At the South Church in Boston, August 14, 1746, Being the Day of General Thanksgiving for the Great Deliverance of the British Nations By the Glorious and Happy Victory Near Culloden*. Boston, 1746.

Rankin, S. W. "Wesley and War: Guidance for Modern Day Heirs?" *Methodist Review: A Journal of Wesleyan and Methodist Studies* 3 (2011): 101–39.

Ready, Milton. "The Georgia Trustees and the Malcontents: The Politics of Philanthropy." *The Georgia Historical Quarterly* 60, no. 3 (1976): 264–81.

Reese, Trevor R. *The Clamorous Malcontents: Criticisms & Defenses of the Colony of Georgia, 1741–1743*. Savannah: The Beehive Press, 1973.

Richardson, John. "Imagining Military Conflict during the Seven Years' War." *Studies in English Literature 1500–1900* 48, no. 3 (2008): 585–611.

Richter, Daniel K. *Facing East from Indian Country: A Native History of Early America*. Cambridge: Harvard University Press, 2001.

Schlenther, Boyd Stanley. *Queen of the Methodists: The Countess of Huntingdon and the Eighteenth-Century Crisis of Faith and Society*. Durham: Durham Academic Press, 1997.

———. "Religious Faith and Commercial Empire." In *The Oxford History of the British Empire*. Volume 2: *The Eighteenth Century*. Edited by Peter J. Marshall. Oxford: Oxford University Press, 1998.

Schmidt, Leigh Eric. "'A Second and Glorious Reformation': The New Light Extremism of Andrew Croswell." *The William and Mary Quarterly: A Magazine of Early American History and Culture* 43, no. 2 (1986): 214–44.

Secker, Thomas. *The Autobiography of Thomas Secker, Archbishop of Canterbury*. Lawrence: University of Kansas Libraries, 1988.

Seward, William. *Journal of a Voyage from Savannah to Philadelphia, and from Philadelphia to England*. London, 1741.

Seymour, Aaron Crossley, and Jacob Kirkman Foster. *The Life and Times of Selina: Countess of Huntingdon*. London: W. E. Painter, 1839.

Silver, Peter Rhoads. *Our Savage Neighbors: How Indian War Transformed Early America*. New York: W. W. Norton, 2008.

Smith, Josiah. *The Character, Preaching, &c. Of the Rev. Mr. George Whitefield*. Boston: Rogers for Edwards and Foster, 1740.

Smith, Julia Floyd. *Slavery and Rice Culture in Low Country Georgia, 1750–1860*. Knoxville: University of Tennessee Press, 1985.

Smith, Lisa. *The First Great Awakening in Colonial American Newspapers: A Shifting Story*. Lanham: Lexington Books, 2012.

Smith, Mark. "The Hanoverian Parish: Towards a New Agenda." *Past & Present* 216, no. 1 (2012): 79–105.

Smith, Mark Michael, ed. *Stono: Documenting and Interpreting a Southern Slave Revolt*. Columbia: University of South Carolina Press, 2005.

Smith, William. *A General Idea of the College of Mirania*. New York: J. Parker and W. Weyman, 1753.

The State of Religion in New England, Since the Reverend Mr. George Whitefield's Arrival There. Glasgow, 1742.

Steele, Ian K. *The English Atlantic, 1675–1740: An Exploration of Communication and Community*. New York: Oxford University Press, 1986.

Stephens, Thomas. *A Brief Account of the Causes That Have Retarded the Progress of the Colony of Georgia in America*. London, 1743.

———. *The Hard Case of the Distressed People of Georgia*. London, 1742.

Stephens, William. *A Journal of the Proceedings in Georgia*. 2 vols. Ann Arbor: University Microfilms, 1966.

———. *A State of the Province of Georgia: Attested Upon Oath in the Court of Savannah, November 10, 1740*. London, 1752.

Stephens, William, and Allen D. Candler. *A Journal of the Proceedings in Georgia, Beginning October 20, 1737. By William Stephens, Esq; to Which is Added, a State of That Province, as Attested Upon Oath in the Court of Savannah, November 10, 1740*. Atlanta: Franklin Print. and Pub. Co., 1906.

Stone, Lawrence. *An Imperial State at War: Britain from 1689 to 1815*. London: Routledge, 1994.

Stout, Harry S. *The Divine Dramatist: George Whitefield and the Rise of Modern Evangelicalism*. Grand Rapids: Eerdmans, 1991.

———. "Religion, Communications, and the Ideological Origins of the American Revolution." *The William and Mary Quarterly: A Magazine of Early American History* 34, no. 4 (1977): 519–41.

Sweet, Julie Anne. "William Stephens versus Thomas Stephens: A Family Feud in Colonial Georgia." *The Georgia Historical Quarterly* 92, no. 1 (2008): 1–36.

Tailfer, Patrick, Hugh Anderson, and Da. Douglas. *A True and Historical Narrative of the Colony of Georgia.* Charles-Town, SC: Printed for P. Timothy, 1741.

Tracy, Joseph. *The Great Awakening: A History of the Revival of Religion in the Time of Edwards and Whitefield.* Boston: Charles Tappan, 1845.

Tyerman, Luke. *The Life of the Rev. George Whitefield, B.A., of Pembroke College, Oxford.* 2 vols. London: Hodder and Stoughton, 1876–1877.

Tyson, John R., and Boyd Schlenther. *In the Midst of Early Methodism: Lady Huntingdon and Her Correspondence.* Lanham: Scarecrow Press, 2006.

Valeri, Mark. *Heavenly Merchandize: How Religion Shaped Commerce in Puritan America.* Princeton: Princeton University Press, 2010.

Walls, Andrew F. *The Missionary Movement in Christian History: Studies in the Transmission of Faith.* Maryknoll: Orbis Books, 1996.

Ward, W. R. *The Protestant Evangelical Awakening.* New York: Cambridge University Press, 1992.

———. *The Protestant Evangelical Awakening.* Cambridge: Cambridge University Press, 2002.

Wesley, John. *The Works of the Reverend John Wesley: First American Complete and Standard Edition.* New York: J. Emory and B. Waugh, 1831.

———. *The Works of the Rev. John Wesley: With the Last Corrections of the Author.* 12 vols. London: Wesleyan Conference Office, 1872.

Westerkamp, Marilyn J. *Triumph of the Laity: Scots-Irish Piety and the Great Awakening, 1625–1760.* Oxford: Oxford University Press, 1988.

Wheeler, Rachel M. *To Live Upon Hope: Mohicans and Missionaries in the Eighteenth-Century Northeast.* Ithaca: Cornell University Press, 2008.

Whitefield, George. *A Brief Account of Some Lent and Other Extraordinary Processions and Ecclesiastical Entertainments Seen Last Year at Lisbon: In Four Letters to an English Friend.* London: W. Strahan, 1755.

———. *A Brief Account of the Rise, Progress, and Present Situation of the Orphan-House in Georgia.* 1746.

———. *Britain's Mercies and Britain's Duty.* Boston: S. Kneeland and T. Green, 1746.

———. *A Continuation of the Account of the Orphan-House in Georgia, From January 1740/1 to June 1742.* Edinburgh: T. Lumisden and J. Robertson, 1742.

———. *Journals.* Meadow View: Quinta Press, 2000.

————. *A Letter to the Reverend Dr. Durell, Vice-Chancellor of the University of Oxford; Occasioned By a Late Expulsion of Six Students From Edmund-Hall*. Boston, 1768.

————. *The Nature and Necessity of Our New Birth in Christ Jesus, in Order to Salvation*. London, 1737.

————. *Sermons of George Whitefield*. Peabody: Hendrickson, 2009.

————. *Sermons on Various Subjects*. 2 vols. Philadelphia: B. Franklin, 1740.

————. *A Short Address to Persons of All Denominations, Occasioned By the Alarm of an Intended Invasion*. London, 1756.

————. *Three Letters from the Reverend Mr. G. Whitefield*. Philadelphia, 1740.

————. *The Works of George Whitefield, Additional Sermons*. Meadow View: Quinta Press, 2000.

Wilson, Kathleen. *A New Imperial History: Culture, Identity, and Modernity in Britain and the Empire, 1660–1840*. New York: Cambridge University Press, 2004.

Winner, Lauren F. *A Cheerful and Comfortable Faith: Anglican Religious Practice in the Elite Households of Eighteenth-Century Virginia*. New Haven: Yale University Press, 2010.

Wood, Betty. "A Note on the Georgia Malcontents." *The Georgia Historical Quarterly* 63, no. 2 (1979): 264–78.

————. *Slavery in Colonial Georgia, 1730–1775*. Athens: University of Georgia Press, 1984.

————. "Thomas Stephens and the Introduction of Black Slavery in Georgia." *The Georgia Historical Quarterly* 58, no. 1 (1974): 24–40.

Index

Titles published in the

LIBRARY OF RELIGIOUS BIOGRAPHY SERIES

Orestes A. Brownson: American Religious Weathervane
by Patrick W. Carey

The Puritan as Yankee: A Life of Horace Bushnell
by Robert Bruce Mullin

Emblem of Faith Untouched: A Short Life of Thomas Cranmer
by Leslie Williams

Her Heart Can See: The Life and Hymns of Fanny J. Crosby
by Edith L. Blumhofer

Emily Dickinson and the Art of Belief
by Roger Lundin

A Short Life of Jonathan Edwards
by George M. Marsden

Charles G. Finney and the Spirit of American Evangelicalism
by Charles E. Hambrick-Stowe

William Ewart Gladstone: Faith and Politics in Victorian Britain
by David Bebbington

Sworn on the Altar of God: A Religious Biography of Thomas Jefferson
by Edwin S. Gaustad

Abraham Kuyper: Modern Calvinist, Christian Democrat
by James D. Bratt

The Religious Life of Robert E. Lee
by R. David Cox

Abraham Lincoln: Redeemer President
by Allen C. Guelzo

The First American Evangelical: A Short Life of Cotton Mather
by Rick Kennedy

Aimee Semple McPherson: Everybody's Sister
by Edith L. Blumhofer

Damning Words: The Life and Religious Times of H. L. Mencken
by D. G. Hart

Thomas Merton and the Monastic Vision
by Lawrence S. Cunningham

God's Strange Work: **William Miller** *and the End of the World*
by David L. Rowe

Blaise Pascal: *Reasons of the Heart*
by Marvin R. O'Connell

Occupy Until I Come: **A. T. Pierson** *and the Evangelization of the World*
by Dana L. Robert

The Kingdom Is Always but Coming: A Life of **Walter Rauschenbusch**
by Christopher H. Evans

Francis Schaeffer *and the Shaping of Evangelical America*
by Barry Hankins

Harriet Beecher Stowe: *A Spiritual Life*
by Nancy Koester

Billy Sunday *and the Redemption of Urban America*
by Lyle W. Dorsett

Assist Me to Proclaim: The Life and Hymns of **Charles Wesley**
by John R. Tyson

Prophetess of Health: A Study of **Ellen G. White**
by Ronald L. Numbers

George Whitefield: *Evangelist for God and Empire*
by Peter Y. Choi

The Divine Dramatist: **George Whitefield** *and*
the Rise of Modern Evangelicalism by Harry S. Stout

Liberty of Conscience: **Roger Williams** *in America*
by Edwin S. Gaustad